STAYING ALIVE
A SURVIVAL MANUAL FOR THE LIBERAL ARTS

STAYING ALIVE

A SURVIVAL MANUAL FOR THE LIBERAL ARTS

L.O. Aranye Fradenburg

edited by Eileen A. Joy

with companion essays by Donna Beth Ellard, Ruth Evans, Eileen A.
Joy, Julie Orlemanski, Daniel C. Remein & Michael D. Snediker

punctum books ∗ brooklyn, ny

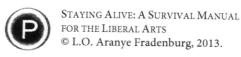

First published in 2013 by
punctum books
Brooklyn, New York
http://punctumbooks.com

punctum books is an open-access independent publisher
dedicated to radically creative modes of intellectual inquiry and writing across a whimsical para-humanities assemblage. punctum indicates thought that pierces and
disturbs the wednesdayish, business-as-usual protocols of
both the generic university studium and its individual
cells or holding tanks. We offer spaces for the imp-
orphans of your thought and pen, an ale-serving church
for little vagabonds. We also take in strays.

ISBN-13: 978-0615906508
ISBN-10: 0615906508

Cover Image: *Nauerna — ladder* (2010), by Ellen Kooi;
with permission of the artist.

Facing-page drawing by Heather Masciandaro.

for Chuck Young

ACKNOWLEDGMENTS

I want to thank Eileen Joy and punctum books for the care and attention they gave this book, and the BABEL Working Group for inspiring its more adventurous features, such as they are. Julie Carlson and Laurence Rickels have helped me with so much of the thinking in *Staying Alive* that I can never thank them enough. I'm also grateful to the Literature and the Mind community at the University of California, Santa Barbara, especially Dominique Jullien, Ken Kosik, Vera Tobin, Jan Caldwell, Kay Young, Cheryl Lynn, Jonathan Forbes and Paul Megna, for their support, encouragement and tutelage. Noelle Batt has been a friend to this book in more ways than she knows. I began learning about neuroscience and evolutionary psychology while in training at the New Center for Psychoanalysis, Los Angeles, and especially want to thank Mark Leffert and my instructors Regina Pally and Harry Brickman for pointing me in so many fruitful directions. Finally, loving thanks to Meiram Bendat and Dahlia Russ for giving me many good reasons to stay alive.

Aranye Fradenburg

The Publisher wishes to thank Aranye Fradenburg for her courage in climbing aboard punctum's ship of fools, and for her tireless advocacy for the humanities and the artful life of the mind. We are happy to toil in the vineyard of her glow. We are also indebted to her for the contributions she made to the design and editing of the book. From beginning to end, *Staying Alive* was a true collaboration, the work of many hands, and we wish to thank A.W. Strouse, especially, for his help with the Index and with proofreading the volume. Thanks are also due to Donna Beth Ellard, Ruth Evans, Julie Orlemanski, Dan Remein, and Michael Snediker, for agreeing, in the midst of terrifically busy schedules and other writing commitments, to co-compose with us.

Eileen A. Joy

TABLE OF CONTENTS

Hands Off Our *Jouissance*
The Collaborative Risk of a
Shared Disorganization

Eileen A. Joy

Do we really mean to take shelter from our *jouissance* in
the order of utility, to become "a branch of the service of
goods," in the mistaken hope that the "human sciences"
will be rewarded for doing so?

    L.O. Aranye Fradenburg, "Group Time, Catastrophe,
Periodicity"

As for what motivated me, it is quite simple . . . . It was
curiosity—the only kind of curiosity, in any case, that is
worth acting upon with a degree of obstinacy: not the
curiosity that seeks to assimilate what it is proper for
one to know, but that which enables one to get free of
oneself. After all, what would be the value of the passion
for knowledge if it resulted only in a certain amount of
knowledgeableness and not, in one way or another and
to the extent possible, in the knower's straying afield of

> himself? There are times in life when the question of
> knowing if one can think differently than one thinks,
> and perceive differently than one sees, is absolutely nec-
> essary if one is to go on looking and reflecting at all. . . .
> [W]hat is philosophy today . . . if it is not the critical
> work that thought brings to bear on itself? In what does
> it consist, if not in the endeavor to know how and to
> what extent it might be possible to think differently, in-
> stead of legitimating what is already known?
>
> Michel Foucault, *The Use of Pleasure*

> We are beings who can neither live nor die without art-
> ful signification.
>
> L.O. Aranye Fradenburg, "The Liberal Arts of
> Psychoanalysis"

I SIT IN ONE OF THE DIVES / ON FIFTY-SECOND STREET /
UNCERTAIN AND AFRAID

In 1981, Michel Foucault gave an interview in the French
gay press, *Le gai pied* (he had mistakenly believed his
identity would be cloaked, but the interview concluded
with "Merci, Michel Foucault"), in which he freely sketched out
what he saw as homosexuality's "historic occasion to reopen
affective and relational virtualities, not so much through
the instrinsic qualities of the homosexual, but due to the
biases against the position he occupies; in a certain sense,
diagonal lines that he can trace in the social fabric permit
him to make these virtualities visible" (Foucault 1996a,
311). More important, Foucault believed, than the questions of "who am I?" and "what is the secret of my desire?" would be to ask, "What relations, through homosexuality, can be established, invented, multiplied, and modulated?"
(Foucault 1996a, 308). It is important to note that, for
Foucault, the possibly utopic potential of homosexuality
would be available to anyone, gay or straight or whatever,
who might experiment with new "affective intensities," new
friendships, and new modes of living that could "yield intense

relations not resembling those that are institutionalized" (Foucault 1996a, 310).

It was at this same time, and following from his ongoing work on the history of sexuality (but with what can be described as a significant, and often overlooked, detour within that work),[1] that Foucault became interested in rehabilitating ascesis, and ascetics, as a practice of the care of the self:

> the work that one performs on oneself in order to transform oneself or make the self appear which, happily, one never attains. Can that be our problem today? We've rid ourselves of asceticism. Yet it's up to us to advance into a homosexual ascesis that would make us work on ourselves and invent—I do not say discover—a manner of being that is still improbable. (Foucault 1996a, 309–310)[2]

Foucault was at pains in many of his lectures to distinguish care of the self from knowledge of the self (i.e., the Delphic dictum: "know thyself"), partly because he did not believe in an ascetic praxis in which the ultimate aim was to "discover" and perhaps also regulate, surpass, and even renounce a self that was always already there (a preoccupation of later Christian culture, to be sure); rather, ascesis would name a set of practices or daily exercises (as in late classical Stoicism) aimed at what David Halperin

---

[1] See, for example, Davidson (1994), Deleuze (1986), and Tuhkanen (2005/06).

[2] In 1981, when Foucault gave this interview, he had already embarked on a series of lectures that he would continue (until his untimely and tragic death in 1984) at the Collège de France, the University of Vermont, UC-Berkeley, New York University, and other sites on the hermeneutics of the subject, technologies of the self, care of the self, and freedom; see Martin at al. (1988), Foucault (1996b), Foucault (1999), Foucault (2001), and Foucault (2005).

has described as a continual process of becoming-queer: "an identity without an essence, not a given condition but a horizon of possibility, an opportunity for self-transformation, a queer potential" (Halperin 1995, 79). One never arrives at the self, but instead, continuously works upon processes of self-transformation. This is, importantly, an aesthetic project, an "art of living," a "style of life," a *tekhnē* aimed at producing a self-always-becoming as a "beautiful and good work" (Foucault 2005, 424).

This work upon the self that one "happily never attains," which is also a concern for and care of the self, has something to do with freedom as well—a term not often associated with Foucault's thought, especially by those who oversimplify his entire ouevre as being only about the ways in which various structures and techniques of power produce knowledge and individuals, with apparently no escape route out of the power-knowledge nexus. And yet much of Foucault's late writings were precisely concerned with "the definition of practices of freedom" and ethics as "the conscious practice of freedom" (Foucault 1996b, 433, 434)—with freedom here to be distinguished from the idea of liberation (the setting free of selves that have supposedly always been there and were simply repressed, in hiding, etc.). For Foucault, freedom was "the ontological condition of ethics" and ethics is "the form that freedom takes when it is informed by reflection" (Foucault 1996b, 435).[3] And what this also means is that, for Foucault (as well as the late classical writers, such as Epictetus, Seneca, and Marcus Aurelius, whom he was reading at the time), ethics is a practice (an ascetics, or set of *exercises*) of freedom that revolves around the fundamental imperative: "Take care of yourself." One of the tragedies, I would argue, of social and cultural life in the

---

[3] It is important to note here that, for Foucault, as for the ancient Greek writers he was studying, an *ethos* named modes of being and behavior—of *living*—as opposed to naming some sort of prescriptive morality.

present (and of gay life, more narrowly), is that we have never really taken up, collectively, Foucault's call to work on ourselves in order to invent improbable manners of being, new modes and styles of living, polymorphous affective intensities, and new relational virtualities and friendships. Instead, as Joshua Glenn has written,

> [e]verything today encourages us to see the dark side, the folly, the impossibility, not just of utopia but of an anti-anti-utopian social order where we'd have a project in common besides selling our commodified labor, intellectual or otherwise. Everything encourages us to think we face a choice between detached houses in a row, where we cook our dinners in private, or else the gulag. . . . Sure, the company of misfits would make you feel bad sometimes; but it also feels bad to have nothing to look forward to but marriage, work and TV. (Glenn 2009)

Some of us *have* devoted much of our lives to cultivating new relational modes and the company of misfits (an agonistic yet joyful venture, to be sure, in which we exult in the exquisite difficulties of becoming-with-others), but when I re-read Foucault's 1981 interview, as I often do, I mourn that, as Adam Phillips has written, we have "not had the courage of [our] narcissism"—we have not found "a version of narcissism that is preservative at once of survival and pleasure," which "would be to have the courage of one's wish for more life rather than less" (Phillips 2008, 98).

ACCURATE SCHOLARSHIP / CAN UNEARTH THE WHOLE OFFENCE / FROM LUTHER UNTIL NOW / THAT HAS DRIVEN A CULTURE MAD

It can be argued that the entire oeuvre of Aranye Fradenburg has been concerned with this sort of courage for "more life rather than less" (with all of its attendant risks, its sufferings as well as its joys), and with the sort of *queer* work that Foucault called for—this "techne" or disciplining of the self as a "beautiful and good work"—and moreover, with this *care* of the self, and thus her work, "composed of eros and dust," has served as a sort of lighthouse for Auden's "affirming flame."[4] This work (this *career*) culminates now in *Staying Alive*, a book that can be described in précis as an elegant and erudite defense of the humanities (and more largely, of the public university, with all of its ruly and unruly knowledge disciplines) as the very site *par excellence* of the practices of the care of the self, and of *other selves* (for Fradenburg, as literary-historical scholar *and* psychoanalyst, attends more than Foucault ever did to the arts of intersubjectivity and therapeutic care that contribute to a more general *eudaimonia*, or flourishing). This is to speak, as Fradenburg does here and elsewhere, of the university as reservoir and generator of styles of living and selves (and groups) as works of art and desiring-assemblages (ever contingent packs and multiplicities, always on the move, and creating "break-flows out of which desire" continuously pours forth),[5] without which, our lives (intellectual *and* personal, and who can tell the difference sometimes?) would be vastly impoverished.

Indeed, there has been no voice within premodern studies more insistent on the subject of the ways in which disciplinarity, desire, enjoyment, work, groupification, and care of the self intersect in always risky (and even melancholy), yet necessary and productive fashion, and with the ways in which aesthetics, signifying, intersubjectivity (intimate *and* ex-

---

[4] From W.H. Auden, "September 1, 1939": "Defenseless under the night / Our world in stupor lies; / Yet, dotted everywhere, / Ironic points of light / Flash out wherever the Just /Exchange their messages: / May I, composed like them / Of Eros and of dust, / Beleaguered by the same / Negation and despair, / Show an affirming flame" (Auden 1979, 95–97).

[5] Deleuze and Guattari 1983, 37.

timate), and self- and world-building are importantly enmeshed. Fradenburg's work has never been just about medieval studies, although it may appear as such to some—rather, it has always concerned itself with living and enduring, with creaturely attachments to meaning-making as a form of thriving and flourishing, as well as with the ways in which institutional and disciplinary life (university life) are bound up with desires that are "unaccountable" and "always on the move" (Fradenburg 2002b, 64), despite all of the attempts of the university's managerial technocrats (and methodologically uptight scholars) to say otherwise. Fradenburg insists that we can never fully know ourselves (personally or institutionally), and therefore unknowing becomes (*has* to become) an important component of *what we do in here*. In this sense, Fradenburg's entire body of work fleshes out what Geoffrey Bennington has claimed (by way of Derrida) is the primary work of the University—that it has "a responsibility to foster events of thought that cannot fail to unsettle the University in its Idea of itself" (Bennington 2010, 28; see also Derrida 2002). Indeed, the future (our personal futures, our group futures, our institutional futures) is not really possible without *not knowing for sure*, and as Fradenburg argues further,

> To be able to anticipate, plan, project a future or into a future, we have to *not* know for sure, because we have to suspend judgment even while exercising it, knowing that we don't know (everything). Ethics—and ultimately psychoanalysis—emerges from a willing of this suspension, a paradoxical knowing of non-knowing. (Fradenburg 2009, 96; my emphasis)

Fradenburg's work is, *pace* Bennington, an "event of thought" that draws important attention to "the contingency and changefulness of living" (Fradenburg 2011a, 596), and outside of premodern studies, her thinking and writing sits alongside the work of theorists such as Lauren Berlant whose work pays important attention to "the *emotional time* of being-with, time where it is possible to value floundering around with others whose attention-paying to what's happening is generous and makes live-ness possible as a good, not a threat" (Berlant 2011, 85–86).[6]

Refusing to jettison loose and fuzzy pleasures in favor of a supposedly austerely rigorous disciplinarity (where one opts for supposedly objective truths over subjective, or increasingly, intersubjective feelings and pleasures) and vice versa, Fradenburg has insisted in her work, over and over again, that enjoyment and disciplinarity have a critical relationship, one that we who are situated within the university decouple at our peril. As she wrote in her book *Sacrifice Your Love: Psychoanalysis, Historicism, Chaucer,*

> Discipline does not teach us the identity of pleasure with the good; rather, it drags desire out into the open, pours gasoline on it, and sets it on fire, which is why it so easily becomes desire's object as well as its means. (Fradenburg 2002b, 7)

For Fradenburg, the "passional and technical coincide in the register of our *jouissance*," and most importantly, discipline "enhances *jouissance*; it multiples and extends its

---

[6] I would note here, too, as an aside, that Fradenburg's more recent focus on the ways in which scientific method and the humanistic arts of interpretation, as she writes in this volume, "actually enhance one another (in practical as well as theoretical ways)," admirably takes up Abraham Maslow's call in the 1960s for "rehumanizing (and trans-humanizing) science" and for biology to "shake itself loose from a pure physical-chemical re-ductiveness" (Maslow 1966, ii). Indeed, what *Staying Alive* demonstrates is that, more recently, the sciences themselves, such as neuroscience, are "now establishing, however (at times) unintentionally, the importance of artistic and humanist train-ing to mental functioning."

possibilities, its potential for the remaking of identities" (Fradenburg 2002b, 252, 7).[7] Put another way, desire and the sorts of passions and compulsions that lead to certain intensely ecstatic experiences are integral to the work of the academy, which often does not admit the importance of (disorganized) subjective life to its "proper objects" of study. I use the term "disorganized" here purposefully, and have lifted it from Lauren Berlant's essay "Starved" (cited above), where Berlant writes that what we are "starved" for right now (in social life) is not necessarily sex or romantic intimacy, but something *like sex*, or *like affect*—in short, "the collaborative risk of a shared disorganization" (Berlant 2011, 86). We might reflect, too, that the university is one important form of social life—it is not just a place where we study, think, and develop knowledge apart from our "real lives." The university *is* a form of life, a *habitus*, and we live (and desire and agonize) there with others. As Donna Beth Ellard writes in this volume, the university can sometimes "feel as inaccessible as a luxury estate in Montecito," yet Fradenburg's work here in this volume "offers theory and praxis for staying alive, personally and professionally, by encouraging living practices that double as reading practices."

Within the setting of the university, with its disciplines that often jostle against and compete with each other for ever-dwindling resources, and within specific disciplines themselves, where different groups of scholars often square off against each other over methodological and other divides,

---

[7] In *Sacrifice Your Love*, Fradenburg defines *jouissance* (an almost unbearable intensity that is also a transgressive excess of pleasure) this way: "*Jouissance* is the point at which pleasure and pain crisscross, when there are no more objects, and the only thing left for desire to desire is the unknowable beyond of insentience. With the loss of its objects, the *I* also loses its self-presence—or, at least, the vulnerability of its self-presence becomes felt experience. Pleasure protects us from *jouissance* by delivering as much *jouissance* as the *I* can bear and still be there to bear it" (Fradenburg 2002b, 18).

Fradenburg's thinking becomes vitally important for seeing how

> [g]roup desire makes what we call knowledge. *There is*
> *no other kind of knowledge than this; this is what*
> *knowledge is and we make it.* It is neither illusory
> nor objective; it is an artifact, carefully crafted,
> tested, debated, within groups, between groups,
> over time, and across cultures. (Fradenburg 2002b,
> 10; her emphasis)

Because of the ways in which Fradenburg has always insisted on the productive (if also agonistic) enmeshment of
desire and discipline, I catch in her writings an echo with
Jonathan Lear's argument, in "Eros and Unknowing" (a
beautiful reading of Plato's *Symposium*), that we should
not, in our intellectual life, "leave the human realm behind," but should

> get deeper into it—its smells, feels, textures, and
> the imaginary feelings we give to them. Whatever
> 'higher' or 'deeper' meanings there may be, they
> do not transcend human life, but lie immanent in
> it. The body, its drives, and the bodily expression
> of mind all lend vitality to 'higher' mental func-
> tions and to social life. It is to this particular sub-
> jectivity with which we are pregnant; and it is from
> this that we give birth in beauty. (Lear 1998, 166)

As Fradenburg herself has more recently argued, "The
embodied, and therefore affective, nature of cognition is
not a figment of the psychoanalytic imagination, but is
asserted everywhere in contemporary neuroscience." As
to beauty, and its importance, "[a]esthetic form is a spell-
binding (or not) attempt to transmit and circulate affect,
without which not much happens at all" (Fradenburg
2010, 66). Further, aesthetic experience "is grounded in,
indeed is the ground of, 'attachment,' and we do not be-

come 'human' without it" (Fradenburg 2010, 67).

In addition to demonstrating, throughout her work, the ways in which knowledge is shaped by the continual (and risky) dance between enjoyment (affect, feeling, and drive) and discipline (the rigors and constraints of study and work), especially with relation to the work of the signifier and signification (the primary *matter* of the humanities, but also of the biological sciences),[8] Fradenburg's work has also everywhere affirmed (perhaps in a lighter mood) the importance of play, over necessity, as the mother of invention (see, for example, Fradenburg 2011a, 597), where "[p]lay is about signifying and therefore about becoming," and becoming "in turn is about process, in particular about processes of transformation of states of mind and body" (Fradenburg 2011b, 57). Further,

> Interpretation and relationality depend on one another because all relationships are unending processes of interpretation and expression, listening and signifying. In turn, sentience assists relationality: we can't thrive and probably can't survive without minds open to possibility, capable of sensing and interpreting the tiniest shifts in, e.g., pitch and tone. (Fradenburg 2011a, 602)

Ultimately, "[p]lasticity, stylistics, enrichment are not embellishments of living process but are inherent in it" (Fradenburg 2011b, 45), and thus the humanities play an important role in helping us to develop certain arts of living and aliveness that not only allow us to want *more*

---

[8] As Fradenburg puts it in *Sacrifice Your Love*, "our *jouissance* extends itself by means of the signifier's power to (re)distribute life and death" (Fradenburg 2002b, 63). And in "Living Chaucer" she reminds us that, "scientific signifiers have the same wayward intersubjective, intertextual, intergenerational lives as do 'literary' signifiers" (Fradenburg 2011b, 47).

rather than *less* life, but also help us to develop a repertoire for what Sara Ahmed has called "the politics of the
hap," which is "about opening up possibilities for being in
other ways, of *being perhaps*," and about working "toward
a world in which things can happen in alternative ways"
(Ahmed 2010, 222; my emphasis). This is a critically important project in an era where neoliberal capital turns
our dreams and other forms of resistance into commodities in the space of a nanosecond, and where our every
move is surveyed, digitized, and sold as data to whoever
wants to purchase the information necessary to plot our
moves in advance of our arrival at desires we no longer
own. Should the university not be, on some level, a haven
for resistance to such techno-capture of every aspect of
our lives? Will success (and happiness) only be measured
by the dollars we pile up and the gadgets for distraction
we accumulate, or shall we wish, rather, for a laboratory-
imaginarium in which one's life (and all of knowledge)
undergoes processes of invention and re-invention (without end) in the company of like-minded seekers who value surprise and unsettlement over certain answers? Such
is one image, for me, of an ideal university, and while few
would argue that the university today is not broken in
some sense (it is not ideal, in other words, in Fradenburg's or anyone else's terms), as Michael Snediker writes
in this volume, Fradenburg's emphasis on "our swerving
attention to the fuzzy world we're making takes some
sting out of this being the case."

It is important to note here as well that, for Fradenburg, the university—and the humanities, more particularly—is a *shared*, intersubjective project, and the signifier
(for example, poetry) has played no little part in a form of
sociability (and even companionability) that is critical for
self-transformation and progressive social change: "symbols enable living process" and what "enables us to risk
change is the feeling that we are understood and (there-

fore) accompanied" (Fradenburg 2011b, 45, 60).[9] As Fradenburg has argued in many places, play and shared attention are so important to so many species, including humans, that they may even be an end in themselves, and this is something the humanities and sciences have in common that they do not always readily acknowledge or *see*. As Ruth Evans explains about Fradenburg's method in this volume, "[i]t's not a choice between a scientific explanation on the one hand and a semiotic one on the other; we need both." We might call this sort of play and shared ludic attention *learning*, or the university: the endless (playful, but also at times, sorrowful) processes we must commit ourselves to, with their open-ended and poetic and rowdy mutliplicity of perspectives, and their cultivation of the non-utilitarian arts of life, which may have more to do with personal and social well-being than we have previously imagined. Or, as Daniel Remein writes in this volume, "Many artifacts indeed do represent, or mimic, or encode—but some ornaments just decorate, an appointment for which they are no less needful in the physical wonder of sentience." For these, and many other reasons, Fradenburg's work has long hailed us to a cross-temporal pedagogical-artistic project that asks us, not just to innovate our scholarship accordingly, but to reclaim the humanities itself as the site of desire and knowledge, of care and attachment, of new relational modes, and thus, of love itself. Put another way, her work creates a space similar to the meeting-places of the cities of ancient philosophy, such as the banquet hall in Plato's

---

[9] It should be noted here as well that the longest possible historical perspectives upon processes of signification (such as those crafted by Fradenburg in her work as a premodernist) are critical, for as she has also written, "Signifiers are remarkably mutable, but they can also be very persistent—and persistent does not mean timeless. Signifiers enable repetitions, revivals, and resurgences; they mark the spot where things have gone missing, hence where we begin to look for them (again)" (Fradenburg 2009, 89).

Symposium, which "are the sites of a metaphysical sociability sympathetic to the beneficent madness of love"
(Bersani 2008, 81).

DEFENCELESS UNDER THE NIGHT / OUR WORLD IN STUPOR
LIES; / YET, DOTTED EVERYWHERE, / IRONIC POINTS OF
LIGHT FLASH OUT

The three terms most richly productive (and ubiquitous)
in Fradenburg's work of the past fifteen or so years—even
as she has moved from a focus on literary narrative and
poetics (especially Chaucer) and on "discontinuist" histories (national, courtly, aesthetic, sexual, queer, psychoanalytic, and so on) to what I would call a more public
intellectual mode of writing about the arts more broadly,
under the aegis of various neuro-cognitive, biological,
anthropological, and psychoanaytic discourses and practices[10]—are probably (and as elaborated above) desire,
discipline, and *jouissance* (with various associated terms
never far behind, such as love, enjoyment, wonder, beauty, excess, sublimity, feeling, sentience, affect, violence,
pain, anxiety, loss, separation, suffering, trauma, and

---

[10] Although it has to be noted here that Fradenburg's longstanding romance and companionship with Chaucer never ends, and
as she wrote in her recent essay "Beauty and Boredom in the
Legend of Good Women," much of her work has been concerned
with seeing more clearly the tragic side of Chaucer's work, while
also attending to its therapeutic comedy (Fradenburg 2010, 74;
see also Fradenburg 1999). This resonates with Fradenburg's
own writings which, although resolutely insistent on the necessity of enjoyment, feeling, pleasure, and aliveness (on, frankly,
refusing to let go of our desires or to have them "disciplined"
away by various Others, to stop moving—which is to say, to stop
living), are also everywhere suffused with the notice and marks
of melancholic longing, "angsting," the various endangerments
of vulnerability, and the spectres of loss, mourning, and death.
Her work thus possesses a dark and complex beauty that (thankfully) does not lend itself to easy calculations. See, especially, in
this vein, Fradenburg (2009).

death, among others), which in turn are always related to "techniques of living" (Fradenburg 2002b, 4, 9). In essence, no matter which text of hers we might be reading, Fradenburg seems to be always talking about something she says more explicitly in "Group Time: Catastrophe, Periodicity, Survival," where she wrote that "enjoyment is the matrix of knowledge, and knowledge is not diminished thereby." Further, "Interpretation and explanation are activities central to libidinal structuration and vice versa. . . . We thereby reclaim our technical work [the humanities, for example] as the work of desire, and desire as that which makes the world" (Fradenburg 2002a, 232).[11]

There is probably no better introduction than the lines cited above to the current work you are now holding in your hands (or viewing on a retina or liquid display screen), which joins a growing body of work on the state(s) of the University, best described as critical self-reflections and public intellectual polemics on the state(s) of higher education by those who know it very well from firsthand experience, either as tenured professors, college administrators, adjunct instructors, or graduate students and members of the ever-growing academic precariat[12]

---

[11] In this respect, I see real affinities and important (heretofore un-noted) linkages between Fradenburg's thinking and that of Jane Bennett in her book *The Enchantment of Modern Life* (2001), especially with regard to Bennett's argument in that work that the will to social justice is "sustained by periodic bouts of being enamored with existence." Further, "[a]ffective fascination with a world thought to be worthy of it may help to ward off the existential resentment that plagues mortals, that is, the sense of victimization that recurrently descends upon the tragic (or absurd or incomplete) beings called human." Ultimately, for Bennett, "one of the tasks proper to ethics is to enjoy the world" (Bennett 2001, 12, 13).

[12] Aaron Bady springs most notably to mind in this latter category—see his collected writings at his zunguzungu blog at *The New Inquiry*: http://thenewinquiry.com/blogs/zunguzungu/—although it

(occasionally critiques of the university also come from think tanks and policy institutes, mainstream journalism, cultural criticism, and the like). These reflections can be narrow-mindedly conservative—Allan Bloom's *The Closing of the American Mind* (1987) and Dinesh D'Souza's *Illiberal Education* (1991) spring to mind, as does David Horwitz's *The Professors: The 101 Most Dangerous Academics in America* (2006)—or they can be more progressively liberal, such as Marc Bousquet's *How the University Works* (2008), which addresses labor inequities in higher education; Derek Bok's *Universities in the Marketplace* (2003), which outlines the commercialization of the university and its disciplines; Christopher Newfield's *Unmaking the Public University* (2011), which shows how unequal access to higher education for Americans is a result of conservative campaigns to thwart the university's democratizing functions; and Benjamin Ginsberg's *The Fall of the Faculty* (2011), which demonstrates the detriments to higher education that have been caused by the rise of "all-administrative" universities, just to name some of the more notable examples of the past ten or so years.[13]

The most compelling and philosophically provocative work in this vein up until now, for me, has been Bill Readings' *The University in Ruins* (published two years after Readings' untimely death in 1994), partly because it offers a vision of a university-to-come (or an always un-

---

should be noted that in the past five or so years there has been a veritable explosion of weblogs authored by graduate students and post-grads, contingent faculty, and members of the academic precariat that are focused on what might be called the ills and travails of higher education and the increasing lack of equitable access to the university, whether as student or faculty member.

[13] And in the vein of horrifically depressing accounts of the dismantling of public higher education, by way of the UK system, especially in terms of access, quality of instruction, and research funding, see McGettigan (2013), and for the implications of what is happening in the UK for US system, see Newfield's (2013) review of McGettigan's book.

realized-yet-possible institution) that I feel I can believe in and work on behalf of, and with which Fradenburg's current work has no little solidarity. In his book, Readings argued that, partly due to certain processes of transnational globalization, whereby "the rule of the cash nexus" has replaced "the notion of national identity as a determinant in all aspects of social life," the University (capitalized to indicate its historical status as an idealized institution) has become a "transnational bureaucratic corporation" and "the centrality of the traditional humanistic disciplines to the life of the University is no longer assured" (Readings 1996, 3). Because "the grand narrative of the University, centered on the production of a liberal, reasoning subject, is no longer available to us," it is "no longer the case that we can conceive the University within the historical horizon of its self-realization" (Readings 1996, 9, 5). Readings prefers the term "post-historical" over "postmodern" for the contemporary University, "in order to insist on the sense that the institution has outlived itself, is now a survivor of the era in which it defined itself in terms of the project of the *historical* development, affirmation, and inculcation of national culture" (Readings 1996, 6; his emphasis). Ultimately, the University is "a *ruined* institution, one that lost its historical *raison d'etre*," but which nevertheless "opens up a space in which it is possible to think the notion of community otherwise, without recourse to notions of unity, consensus, and communication" (Readings 1996, 19, 20; his emphasis). This is a space, moreover, where the University "becomes one site among others where the question of being-together is raised, raised with an urgency that proceeds from the absence of the institutional forms (such as the nation-state), which have historically served to mask that question" (Readings 1996, 20).

Indeed, the University, however "ruined," must strive, in Readings' view, toward building a "community that is not made up of subjects but *singularities*": this community would not be "organic in that its members do not share an immanent identity to be revealed," and it would not be "directed toward the production of a universal subject of history, to the cultural realization of an essential human nature" (Readings 1996, 185). Rather, this would be a community "of dissensus that presupposes nothing in common," and that "would seek to make its heteronomy, its differences, more complex" (Readings 1996, 190). In this scenario, the post-historical University would be "where thought takes place beside thought, where thinking is a shared process without identity or unity"—this is ultimately "a dissensual process; it belongs to dialogism rather than to dialogue," and instead of a new interdisciplinary space that would reunify the increasingly fragmented disciplines, there would be a "shifting disciplinary structure that holds open the question of whether and how thoughts fit together" (Readings 1996, 192).

Readings' thinking accords well with Derrida's in his essay "The University Without Condition," where Derrida argued for a "new humanities" and "unconditional university" that would "remain an ultimate place of critical resistance—and more than critical—to all the powers of dogmatic and unjust appropriation" (Derrida 2002, 204). This unconditional university, further, would provide harbor for "the principal right to say everything, even if it be under the heading of fiction and the experimentation of knowledge, and the right to say it publicly, to publish it" (Derrida 2002, 205). The humanities would have a privileged place in this unconditional university, because the very principle of unconditionality "has an originary and privileged place of *presentation*, of manifestation, of safekeeping in the Humanities. It has there its space of discussion and reelaboration as well" (Derrida 2002, 207).

Although Readings' argument in *The University in Ruins* has been subject to carefully considered counter-critique,[14] it remains today, I would argue, a powerful

---

[14] See, for example, LaCapra (1998), where he argues that the

spur to thought and action for those of us working within or on behalf of the public university who are concerned with the future of humanistic teaching and scholarship, and with the increasing numbers of persons who are being treated as the "bare life" of the academy—our non-tenure-track instructors, for example, but also our students. These are also the lives for which we must "take care." While Readings gave us a highly trenchant critique of the ways in which the American university has become a transnational bureaucratic-managerial corporation, thus disrupting and weakening the role of traditional humanistic disciplines (and we might pause to consider how prescient he was), more importantly, he also suggested ways in which this situation might (perversely? positively?) open new (heterotopic and post-historical) spaces "in which it is possible to think the notion of community otherwise": this community would not be "organic in that its members do not share an immanent identity to be revealed," and it would not be "directed toward the production of a universal subject of history, to the cultural realization of an essential human nature" (Readings 1996, 185). One might argue (and I will) that Readings' ultimate hope for the University as a space in which the question of "being-together" and disciplinarity itself would be permanently en-

---

contemporary American academy is not as much a "transnational bureaucratic corporation" as it "is based on a systematic, schizoid division between a market model and a model of corporate solidarity and collegial responsibility" (LaCapra 1998, 32). Further, LaCapra argues that Readings' insistence on the fact that "the older ideals of culture, *Bildung*, the liberal subject-citizen, and the nation-state are no longer relevant" in the contemporary academy belies the fact, in LaCapra's view, that these things were always phantasms or idealizations, "made to cover a much more complex and changing constellation of forces that varied with nation, region, and group" (LaCapra 1998, 38, 39). LaCapra also wonders, "with respect to the present," if "culture, ideology, and the nation-state are as evacuated or obsolete as Readings believes" (39). See also Royle (1999) and LaCapra (1999).

tangled and left purposefully open and unsettled, and where we would work to make our heteronomic differences more complex, has never really been put into serious practice. It would be too open-ended, of course, too experimental, risky, and perhaps, non-practical (and really messy in terms of administration), and yet, nothing strikes me as so necessary. Happily, Fradenburg's new work takes up the mantle of Readings' hope and extends it with important new research and reflection on the importance of the humanities' role in the arts of intersubjectivity so critical for making anything happen at all, and for a vision of the university as a shared (if dissensual) enterprise.

A lot has happened since Readings' book was published—his critique certainly appears dead-accurate and the "ruinous" situation he sketched, especially in terms of the university's corporate-managerial structure and the concomitant assaults on the humanities, has intensified. And since the financial crises of 2008 onward, the idea (long-valued) that the university should be an important public (and publicly-funded) concern, especially for its vital role in securing various forms of social egalitarianism and a broad-based meritocracy for the greatest numbers of persons possible (not to mention, in order to enhance cognitive and technical innovations of all varieties, for the pure advancement of knowledge and practices of making, regardless of cost-based outcomes), no longer appears to be either viable or what might be termed a common concern. All across the country, states are slashing university budgets and expecting institutions of higher education to figure out more and more ways to pay for themselves, and to be "profitable," whatever that might mean—MOOCs, or Massive Open Online Courses, are one prominent and lamentable outcome of this type of thinking (see, for example, Bady 2013a). This may be an oversimplification (because I can't do justice in this Prelude to all of the myriad examples in Fradenburg's book, which itself supplies plenty), but let's just say that the foregoing state of affairs has led to all sorts of jockeying within the university today to both winnow down and/or eliminate disciplines that appear non-utilitarian or to dress up traditionally philosophical disciplines (such as literary studies) in more utilitarian and applications-based clothing. In addition, protocols of oversight and accountability have intensified to the point of leaving faculty little time and room to actually do the work they were hired to do: teach and research and mentor, and direct and innovate their own curricula and disciplinary collaborations. Most harmful of all, and in direct proportion to the budget-slashing maneuvers of state legislatures (and the dearth of progressive federal amelioration of such), tuition and student debt levels are at unsustainably crippling levels, and the ranks of tenure-track faculty have shrunk to something around thirty percent of all teaching positions (see, for example, June 2012 and Editors 2012).

The university system in the state of California, where Fradenburg works as a professor of English, clinical psychoanalyst, and educational activist, has represented an important battleground in this current situation, partly because the state's economic woes have been so severe since 2008 (and more importantly, because of Governor Jerry Brown's and former UC President Mark Yudof's dismantling of the UC Master Plan, whereby all eligible California citizens had been entitled to a place within the University of California, regardless of means),[15] but also because the state has long been internationally admired for its public research institutions (their quality and also their broad access) and also has a long and enduring history of faculty and student activism on behalf of the notion of a free, open, democratic, and public university.[16] Fraden-

---

[15] See "Brown and Yudof Bail on the Master Plan," *KeepCaliforniasPromise.org*, July 1, 2012: http://keepcaliforniaspromise.org /2628/brown-and-yudof-bail-on-the-master-plan.

[16] See, for recent examples, Bady (2013b), Michael Meranze and Christopher Newfield's blog *Remaking the University* (http://

burg herself has long been an outspoken activist on behalf
of the public humanities (and against administrative mal-
feasance in all of its guises), but she has been extremely
busy since 2008 helping to organize and lead critical and
activist interventions within the UC system: she founded
the group 'Saving UCSB' and organized a faculty walkout
at UC-Santa Barbara in 2009, and among many other
activities too numerous to mention here, she is a tireless
letter writer and public speaker on behalf of academic
freedom, the value of the humanities, and the importance
of open access to public higher education.

Thus we are fortunate that Fradenburg has decided to
devote an entire monograph, *Staying Alive*, to an insight-
ful and laser-like diagnosis of the various neoliberal and
technocratic forces currently assailing and undermining
the public university, and to a fierce polemic on behalf of
the humanities as *the* critical site for fostering forms of
artfulness critical to the future of the keeping open of the
question of our "being-together," both within the institution and outside of it. And she has generously decided to
publish it with an open-access and para-academic press
(punctum books), because she agrees (thankfully) that
work within the humanities, and especially public intellectual work, needs to have the widest purchase possible
upon the public commons and should not be kept locked
behind corporatized and other paywalls. And in the spirit
of collaboration that we at punctum and the BABEL
Working Group certainly hold dear, she has crafted the
book to include companion "fugue" essays by myself (this
Prelude), Donna Beth Ellard, Ruth Evans, Julie Orlemanski, Daniel C. Remein, and Michael D. Snediker, so that

---

utotherescue.blogspot.com/), Robert Samuels's blog *Changing
Universities* (http://changinguniversities.blogspot.com/), and California
Scholars for Academic Freedom (http://cascholars4academicfreedom.
wordpress.com/), just to cite a few examples of UC's robust
student and faculty advocacy and activism on behalf of the public university.

the book is part-scholarly monograph, part-poetic-activist desiring-assemblage. The four chapters by Fradenburg can be read as a complete book (or "monograph"), and they can be read individually as stand-alone, broadsheet-style polemics. Each "fugue" chapter can be read in tandem with the chapter by Fradenburg to which it responds—a work in "two voices," as it were—or as a "flight" that "chases" after Fradenburg's thought, or as a well-lit "connecting passage" between the small yet expansive "rooms" (the "stanzas") of her writing (all associated meanings of "fugue," in music and beyond). Similar to what Deleuze and Guattari said about their work together, "Since each of us was several, there was already quite a crowd. . . . We have been aided, inspired, multiplied" (Deleuze and Guattari 1987, 3, 4). Again, this book is "an assemblage. It has nothing to do with ideology. There is no ideology and never has been" (Deleuze and Guattari 1987, 5). Rather, this is a (loving) labor of becoming-world.

Ultimately, and as outlined in detail above, *Staying Alive*—as a labor of public intellectual advocacy for the humanities, and the public university more largely—does not represent a departure for Fradenburg's oeuvre, for she has always been concerned with defining and valuing the work (and importantly, the *jouissance*) of the liberal arts against the "order[s] of utility." To briefly revisit her book *Sacrifice Your Love*, in the Epilogue to that work, Fradenburg discussed the importance of resisting, from within the humanities, the "utilitarian rhetorics that sustain the *jouissance* of capitalism," and she urged us to take up

the question of the *jouissance* of the academy, rather than assuming it is our task to discipline *jouissance* out of the academy. For one thing, we cannot discipline *jouissance* out of the academy, because discipline is always permeated with enjoyment. So why give ground on our enjoyment? (Fradenburg 2002b, 247)

Why, indeed? In fact, in her more recent forays into cognitive studies, animal behavioral research, neuroscience, evolutionary biology, biosemiotics, and the like (all of which disciplines inform the arguments of this book, along with psychoanalysis and literary-historical analysis, and cultural critique), Fradenburg has amassed an incredible body of scientific and other evidence for why we should not only *not* "give ground" on this enjoyment (with all of its positive *and* negative implications—i.e., enjoyment is a messy affair but no less necessary for life as a result), but also for the ways in which living itself is an art and the humanities provide the deepest reservoir of the non-utilitarian, excessive, ornamental artfulness so necessary, not just for surviving, but for thriving in this world. Contrary to recent polemics that simply urge the humanities to become more scientistic or technology-focused, to demonstrate their utility or even trophy their uselessness, *Staying Alive* does something remarkably different: it argues for the humanism of a new scientific paradigm based on complexity theory and holistic and ecological approaches to knowledge-making. It urges us to take the further step of realizing not only that we can promote and enhance neuroplastic connectivity and social-emotional cognition, but also that the humanities have always already been doing so. In this sense, Fradenburg's work and thought exemplifies what Michael O'Rourke has called a queerly "roguish relationality" that is open to "an infinite series of [disciplinary] encounters," which is also an opening to futurity (O'Rourke 2006, 36).

As Fradenburg writes in this volume, "Nature always exceeds itself in its expressivity"—which is to say artfulness is necessary for adaptation and innovation, for forging rich and varied relationships with other minds, bodies and things, and thus, again, for thriving—whether in the boardroom or the art gallery, the biology lab or the recording studio, the alley or the playground, the book or the dream. Bringing together psychoanalysis, science, aesthetics, and premodern literature (from Virgil to Chaucer to Shakespeare), Fradenburg offers a bracing polemic against the technocrats of higher education and a vibrant new vision for the humanities as both living art and new life science. For me, especially, the book matters so profoundly, because—even if not overtly—it takes up and further exemplifies the necessity of Bill Readings' vision of the university as a critical site for play, for non-utilitarian experimentation, for keeping knowledge unsettled, where, in Readings' words (again), "thinking is a shared process without identity or unity." And it further exemplifies the case for the critical value of the type(s) of intersubjectivity crafted through artful processes of signification that I really believe are the only route out of the greed, selfishness, fear of the Other, and violence that currently grips our world. And thus Fradenburg's work also shares with Leo Bersani a deep and abiding investment in the question of whether the work of art might be able to "deploy signs of the subject in the world that are not signs of interpretation or of an object-destroying *jouissance*, signs of . . . correspondences of forms within a universal solidarity of being" (Bersani 2010, 142).

What this book also demonstrates—along with the important body of work known as "university studies" that this book now joins—is that those of us who work within the humanities must commit some of our most valuable resources (primarily, our always-encroached-upon time, and some part of our inner emotional lives) to academic activism, whether through letter writing, blog polemics, organized protests and strikes, collectivist agitation and intervention, mutual aid initiatives, and books such as these. We cannot just bide our time within the university, hoping things will get better, or even assuming they will ("all storms pass" is what many people seem to believe). The powers-that-be always want you to be patient and wait for things they never intend to give you (Martin Luther King Jr.'s "Letter From Birmingham Jail" never ceases to be instructive on this point). As long as we have shelter of any kind, and are willing to make room in that shelter for those more vulnerable than we are, there is no reason to wait. Do we want to know what kind of university we want? Let us simply enunciate our institutional and disciplinary desires, as this book does, and in makeshift shelters. We are in Lear's company now, and we have to seize hold of the university—as an institution, but also as a *public trust*—as our concern, and we must be willing to fight for that concern. As Julie Orlemanski writes in her contribution to this volume,

> Academic-activist writings not only deliver dispatches from the numerous battlegrounds of higher education. They also call upon those who care to read them—those who might defend the institutional homes of speculation, imagination, and historical understanding. These writings are the communiques that circulate within the "army of lovers" and also pass beyond them, to unpresupposed outposts and new readers. . . . mobilizing reflections about learning in the present.

THE SPACE IN WHICH WE LIVE, WHICH DRAWS US OUT OF OURSELVES, IN WHICH THE EROSION OF OUR LIVES, OUR TIME AND OUR HISTORY OCCURS, THE SPACE THAT CLAWS AND GNAWS AT US . . . A HETEROGENEOUS SPACE

In some sense, this book constructs what Hakim Bey called a "temporary autonomous zone": a site where some of us might gather (as authors and readers, friends and strangers, teachers and students, lovers and fighters) to practice our work as rogue agents in search of new means for the development of a certain institutional *amour fou* and "clockless nowever," a "politics of dream, urgent as the blueness of the sky" (Bey 1985). The fact of the matter is—whether we inhabit student desks, tenure lines, adjunct positions, or post-/never-graduate, somewhere-other-than-here positions—now might be the time to take a bit more seriously the development of new and alternative spaces (both within and without the university) for learning, for inquiry, and for knowledge-culture production. It turns out (and didn't we already know this?) that the future actually has to be constructed, and let's remind ourselves that this is the work of the present, and we need to enlarge our scope of collaboration beyond our specific institutions (if we have institutional homes), beyond our disciplines, beyond our so-called position and rank (faculty vs. adjunct, professor vs. student, etc.), and beyond the University proper. The real University should comprise everyone who wants to be a part of it, whether or not they have an official position or desk. And it will be in this work—the present-ing of the future, the future-ing of the present—that we will *manifest* ourselves. For this volume of Fradenburg's is also a collective manifesto, and it is to manifesting ourselves (making ourselves *more present* to each other, which is to also say, more *responsible* to each other) in some sort of collective endeavor that works on behalf of the future without laying any possessive claims upon it, that we might craft new spaces for the University-at-large, which is also a University that *wanders*, that is never just *some*where, dwelling in the partitive—*of* a particular place—but rather, seeks to be everywhere, always on the move, pandemic, uncontainable, and yes, precarious, always at risk, while always being *present/between us* (manifest). At the same time, we insist on perversely-hopefully laying claim to specific institutions and subject areas—the University of California, or premodern studies, for example—as collocations of objects and trajectories of thought that we desire to hold *close* to us, while also placing them in certain perpetual tensions with everything else (even ourselves).

Manifestos can be hackneyed, and even dangerous, especially when they assume a ground-clearing maneuver (i.e., whatever exists now must be destroyed to make way for the new), but I think we increasingly need them, because they help us to outline our commitments and desires in a writerly action that *presences* those commitments and desires. That is Step 1. Step 2 would be doing something about it, and here again Fradenburg's career, as scholar, public intellectual, and activist, is exemplary. In the manifesto (albeit, the manifesto that does not desire the violence of erasing the past or the Other), we express in an always-fleeting yet still phenomenologically palpable present a radical form of desire that seeks an alteration of the status quo, and while the manifesto often looks silly and hyperbolic and always unaware of the demise of its (vain?) hopes in the future (the retrospective-melancholic view), there is something *sincere* about it. It presents a radical opening to (or window upon) the risk of a fragile yet necessary honesty. We could do worse than to be honest with each other. We could do worse than to actually want things that we haven't been told in advance to want. This is also a matter of contributing to the political imaginary that some believe is withering away (see, for example, Srnicek and Williams 2013 and Wark 2013). This volume is an important contribution, I want to argue, to the political imaginary.

* * *

Is it possible that "heterotopia" might be one term (or route) by which to rethink the space of the university as both "closed" and productively "open" to alternative knowledge practices, inventive lives, and new relational modes that would allow us to *take care*—of ourselves, of others, and of this fragile institution we call a university, that has no little relation to the world? For Foucault, who coined the term, a heterotopia (which might be a psychiatric hospital, a cemetery, a mirror, a theater, a colony, a museum, a brothel, a library, a garden, and I will say, a university) "is capable of juxtaposing in a single real space several spaces, several sites that are themselves incompatible," and thus opens onto "heterochrony" (Foucault 1986, 25, 26). Further, heterotopias "always presuppose a system of opening and closing that both isolates them," but also "makes them penetrable" (Foucault 1986, 26). The university seems an apt example in Foucault's schema, for it both exists apart (in some important respects) from the nations, provinces, and cities within which it resides, as a sort of independent "colony," and also comprises within itself separate spheres, or little other worlds—departments, schools, disciplines, and the like. In addition, because of its geographical placement, often either directly within urban centers or adjacent to them, and also its public functions, the university is somewhat permeable to the Outside, while also performing certain gatekeeping functions (these are lamentable, I might add). It is both set apart, comprising its own miniature heteroverses, and also woven into the fabric of the polis, which it reflects, like a cracked mirror.

Perhaps, like Foucault's favorite example of a heterotopia, the ship—even the pirate ship—the university might be reconceptualized as "a floating piece of space, a place without a place, that exists by itself, that is closed in on itself and at the same time is given over to the infinity of the sea and that, from port to port, from tack to tack, from brothel to brothel" goes in search of "the most precious treasures"—in short, the university as "the greatest reserve of the imagination," the heterotopia *par excellence*, without which, as Fradenburg demonstrates here in this volume, "dreams dry up, espionage takes the place of adventure, and the police take the place of pirates" (Foucault 1986, 27). In which case, let us set sail.

London and Washington, DC

REFERENCES

Ahmed, S. (2010). *The Promise of Happiness*. Durham: Duke University Press.

Auden, W.H. (1979). *Selected Poems: Expanded Edition*, ed. E. Mendelson. New York: Vintage Books.

Bady, A. (2013a). "The MOOC Moment and the End of Reform." *zunguzungu* [weblog], *The New Inquiry*, May 15: http://thenewinquiry.com/blogs/zunguzungu/the-mooc-mo ment-and -the-end-of-reform/.

Bady, A. (2013b). "Bartletby in the University of California: The Social Life of Disobedience." *zunguzungu* [weblog], *The New Inquiry*, May 3: http://thenewinquiry.com/blogs/zun guzungu/bartleby-in-the-university-of-california-the-social-life-of-disobedience/.

Bennett, J. (2001). *The Enchantment of Modern Life: Crossings, Attachments, Ethics*. Princeton: Princeton University Press.

Bennington, G. (2010). "Foundations." In *Not Half No End: Militantly Melancholic Essays in Memory of Jacques Derrida*, 19–34. Edinburgh: Edinburgh University Press.

Berlant, L. (2011). "Starved." In *After Sex? On Writing Since Queer Theory*, eds. Janet Halley and Andrew Parker, 79–90. Durham: Duke University Press.

Bersani, L. (2008). "The Power of Evil and the Power of Love." In L. Bersani and A. Phillips, *Intimacies*, 57–87. Chicago: University of Chicago Press.

Bersani, L. (2010). "Psychoanalysis and the Aesthetic Subject." In *Is The Rectum a Grave? And Other Essays*, 139–153.

Bey, H. (1985). *The Temporary Autonomous Zone, Ontological Anarchy, Poetic Terrorism*. Brooklyn: Autonomedia.

Davidson, A. (1994). "Ethics as Ascetics: Foucault, the History of Ethics, and Ancient Thought." In *The Cambridge Companion to Foucault*, ed. G. Gutting, 115–140. New York: Cambridge University Press.

Deleuze, G. (1986). *Foucault*, trans. S. Hand. Minneapolis: University of Minnesota Press.

Deleuze, G. and F. Guattari (1983). *Anti-Oedipus: Capitalism and Schizophrenia*, trans. R. Hurley, M. Seem, and H.R. Lane. Minneapolis: University of Minnesota Press.

Deleuze, G. and F. Guattari (1987). *A Thousand Plateaus: Capitalism and Schizophrenia*, trans. B. Massumi. Minneapolis: University of Minnesota Press.

Derrida, J. (2002). "The University Without Condition." In *Without Alibi*, ed. and trans. P. Kamuf, 202–237. Stanford: Stanford University Press.

Editors of *Speculations* and *continent*. (2012). "Discussions Before An Encounter." *continent*. 2.2: 136–147.

Foucault, M. (1985). *The Use of Pleasure, Volume 2: The History of Sexuality*, trans. R. Hurley. New York: Random House.

Foucault, M. (1986). "Of Other Spaces." *Diacritics* 16.1: 22–27.

Foucault, M. (1996a). "Friendship As a Way of Life." In *Foucault Live (Interviews, 1961-1984)*, ed. S. Lotringer, 308–312. New York: Semiotext(e), 1996.

Foucault, M. (1996b). "The Ethics of the Concern for Self as a Practice of Freedom." In *Foucault Live*, 432–449.

Foucault, M. (1999). *Religion and Culture*, ed. J.R. Carrette. New York: Routledge.

Foucault, M. (2001). *Fearless Speech*, ed. J. Pearson. Los Angeles: Semiotext(e).

Foucault, M. (2005). *The Hermeneutics of the Subject: Lectures at the Collège de France, 1981-82*, ed. A.I. Davidson, trans. G. Burchell. New York: Palgrave Macmillan.

Fradenburg, L.O. (1999). "'My Worldes Blisse': Chaucer's Tragedy of Fortune." *South Atlantic Quarterly* 98.3: 563–592.

Fradenburg, L.O.A. (2002a). "Group Time: Catastrophe, Survival, Periodicity." In *Time and the Literary*, eds. K. Newman, J. Clayton, and M. Hirsch, 211–238. New York: Routledge.

Fradenburg, L.O.A. (2002b). *Sacrifice Your Love: Psychoanalysis, Historicism, Chaucer*. Minneapolis: University of Minnesota Press.

Fradenburg, A. (2009). "(Dis)continuity: A History of Dreaming." In *The Post-Historical Middle Ages*, eds. Elizabeth Scala and Sylvia Frederico, 87–115. New York: Palgrave Macmillan.

Fradenburg, L.O.A. (2010). "Beauty and Boredom in *The Legend of Good Women*." *Exemplaria* 22.1: 65–83.

Fradenburg, A. (2011a). "FRONTLINE—The Liberal Arts of Psychoanalysis." *The Journal of the American Academy of Psychoanalysis and Dynamic Psychiatry* 39.4: 589–609.

Fradenburg, L.O.A. (2011b). "Living Chaucer." *Studies in the Age of Chaucer* 33: 41–64.

Glenn, J. (2009). "The Argonaut Folly." *HiLoBROW.com*, June 10: http://hilobrow.com/2009/06/10/argofolly-1/.

Halperin, D. (1995). *Saint Foucault: Toward a Gay Hagiography*. New York: Oxford University Press.

June, A.W. (2012). "Adjuncts Build Strength in Numbers." *The Chronicle of Higher Education*, November 5: http://chronicle.com/article/Adjuncts-Build-Strength-in/135520/.

LaCapra, D. (1998). "The University in Ruins?" *Critical Inquiry* 25: 32–55.

LaCapra, D. (1999). "Yes, Yes, Yes, Yes . . . Well, Maybe: Response to Nicholas Royle." *Critical Inquiry* 26: 154–158.

Lear, J. (1998). "Eros and Unknowing: The Psychoanalytic Significance of Plato's *Symposium*." In *Open Minded: Working Out the Logic of the Soul*, 148–166. Cambridge, MA: Harvard University Press.

Martin, L.H., H. Gutman, and P.H. Hutton, eds. (1988). *Technologies of the Self: A Seminar with Michel Foucault*. Amherst: University of Massachusetts Press.

Maslow, A. (1966). *The Psychology of Science: A Reconnaissance*. New York: Harper & Row.

McGettigan, A. (2013). *The Great University Gamble: Money, Markets and the Future of Higher Education*. London: Pluto Press.

Newfield, C. (2013). "The Counterreformation in Higher Education" [review of A. Mcgettigan's *The Great University Gamble*]. *LA Review of Books*, October 19: http://lareview ofbooks.org/review/the-counterreformation-in-higher-educ ation.

O'Rourke, M. (2006). "The Roguish Future of Queer Studies." *SQS* [Journal of Queer Studies in Finland] 2: 22–47.

Phillips, A. (2008). "On a More Impersonal Note." In Leo Bersani and Adam Phillips, *Intimacies*, 89–117. Chicago: University of Chicago Press.

Readings, B. (1994). *The University in Ruins*. Cambridge, MA: Harvard University Press.

Royle, N. (1999). "Yes, Yes, the University in Ruins." *Critical Inquiry* 26: 147–153.

Srnicek, S. and A. Williams (2013). "#ACCELERATE: Manifesto for an Accelerationist Politics," Accelerationism [weblog], May: http://accelerationism.files.wordpress.com/2013/05/will iams-and-srnicek.pdf.

Tuhkanen, M. (2005/06). "Foucault's Queer Virtualities." *rhizomes* 11/12: http://www.rhizomes.net/issue11/tuhkanen.html#a3.

Wark, M. (2013). "#Celerity: A Critique of the Manifesto for an Accelerationist Politics," *Speculative Heresy* [weblog], May: http://speculative heresy.files.wordpress.com/2013/05/wark-mckenzie-celerity.pdf.

1: Driving Education

A Crash Course

> We must . . . provide resources and guidance to an elite
> which can take up anew the task of enculturation. . . .
> The coming age of such elites has provided the current
> leadership of the conservative revival. . . . [T]he con-
> servative movement is now mature enough to sustain a
> counter-offensive on that last Leftist redoubt, the college
> campus.
>
> T. Kenneth Cribb, Heritage Foundation Lecture

Today, all around the world, the future of the humanities
stands on the edge of a knife. The value of the liberal
arts—its generous range of subjects and methods, its emphasis on teaching students how to think—seems to have
plummeted; what's wanted instead is technical education
and job training *avant le fait*, or rather, what's wanted is
the prestige of a liberal arts degree for programs that are
normally to be found in vocational, technical and online

schools, from ITT to M.I.T. If there are not enough, or not good enough, opportunities in the U.S. for technical and job training, one wonders why we don't focus on improving the institutions already engaged in that work, or create new ones, instead of complaining that liberal arts institutions do not do what they were never meant to do. Since there is no sign of that kind of rationality on the horizon, in Europe or America at least, perhaps we could be forgiven for suspecting that attacks on higher education mean to make the liberal arts scarce, not to address scarce or incompetent technical training. What makes the liberal arts so threatening? Is it simply because their utility is so difficult to quantify? (Which, of course, does not mean they have none; neither are many sought-after and well-advertised commodities obviously useful, like expensive soccer uniforms for five-year-olds, or monumental death-ray televisions.) Is it because they produce exactly the kind of citizenry *needed* in today's "knowledge economy"—broadly educated people, who do not fear expertise since they have the fundamental knowledge and analytical agility needed to explore its claims (see Nussbaum 2010)? Whatever the reasons—and many will be explored in this chapter and throughout this book—we must continue to uphold the value of exploration, knowledge production, and deliberation. This is, after all, a country (the U.S.) that advertises freedom of speech and assembly and *habeas corpus*—even if the latter no longer pertains to American citizens who are tagged as 'enemy combatants,' and even if our universities have once again become practice grounds for new, and very very old, exercises of emergency powers (see Hedges 2012).

The fetishizing—and profitability—of security goes on apace in our time, and on campuses may well do so until the injudiciousness of some Chancellor somewhere, perhaps Linda Katehi of the University of California-Davis, orders measures that result in the deaths of students, as happened many years ago at Kent State. Universities are now contracting private security forces (in the case of the

University of California, Kroll Security) that carry destructive weaponry vastly out of proportion to any possible threat posed by unarmed protesters.[1] "Security services" promise to keep the peace, but their actual efficacy is the creation of *in*security—a state of mind actively solicited by the defense industry in general. (One wonders, sometimes, what the Pentagon is thinking, or if it's thinking at all; it has historically been the case, in British history at least, that the leaders and communities who engage mercenary armies not only cannot manage them, but usually fall prey to them.) The increasing use of such services by university administrators—including the outsourcing of employee surveillance techniques and payroll and "human resource" management—is both sign and instance of contemporary capitalism's attempts to redesign the very experience of mind for the knowledge economy.

In 2011, the UC-Davis Academic Senate demanded the resignation of Linda Katehi because of brutal "police" treatment of students and faculty who were protesting fee hikes (as everyone knows, UC fees have risen exponentially, driving the young into further debt and barring thousands of middle- and working-class students from access to one of the best systems of higher education in the world). After the incident, Katehi apologized for failing to communicate more clearly to security forces that the protesters were not to be harmed, and initiated an "investigation," conducted by none other than Kroll Se-

[1] Kroll Security is eager to assist in the militarization of everyday life. Their 2011 forecast of security trends "predicted" that, "Incident Response Teams will get a permanent seat at the table when it comes to standard business operations. Historically, incident response teams were made of employees from across the organization. . . . [But] to remain competitive in today's market companies need to upgrade incident response teams to day-to-day operations. Effective incident response teams can include a team of outside consultants (via a third party) hired for 24/7 incident response support" (see PRWEB 2011).

curity, that found no evidence of abuse of authority. But Katehi still insisted on pressing very serious charges against a dozen protesters arrested for "blocking access" to (i.e., standing in front of) university buildings.[2] Was this an atavistic response? A return of the repressed? Katehi was a student at Athens Polytechnic University in 1973 when the Greek military junta sent a tank through the university gates in hopes of crushing, at whatever expense of blood and shame, the massive student protests ongoing therein against their regime. Katehi has refused to clarify whether, at the time, she was pro-democracy or a fascist sympathizer ("I have never been political"), but her complaints about the degradation of Greek higher education during the post-fascist "asylum" period (when all security forces were prohibited from entering university grounds) may give us an indication of her current position on freedom of assembly.[3] It's good to know something about history, though if Katehi and her ilk have their way, only those who can afford private schools and universities will be able to study it.[4]

As a consequence of Greece's recent financial naughtiness, a panel of North American and European technocrats was commissioned to advise the Greek government on how to improve the performance of Greek universities (Ames 2011). Though one of the panel members had a background in religious studies, otherwise not a single

---

[2] Yolo County prosecutors dropped the charges, saying there was "insufficient information" to proceed; see Lee and Fagan (2012).

[3] In case anyone thinks Greek old history is history, the new pro-"austerity" government boasts a number of fascists and neo-Nazis, including at least one former pro-junta Athens Poly student notorious for wielding an axe against the pro-democracy protesters (see Ames 2011).

[4] The appointment of Janet Napolitano as President of the UC system in July 2013 should not have been as big a surprise as it was. Her links to the security industry were, at this point in history, the only credentials she needed.

humanist or artist was included. But Linda Katehi was. Citing the decline of the Greek universities as a central reason for the country's financial woes, the panel argues that "politicization of the campuses—and specifically the politicization of students—represents a beyond-reasonable involvement in the political process. This is contributing to an accelerated degradation of higher education" (International Committee on Higher Education in Greece 2011). In the U.S., of course, reasonableness (being, by definition, open to debate) cannot limit *prima facie* the constitutional right to freedom of expression and assembly—though legal scholar and former UC President Mark Yudof, who appointed Katehi to her Chancellorship, has been a longtime advocate for flexible interpretations of academic freedom (see, for example, Yudof 1987). This theme is repeated throughout technocratic reports on higher education: neither students nor faculty have any business being openly "political," and if they are, what results (it is claimed) is grade inflation and students who spend their time reading the Communist Manifesto instead of studying for their electrical engineering exams. But *where is the evidence* that interest in politics degrades higher education? The freedom to argue and deliberate and then think again—to engage in thoughtful reflection—is vital to the human mind/brain's capacity for innovative thinking and hence to the well-being, financial and otherwise, of the citizenry the panel putatively wants to foster. (Creativity is the result of both "generative and analytical thinking.")[5] The panel's claim that the university is resistant to change may have merit; but it matters which changes are on offer. Not all are good, and few have the inevitability claimed for them by highly interested parties (statements like "tenure is over" are performative utterances, not descriptions of

---

[5] "[C]reativity is a complex thought process that calls on many different brain regions in both hemispheres [of the brain]. Left brain/right brain theories of learning are not based on credible science and are unhelpful in understanding creativity, especially when used to categorize individuals" (Howard-Jones 2010, 160).

present realities). Further, the kind of Thatcherite accountability the panel proposes has already proved, in the UK, to divert an enormous amount of time, energy, and money from the educational and research missions of the universities. According to one of the former directors of the British Library, the Library's administrative costs went up by 60% when Thatcher's "reforms" were implemented. Strangely, no one seems to think accountability should account for itself; but it is not at all apparent that massive investment therein is producing a better academic "product." Independent audits are in order here, too.

We are witnessing technocratic "capture," in the Deleuzo-Guattarian sense, of academic culture and its campuses, on behalf of an increasingly globally-networked capitalism quite careless of the well-being of any particular nation, including the U.S. Far from depoliticizing the universities, these forces are pursuing a reactionary, top-down, *hyper*-politicization of the university. We might wonder why the world's financial powers would bother. The simplest answer is that power always wants to control and generate what counts as knowledge; we have learned that much from Foucault. Another simple answer is capitalism's unending frenzy for new markets and commodities *irrespective of* effectiveness. The best studies of online education show that it is most effective in the context of live classroom education; by itself, it compounds the difficulties of the very at-risk students (including males of all ethnicities) that its proponents claim to be serving (see Xu and Jaggers 2013a, 2013b). Investing in online courses outside the context of embodied or "live" classroom education is a mistake financially and a disservice to students, families, and taxpayers. Folly, of course, is nothing new; but it is sobering to witness how aggressively and mendaciously it can now be marketed.

Universities have served historically not only as purveyors of hegemonic ideologies but also as significant points of resistance to capture and mystification. Campus unrest, moreover, has been a *global* phenomenon at least since the 1960s, as Joe Califano argued in *The Student Revolution* (Califano 1970).[6] Its international reach is a big problem for the world's financial and state powers, if their habitual overreaction thereto is any indication. But this is not a simple rebellion/repression situation. As noted, while "security" may succeed in intimidating troublemakers, it works just as hard to provoke them (cf. the CIA's fondness for "destabilizing" regimes considered unfriendly to the U.S. and its international interests). The financial powers are doing their best to destabilize academic culture everywhere, through the time-honored method of pauperization—sharply raising fees, starving faculty and student budgets, relying on poorly-paid part-time itinerant lecturers instead of creating more ladder-track faculty positions, legislating on behalf of online for-profit courses, ignoring conflicts of interest, and staffing administrations with grotesquely well-compensated technocrats who often know little to nothing about academic professionalism—all in the name of "solving" the funding crisis they have themselves induced. The desired result is to add both faculty and students to the "precariat"—the ever-growing numbers of people across the globe who teeter on various verges of tenuous and "contingent" employment and thus are vulnerable to exploitation of the most old-fashioned sort (see Butler 2004; Scott 2012).

California Governors seem to be particularly fond of (in)security. Not to be outdone by his predecessors, including himself, Jerry Brown agreed not long ago with former UC President Mark Yudof that the University of California should no longer be obliged to demonstrate compliance with its Master Plan.[7] This was an autocratic end-run around the legislature, the thousands of Califor-

---

[6] The arts faculties and students in medieval universities were also troublemakers; see Lipton 1999, 99, fig. 70 for an image of the medieval arts faculty as a contemporary Babel.

[7] On the Master Plan for Higher Education in California, see: http://www.ucop.edu/acadinit/mastplan/mp.htm.

nians who have petitioned to preserve the Master Plan, the many faculty who have worked diligently (and, of course, *pro bono*) on UC's Commission on the Future, and the UC Council of Faculty Associations' tireless efforts to ensure compliance (see Meister 2012). One of the provisions of the Master Plan is to guarantee a place for every Californian who can meet UC's entrance requirements. As a consequence of Brown's action, however, UC will now be free to admit many foreign as well as out-of-state students without fear of having its feet held to the fire. Not only will this further hamper Californians' access to their own university system; it will likely also further erode public support for higher education. Both Brown and Yudof are well aware that Californian taxpayers have historically reacted badly to increases in the numbers of out-of-state students. Brown's unilateral setting-aside of the Master Plan amounts to a decision to cut UC loose from considerations of public confidence and the state funding that follows from such. Like many of its counterparts, UC is less and less a public university, and more and more a university that uses taxpayer money (about 20% of its overall funding) to serve ends having little to do with the public good. So what UC will gain in tuition dollars from admitting foreign and out-of-state students, it will almost certainly lose in public confidence and state funds. We can always hope that, instead of perpetuating this vicious circle, Californians will decide to take back their University from the global financial interests it increasingly serves. Having already experienced some blowback from the citizenry on the problem of diminished access, however, Brown and various powers in the California State Assembly are now posing as defenders of the people by trying to impose the outsourcing of online learning modalities from the "public" university to private alternatives (see Chapter 2 in this volume)—in other words, another two turns of the screw, because the action is really one of infiltration.

I am not arguing for parochialism; "diversity," unlike

Udacity,[8] is a precondition for enriched experience of mind and the making of new knowledge. But foreign exchange programs are being *cut* at UC, just like language departments, which would suggest that international diversity is not the motive driving the opening of UC to unprecedented numbers of foreign students. The tuition dollar is a central motive; but internationalizing will also lead to yet more administrators, yet more funding of their corporate salaries and fostering of their ties to global business interests, and more and more diversion of resources away from the departments that actually do the work of teaching and mentoring *all* students. Efficiency and cost-saving are not as high on capitalism's list of priorities as some think; its real goal, where the academy is concerned, is transferring money from faculty, students, parents and taxpayers to administrators who serve interests antipathetic to the vigorous circulation of new and complex ideas. These are the labor costs taxpayers should be worried about.

Internationalizing will also put further pressure on the curriculum, traditionally (in the U.S. at least) a faculty prerogative and responsibility, now under attack from people who have dollars rather than students in mind. The Bologna Process documents recommend that universities across Europe facilitate migration for education by homogenizing their programs of study. But when did migration for education become a higher good than education itself? The Bologna Declaration calls for the "adoption of a system of easily readable and comparable degrees . . . in order to promote European citizens [*sic*] employability [and mobility]. . . . The degree awarded after the first cycle shall also be relevant to the European labor market as an appropriate level of qualification" (European Ministers of Education, "Bologna Declaration," 2003). The implication of these papers on higher education—in-

[8] Udacity is a private, for-profit corporation that offers massive, open online courses (MOOCs); see http://www.udacity.com.

sofar as they hope to identify the problem they purport-edly want to solve, at any rate—is that employment has been compromised in Europe and the U.S. because the universities are failing to produce employable students. Surely that would mean the technical schools are failing even more miserably; and yet they are barely mentioned in current debates about the proper role of higher educa-tion.

But one must demur in any case. If the universities are in fact failing to produce employable students, that is at least in part because the world economy is failing to produce employment of *any* kind, which is hardly the fault of the academy. Trickle-down economics has been shown for the second time in my lifetime to be complete-ly without merit; yet we seem to be surprised, to the point of casting about for scapegoats, that anti-labor policies might have had depressive effects on hiring. The chief factors that have produced the current economic crisis are: 1) the shenanigans of international financiers (espe-cially the big banks); 2) at the turn of the century, Alan Greenspan's famous "bubble"-breaking decision to raise interest rates because the labor market was too "hot," i.e. too many people had jobs; 3) "out-sourcing" of white- as well as blue-collar employment to the rest of the world; and 4) overemployment.[9] It's true that many academics—like many attorneys, doctors, businesspeople, secretaries, factory-workers, farmers, and homemakers—are interest-ed in politics. (This is why industries hire lobbyists, after all; they are well aware of their vulnerability to political developments, and so are a lot of academics.) By compar-ison with the madness of financial capitalism, however, the political awareness of academics has not been much of a factor in, for example, the downfall of the U.S. hous-ing market and the construction industry.

---

[9] "Overemployment" in this case means demanding excessive (and, in the professions, often unpaid) work from one employee instead of simply hiring two.

If nothing else, then, let us consider that unemployment may not necessarily be the fault of the political leanings of the world's universities. We are also entitled to wonder how the (cultural and economic) aggrandizement promised by the Bologna Process could be served by homogenizing European regionalism, since the power of said regionalism to derail the world economy is no more impressive compared to that of the banks than the power of academic political awareness. In truth, contemporary capitalism is happy to regulate everything but itself.

So why does technocracy remain so resistant to the idea that a good liberal arts education helps to produce good employees, especially when it is supported by so much research (neuroscientific and otherwise)? A course of study in classics will have trouble justifying its appropriateness to any labor market; but, at least in the U.S., classics majors (and language and literature majors) have typically gotten better grades in law school, and made law review more often, than students who major in a variety of popular "pre-law" fields (such as economics, political science, and business) (Engell and Dangerfield 1998, 50). Students who pursue occupational majors—like "Security Systems" —are typically outstripped in said occupations by their liberal arts peers, because the latter are capable of making better use of the learning they do on the job. It is all so self-defeating; even if we did decide to evaluate education exclusively on the basis of its ability to produce useful labor, these attempts to rationalize courses of study would not be the way to do it. Good employees need many skills that apply across the board, like the ability to write, read, speak, think, imagine, argue, and put issues into various kinds of perspectives, e.g. local, global, and historical. The objective of "mobility" mentioned in so many of the documents of the Bologna Process does not, as noted, refer to the value of experiencing diverse cultures; it wants to get rid of diversity, in the name of comparability (quantifiability, accountability, etc.), as is true of most of the "flexibilization" (read "homogenization" and "helplessness") falsely heralded by neo-liberal capitalism.

Furthermore, the level of international student mobility thus envisioned may transform student bodies from enfranchised, acculturated, politically aware groups into disenfranchised, deportable, culturally diffident groups with limited investments in the political process, cut off from the legal systems they know best and the families who might complain should their sons or daughters be bashed on the head by Kroll Security. It is, of course, true that job mobility in Europe has created exciting changes in the lives of people and cultures: one can now eat well in the UK; design is more sophisticated. These improvements, however, such as they are, have depended on a real mobility of persons across national borders, not just capital. As long as national boundaries continue to confine labor to local markets, mobility will simply mean statelessness and precarity. One can imagine that insecure "mobility" might be mobilized nonetheless to serve the internationalization of student power. But the risks will be considerable for newly itinerant students. The desire of the authors of the Bologna Protocol and their ilk does not even run to protecting foreign students by organizing them into "nations," as happened in the medieval European universities. Further, top-down, managerial homogenization of courses of study not only threatens what's *special* about a centuries-old university with distinctive traditions and local ties; it also squelches academic freedom and self-governance, wherein the people who actually develop our knowledge of mitochondria or cetaceous intelligence or dark matter decide how these subjects might best be taught, and students are encouraged to pursue, as much as possible, their specific talents and interests. Should we really evaluate our universities on the basis of how many biddable and employable laborers they can graduate? Haven't our universities given us the genome? Lumosity.com? New treatments for autism, and new ways of thinking about it? God particles (the Higgs boson particle)? Haven't they introduced us to synthesizers and digital archives? *To online education?* Is it really demonstrable that universities don't know what they're doing?

Underlying the Bologna Declaration is the assumption that people ought not to be allowed to explore for themselves what they want to learn, teach, be, and do. Again: conservatives and technocrats do love a plan, as long as it's *their* plan.[10] Jesper Hoffmeyer associates "the separation of planning from execution in a master-slave relationship" characteristic of the industrial revolution, with separation of the "genetic master plan (the DNA) from the mundane [and obedient] operations of the cytoplasm"—and finally with the "privileging of digital information," where input and design seem to "dwarf variable outputs in importance" (this privileging usually forgets that language is also a digital sign system) (Hoffmeyer 2008, 79). A few qualifications come to mind—as to whether the separation of plan from execution is particular to the industrial revolution, for example—and it must be said that our freedoms are always limited by the historical and social contexts, including hopes for the future, in which they develop. But while I would not want to devalue conscious decision-making—it is a great gift, acquired at the cost of deep time—our "executive functions" must also respect the freedom of drift, the creativity of open systems, and the ability to tolerate creaturely vulnerability, anxiety, surprise, and wonder (see Jacobs 1985, 221 ff.). These are also great gifts, which make use of other parts of the brain/mind equally important to our surviving and thriving. I am not speaking against "vision"; I am saying that vision must be accompanied by respect for the irreducible complexity and non-conscious aspects of human knowledge-making, sociality, and their histories. The con-

---

[10] See, again, the "Bologna Declaration" (1999) or the Heritage Foundation's 1,093-page public policy blueprint, "Mandate for Leadership: Policy Management in a Conservative Administration" (http://www.heritage.org/about/our-history/35th-anniversary).

tempt for academic freedom of expression *and* govern-ance demonstrated by the new corporate managers of North American public universities is worrying, to say the least, both because of what it reveals about the status of constitutional protections in corporate culture, but al-so because it encroaches upon one of the few institutions left which, because of the nature of the work it does, *culti-vates* power streams that move bottom-up and sideways as well as top-down.

If this treatment of our universities is not intended as capture (or "acquisition"), that is its effect, and it is also a rehearsal for limiting citizens' rights in other contexts. The Government of Quebec recently responded to stu-dent protests against fee hikes by introducing "emergency laws" to close down the universities there. Allan Gilmour, formerly of the Ford Motor Company and now President of Wayne State University in Detroit, has recently, in the course of negotiations with his faculty's union, "pro-posed" that he be granted the right to fire tenured faculty at will, without benefit of peer review and due process, should he decide (for and by himself) that said faculty were "intentionally causing injury to persons and/or damage to property, forcibly interrupting the normal dai-ly teaching, research or administrative operation of the University or directly inciting others to engage in such actions."[11] In 2012, the Office of the President of the Uni-versity of California proposed changes to the Academic Personnel Manual (‡16) that would make faculty subject to "administrative" rather than faculty discipline should they violate "the general rules and regulations and poli-cies of the University; these include, but are not limited to . . . health and safety, and use of University facilities."[12]

---

[11] I am quoting a personal copy of Gilmour's proposal shared with me by Charles Parrish; for an account of the proposal, see Kozlowski and Hicks (2012).

[12] See the University of California, Office of the President's *Academic Personnel Manual* (2012), available here: http://www.ucop.edu/academic-personnel/academic-personnel-policy/.

Campus unrest, modest as it's been in recent years, is being exploited as a pretext for the cultivation of local, national and international states of emergency and "exception," wherein the authority of the law is founded on the power to suspend it when "necessary" (see Agamben 2005). The UC Regents, however, recently agreed (July 13, 2013) to enhance the protection of the faculty's right to speak freely about all administration policies. Many faculty don't know how these protections stand at their schools, but they can easily find out, and make a fuss; most universities don't want to appear to be despotic, so we need to use their concerns about "image" to guarantee as much openness as possible.

Academic freedom has its own history, and its history suggests that "new" criticisms of tenure are actually attempts to turn back the clock. According to John Savage, tenure began

> in response to decades of public discussion of the arbitrary dismissal of faculty members for holding unpopular views. . . . Late in the 19th century, [Benjamin Andrews, President of Brown University] advocated the free coinage of silver as a means to stop deflation in the American economy. This angered members of the Brown Corporation many of whom were creditors benefiting from deflation. . . . Francis Wayland, Brown Corporation member and Dean of the Yale Law School, said that President Andrews' position threatened donations to Brown and that money was the life blood of universities. . . . Prof. Josiah Royce of Harvard . . . [replied] that freedom, not money, is the life blood of the university. . . . But the censorship of unpopular economic ideas did not stop. . . . in the late 1940s, the University of Illinois at Urbana fired a group of untenured economists, all of whom subsequently had distinguished careers, for teaching the "heresy" of Keynesian economics. (Savage n.d.)

The Koch brothers' attempt to weigh in on the hiring of faculty for two endowed chairs in economics at Florida State University is only the latest in a long line of financiers' efforts to cultivate academic compliance with their own economic interests (see Hundley 2011).[13]

Whether students and faculty will develop their potential for global influence is another question. (It has to be said that one of the best arguments *against* the notion that the universities are hotbeds of revolutionary sentiment is that, in the U.S. and the UK, at least, tenured faculty have been so willing to jump on the trains.) As has happened so often in the past, distortions of the perils posed by student and faculty unrest provide distraction from the chaos and pillaging set loose by global capitalism's attempts to capture everything from universities to national governments. What capital wants is immunity from accountability, as Roberto Esposito has argued in *Immunitas* (2001); and it is tired of being held to account by people who actually know something about causal parity or economic behavior. But the more capitalists try to make themselves immune to contagion and otherness, the more vulnerable they will in fact become. Knowledge matters, and reports now coming in from universities offering the kind of online courses favored by Richard Blum, Senator Steinberg and their ilk, are presaging some embarrassment for said ilk: no one signs up for them. Why should anyone, especially the taxpayer, subsidize the University of California's "partnerships" with for-profit companies (such as Coursera and Udacity), when university faculty have always-already been integrating such online offerings into university curricula? Who will reimburse the students and families who spent money seeking "access" to UC through online courses they would, as

---

[13] According to Bruce Benson, Chair of the Florida State University Economics Department, the faculty thereof ultimately worked out a hiring process whereby the Koch brothers' foundation could only approve candidates from a list generated by the department; see Strauss (2011).

studies have predicted, most likely never complete? Maybe such courses really will stay "free" for some time; if so, what's in it for the investors? The answer is data-mining, through mechanisms (like keystroke collection) that undermine students' rights to privacy, including those (if they have any in the first place) of the aforementioned greatly-sought-after foreign students. Capital seeks the freedom to render life precarious, unstable, and in need of "protection," which it will then sell back to us in the form of private security forces, and it also seeks the freedom to shut down quality public educational opportunities in order to conceal the shoddiness of their offerings and then sell them to the disadvantaged.

The rhetoric is always about emergency. Regents with investments in online education drive up tuition costs dramatically while state legislatures refuse to fund low-cost high-quality education for their constituents. Then the State Assembly begins to cry crocodile tears over their constituents' loss of access to high-quality public education, and tries to legislate the adoption of certain textbooks and for-profit online courses as though these were solutions rather than expensive and ineffectual measures profiting no one but the interests responsible in the first instance for the very loss of access being bemoaned. Everybody knows this, but apparently it can never be pointed out too often.

The discourse of crisis is also at work when assaults on academic freedom are leveled (as they so often are) against criticism of Israeli national policies. Here too reasons of "national security" try to legitimate the suspension of academic freedom and civil liberties. The current proliferation of security industries and techniques is thus both pretext and prophylactic. The privatization of security, payroll, employee surveillance, and human resource functions does not mean that anything is going "out" (as in "out"-sourcing); it means, as noted earlier, that something is "coming in" to (infiltrate) the institutions and companies that contract with such companies (see note 1 above). The U.S. government does not "outsource" to Blackwater; Blackwater (and Haliburton) *take over* the functions *and* funding of the Defense Department. This is the action of capture. Bizarrely—but then again, maybe not—Blackwater is trying to obscure its real nature by appropriating the "brand" of the Academy and renaming itself "Academi"; in yet another turn of the screw, it has been sued by a Texas sporting goods company, Academy Ltd., for trademark infringement (Sizemore 2012). So, also, do the for-profit online schooling bosses even more desperately want to acquire the brands of real universities: because those brands still signify integrity.

Altegrity, Inc. (an ironic brand-name, if ever there were one) is the holding company for Kroll Advisory, Kroll OnTrack (recipients of three security contracts from the University of California), HireRight, and USIS (who provide information and security services to the U.S. federal government, such as employee background investigations and biometric capture for the Depts. of Homeland Security and Immigration Services). HireRight's "Drug and Health Screening Services" include "in-house medical, legal and compliance expertise"; that is to say, government agencies and corporations can contract HireRight's personnel to conduct drug (and other kinds of) surveillance on their own employees (see HireRight. com). Joe Califano, Jr., author of the aforementioned *The Student Revolution,* is also the founder of the National Center on Addiction and Substance Abuse at Columbia University (CASA) (the work of which has been much criticized). Califano and one of Altegrity's CEO's, Sharon T. Rowlands, have both served as directors for Automatic Data Processing, Inc., a "business process outsourcing" company (which is in fact a business-process infiltrating company).[14]

Califano, one of LBJ's cronies and former Secretary

---

[14] See the agenda for ADP's annual stockholder meeting in 2000: http://www.investquest.com/iq/a/adp/fin/proxy/audx00.pdf.

of the U.S. Dept. of Health, Education, and Welfare, is also a Director of Willis Group Holdings, the world's third-largest insurance brokerage, specializing in "risk management" and "human resource consulting." Yes, this is the same Joseph Califano Jr. who, while describing the putative takeover of the federal government by Students for a Democratic Society in the 1960s, lamented the resistance of "young scientists" to the development of anti-ballistic missiles "and their involvement on a major scale in opposition to government policy they consider wrong. Business and labor have not yet had their share of anti-government revolutionaries," but "they will," according to Califano—though he also opined that "radicals" had already taken "control [of] Local No. 41 of the American Federation of Government Employees (the union with jurisdiction over . . . most of the Public Health Service": "SDS is willing even to shave in order to bore the corporate and worker establishments from within" (Califano 1970, 88–89). Ah, the Old Mole—very long-lived, it appears.

This is indeed a biopower struggle. Who really threatens our lives and livelihoods? Who promises us salvation by technology? Who gets to exercise the power of life *and* death over other human beings? Not the Black Panthers, who, besides being badass political activists, really did run soup kitchens for the poor, before some of the nation's finest shot them down. Not Lyndon La-Rouche, controversial early critic of speculative capitalism and founder of the American Labor Party in 1973, jailed for mail fraud by the Reagan Administration—a longtime target of conservatives of all stripes (including those in the Democratic Party), as well as seekers after racial justice.[15] But neither is LaRouche what we are seek-

---

[15] LaRouche's inflammatory attack on monetarism in *The Ugly Truth about Milton Friedman* (e.g. Chapter 4, "Oxford Monetarism and Hitler's Vienna," in LaRouche and Goldman 1980) makes for stimulating reading in these economically post-apocalyptic times. LaRouche's politics have always been compli-

ing today, given that he himself is something of a messianic exceptionalist, and that is the form of power under scrutiny in this chapter.

When the CIA is not available, private security and surveillance services have usually been the means by which technocracy and capitalism have gone global, in the form, for example, of the corporate goon squads that "break up" resistance and nascent unionization in South America, Asia and Africa. The current effectivity of risk-and-security biopower has been enhanced beyond the beyond by computerization and the internet,[16] but its basic function—to crush life while appearing to advance it—has changed little, despite the fact that devitalization is inescapably enervation for all. (Epidemiological studies show that a drop in the health and well-being of the poorer members of a given community inevitably means a corresponding drop in the health and well-being of those who can afford to buy good care; see Wheeler 2006). Philippe Carrel's *Handbook of Risk Management* (Katehi is one of the directors of its publishing house, John Wiley & Sons, Ltd.) begins with this sonorous observation: "Risk is the essence of free enterprise in liberal economies" (Carrel 2010, 1). He goes on: "the discipline of managing risk has always existed," at least "[s]ince the eighteenth century's industrial revolution"—a bald statement indeed, given the development of merchant capital, banking, finance and insurance during the Middle Ages, and the global "ventures" of early modern enterprise. But

---

cated and, on the question of race, most unhappy. But these flaws hardly set him apart from many of our recent presidents and presidential candidates. In fact, it makes him an excellent screen for right wing projections. For a sample of the latter, see Copulos (1984); Copulos was the director of energy studies at the Heritage Foundation who advised the Reagan administration on energy resources, especially domestic oil development.

[16] See, for example, Coley and Lockwood (2012), Galloway (2006), Galloway and Thacker (2007), Thacker (2004), and Virilio (2006).

let us not expect too much. The carelessness of Carrel's historical formulations—whereby "always" turns out to be two hundred years—is matched by the fuzzy-mindedness of his appeals to biology and evolutionary theory: "[t]he very few [corporations] that survive, expand and thrive usually evolve at a staggering pace, through organic and inorganic growth, continuously adapting and innovating from core business to new market niche"; "[i]t is the evolution of risks, the unexpected ones in particular, that seems to be pushing the boundaries of innovation by changing the conditions for survival" (Carrel 2010, 1).

But evolutionary theory today—see, for example, Lynn Margulis's (1988) pioneering work on the role of symbiosis in organic change—even the evolutionary theory of many yesterdays ago, does not view the "struggle for survival" or "survival of the fittest" as the prime motor of life's many histories. Darwin's law of "survival of the just-barely-fit-enough," Conrad Pritscher remarks, "makes altruism a virtue. That species which is cooperative, which . . . helps [the weak and disabled] to survive, will attain the greatest degree of variation of characteristics possible in a particular environment and will thus have a better chance of survival *as a species*. . . . Not competition but cooperation is the behavior blessed by evolution" (Pritscher 2010, 226). Carrel's rhetoric means to vitalize business enterprises, as a way of aggrandizing the importance of their births and deaths, and rationalizing the lengths to which they are prepared to go to "survive"; if they're predators, at least they're still down here with the rest of us chickens. But while it is true that few corporations last longer than fifty years—a fact that should have given the U.S. pause when it began glorifying corporate management techniques and "efficiency" in the 1980s—their infrastructures, resources and holdings rarely crumble and vanish like the lost continent of Atlantis.

So who is "they"? I am not speaking of conspiracy; I am speaking of an "emergent" phenomenon, which certainly has concentrations of forces, but no single central point from which domination radiates. Historical complexity, however, does admit of the reverberating power of particular agents. As noted, Linda Katehi has attributed the degradation of higher education in Greece to the period after the fall of the military junta, in the 1980s. It was also in the 1980s that the U.S. right wing propaganda machine found new energy (funded by Richard Mellon Scaife and his ilk; see the epigraph to this chapter), and began to complain about the breakdown of higher education, especially the take-over of the Ivies by liberal faculty who imposed their "distorted views" on future rulers of the world.[17] The *Dartmouth Review*, funded generously by defense industry boss John Olin's (non-profit) foundation, was the first of the Ivies' unofficial "student" newspapers; its student moles made off with faculty members' intellectual property by taping classes without permissions, and defamed faculty in *ad hominem* and quite vulgar fashion (for such pious lasses and lads, anyway; one Women's Studies professor was called, in print, a "quimqueen." The University did nothing because it didn't want to "stoop" to the level of the *Dartmouth Review*, or dignify it with a response. At roughly the same time, in 1986, Lynne Cheney became head of the National Endowment for the Humanities (a post she held until 1993).[18] Oh

---

[17] See the National Committee for Responsive Philanthropy's Report "Targeting the Academy" (available at www.media transparency.org/targeting_academy.htm), Johnson (2003), and Messer-Davidow (1993).

[18] See Nash, Crabtree and Dunn (2000) for an account of Cheney's antics vis-à-vis the National History Standards, and also SourceWatch (Center for Media and Democracy) for a list of articles by and about Cheney: http://www. sourcewatch.org/index.php?title=Lynne_Cheney. "Telling the Truth," her final report as NEH Chair (1992), achieved notoriety for its distortions and fabrications of evidence for the claim that liberal politics were controlling the minds of American academics; see Schwartz (1992).

"dirk and drublie" day, as William Dunbar might have said.[19]

In response to the insouciance of the best-educated generation in American history, the Heritage Foundation included in its right-wing agenda an assault on public education—as Dick Armey put it in the summer 1994 issue of the Foundation's *Policy Review*, "the end of the public school monopoly." Monopoly? No one *has* to go to public school; they just have to go to some kind of school. The whole "voucher" movement in the secondary school system was an attempt to raid the local and national treasuries so that ordinary taxpayers would fund private educations for the wealthy—just as the "corporatization" of public universities means using taxpayer money to fund research for Novartis.[20] Public schools were meant not to "monopolize" anything but to make sure that American children who could not afford private schooling could still get a decent education. Public education began in the U.S. shortly after the nation's founding, beginning in the Northeast (it went countrywide by the 1870s). John Adams—one of the wealthiest and most conservative of our founding fathers—wrote in a letter to John Jebb in 1785 that,

> The whole people must take upon themselves the education of the whole people and be willing to

[19] The reference is to William Dunbar's poem, "In to thir dirk and drublie dayis" (http://www.scottishpoetrylibrary.org.uk/poetry/poems/thir-dirk-and-drublie-dayis).

[20] It is an article of faith amongst scientists that their extramural grants fund their research projects *in toto*, and in fact "bring money into the university" since parts of their grants are taken to fund their "indirect costs" (the cost to the university of supporting said projects). In fact, scientific research relies on University resources beyond what extramural grants can subsidize, for infrastructure development, maintenance, and takedown, as for the admissions, registration, accounting, and many other administrative services on which the sciences depend equally with other disciplines.

> bear the expenses of it. There should not be a dis-
> trict of one mile square, without a school in it, *not
> founded by a charitable individual*, but maintained
> at the public expense of the people themselves.
> (Adams, 1854, 540; my emphasis)

Even in Georgia there were ten grammar schools by 1770, most of which had government funding, and were free for both male and female students. The Far Right's "new" ideas on education are in fact far older than the nation itself and do not respect its founding principles. Perhaps we need a constitutional amendment to clarify that the right to education is on a par in this country with the right to bear arms. Both are crucial means for the citizenry to defend itself against tyranny. At least, that's how the "forefathers" saw it.

A great champion of studying American history, Lynne Cheney has never seemed to think freedom of speech is one of the American freedoms that have made American history worth studying. In the 1990s, her American Council of Trustees and Alumni (ACTA, founded with Joe Lieberman in 1995) published a "report" called "Defending Civilization: How Our Universities Are Failing America." Described by many critics as a "blacklist," the first, unbowdlerized version named the names of professors who professed "anti-American sentiments," such as: suicide bombers are among "the desperate, angry and bereaved"; or, "war created people like Osama Bin Laden, and more war will create more people like him."[21] One wonders what Cheney and Lieberman thought *had* created suicide bombers and the phenomenon of Osama bin Laden. Satan *again*? It is grotesquely absurd to defame as anti-American scholarly attempts to understand (*not* to justify) why human beings do horrible things to other

---

[21] The bowdlerized version, revised and expanded in February 2002, can be accessed here: https://portfolio.du.edu/portfolio/getportfoliofile?uid=85865.

humans.[22] If we don't try to find out the reasons why people become terrorists, and address those reasons, there *will* forever be terrorists. And we have every right to question the nation-state's monopoly on violence; that's why we have the right to bear arms. The violence inflicted on the world by the U.S. government, and its allied mercenaries, defense contractors, arms dealers and security specialists, far outstrips in all categories (quantity, destructive power, non-combatant casualties) that of the worst of terrorist attacks. We have loved the bomb, and profited from it. We also have the distinction of being number one in selling arms to troubled regions of the world. Of course, we do have some significant competitors in Russia, China, France, Germany, and the United Kingdom. The problem is global. There are Olin Industries and Haliburton and "Academi," but also Glock, BAE Systems, IMBEL, Arsenal, Norinco, Soltam Systems, and many many more. All thrive in "crises," because critical moments are the moments in which covert operations—the suspension of the law for the sake of the law—are afforded legitimacy. The points made above are not new, but their relevance is sadly undiminished at a time when privatization (a misnomer for "taxpayer subsidization"), disregard for the Geneva conventions, and the militarization of everyday life have been galloping forward unchecked.

ACTA and the American Enterprise Institute, Lynne Cheney's most recent nests, are funded by, among others, the Scaife foundations (Carthage and Sarah Scaife, both non-profits). Think tanks and foundations give each other a *lot* of money—it is a kind of laundering, the deleterious effects of which on the national fisc far outweigh the public "good" implied by tax-exempt status. (We need, at least temporarily, to withdraw non-profit status—i.e., taxpayer assistance—from all the think tanks, of whatever

---

[22] In fact, the terrorist demographic is typically young men recently transplanted from rural, traditional villages to large towns and cities: see Pape (2005) and Reuter (2004).

political stripe.) Scaife's (non-profit) Allegheny Foundation gave the Heritage Foundation over a million dollars in 2010. Allegheny, in turn, funds the Koch brothers' Bill of Rights Institute; the Center for Equal Opportunity, a right wing think tank opposed to bilingual education; the Free Enterprise Education Foundation, led by Tea Partier John Trombetta; and the Counterterrorism and Security Education and Research Foundation. Another patron of the latter organization is Sheldon Gary Adelson, the self-professed Zionist and casino tycoon (is gambling encouraged in Hebrew Scripture somewhere?), who has traveled to Israel to hawk a DVD warning against the spread of Islam in the West. His company, the Las Vegas Sands Corporation, has been investigated by the Department of Justice for possible violations of the Foreign Corrupt Practices Act, and by the U.S. Attorney's Office in Los Angeles for possible money laundering. He was also the chief bankroller of the 2012 Romney-Ryan presidential campaign (is gambling also encouraged in the Book of Mormon?).[23]

Ronald Reagan, who began his political career and collaboration with J. Edgar Hoover by informing on fellow members of the Screen Actors Guild in the late 1940s, consolidated his political position while Governor of California as the dragonslayer of "student radicals" in the UC system. Despite the fact that McCarthy finally fell because his accusations couldn't be substantiated—perhaps Reagan didn't give him the right information—the latter remained loyal to his idol's smear tactics, and represented California's campuses as full of violent Communist subversives plotting the overthrow of the United States.[24] Re-

---

[23] See the op-ed piece in *The New York Times*, August 17, 2012, "In Thrall to Sheldon Adelson": www.nytimes.com/2012/08/17/opinion/in-thrall-to-sheldon-adelson.html.

[24] Contrary to right-leaning popular accounts of the later twentieth century, hippies, yippies, radicals and Students for a Democratic Society, though powerful change agents, were always in the minority and never in charge of anything except their own

cently, the right-wing California Association of Scholars published a "report," "A Crisis of Competence," blaming the supposed "decline" of the UC system on—no surprise here—"the corrupting effect of political activism" therein.[25] (The arguments and rhetoric of this report are virtually identical to those of the ACTA report and the report of Katehi *et al.* on the decline of education in Greece). Now, it is true that many (certainly not all) university professors believe that we should address urgent issues (like enormous fee hikes and budget cuts) in the classroom, because it is our responsibility to teach our students how to *think about* and *study* these matters, in addition to having feelings and opinions about them. Where else will American youth be asked to read, write, and debate *calmly* and *comprehensively* the very topics controversial enough to diminish our rational capacities in the first place? The skills taught thereby, it is true, have not been too fashionable recently: patience, and self-control. But educating our students to think about their passions, rather than simply giving way to them, does not require apology.

As the above remarks about think tanks have already indicated, the academy is far from being the only hub of mentation, political or otherwise, that accepts taxpayer support. Think tanks of all stripes are far more motivated by partisan political agendas than is the academy, and yet

---

activism. The phenomena of post-1970s avarice, de-regulation, financialization, and immiseration are more properly laid at the feet of the "silent majority" (Nixon's phrase) and their bully heirs, who partied their way through the Vietnam War (immunity again) and achieved a repulsive exemplarity in the father/son Bush presidencies. I do thank George Bush, Sr. for his service in World War II.

[25] California Association of Scholars, "A Crisis of Competence: The Corrupting Effect of Political Activism in the University of California," April 2012 [a report prepared for the Regents of the University of California]: http://www.nas.org/images/documents/a_crisis_of_competence.pdf.

the taxpayer still foots a good part of the bill, if said think tank is a tax-exempt non-profit. "Reports" that link the decline of civilization to the political thoughtfulness of faculty and students are demagogic attempts to blame "decline" on the very people whose *raison d'être* is to *uphold* standards of argumentation and evidence. The problem with educators, from the standpoint of the demagogues, is that our business is the creation of new knowledge and ways of thinking by means of debate, inspiration, scholarship, statistics, mathematics, sound experimental protocols, telescopes, colliders, and so forth. As fond as we may be of certain traditions of learning and not others—a fondness that can certainly fall to the level of prejudice—ultimately our allegiance is neither to conventional nor convenient wisdom. This is why our history has always been one of controversy as well as collusion. We are accused of heresy; people burn our books; dictators send us to the mines, or Siberia, to be re-educated. The Pythagoreans were thrown out of Croton. Socrates had to drink the hemlock. Twenty of Thomas Aquinas's propositions were condemned. The Wycliffites of fourteenth-century England were cultured at Oxford and later burned to death. The Brothers Grimm were thrown out of the University of Gottingen by the Duke of Hanover. Martin Luther King, Jr., PhD in Theology (Boston University) and author of several important books, including *I Have a Dream,* was jailed and also assassinated. And the "September Six" were not only excommunicated by the Mormon Church for studying its history, social policy, and sexually abusive treatment of women and children, they were also fired by Brigham Young University.[26]

---

[26] Knowledge is carefully guarded by the Mormons, according to the former Mormons who spoke to me about this matter. For example, because Mormon men know the secret names of their wives, they can call for them after death to join them in heaven. Mormon women have no comparable power/knowledge. Mormons believe that "the glory of God is intelligence," but this also

As noted, the truth is far more mixed than this description of academic martyrdom would suggest. All institutions are susceptible to the conservatism of social learning; as Michel de Certeau puts it, "each 'discipline' maintains its ambivalence of being at once the law of a group and the law of a field of scientific research" (de Certeau 1988, 61). Academics are now, and always have been, in the grip of the group; and sometimes the research that least interests us concerns ourselves, and how we might better act on behalf of our communities while maintaining our allegiance to "pure" knowledge. It is, therefore, particularly vital at this time in history that we further the self-reflection we so generously propose to others—through, for example, the kinds of teaching and research ongoing at UC-Santa Barbara and many other universities on the public humanities. My colleague Alan Liu has for years devoted himself to finding new ways to be humanist, digitally and otherwise; my colleague Christopher Newfield, author of *Unmaking the Public University* (2011), runs a widely-respected weblog (with Michael Meranze from UCLA) on academic topics, *Remaking the University*; and my colleague Robert Samuels, author of *Why Higher Education Should Be Free* (2013), also maintains a similar weblog, *Changing Universities*.[27] I have taught a number of courses on the public humanities, as Newfield is now doing in the field of critical university studies. All of us have learned from a long line of predecessors (for example, Readings 1997, Engell 1999) and the continuing inspiration of figures like Stanton Glantz

means, "don't delve into the mysteries; the mysteries will take care of themselves."

[27] For more about one of Alan Liu's recent initiatives (with Geoffrey Rockwell and Melissa Terras), see "4 Humanities—Advocating for the Humanities," http://liu.english.ucsb.edu/category/new-media-projects/. See, also, Newfield's and Meranze's weblog, *Remaking the University*, http://utotherescue.blogspot.com/, and Samuels's weblog, *Changing Universities*, http://changinguniversities.blogspot.com/.

(UC-San Francisco, School of Medicine), an important advocate for the effects of secondhand smoke and for tobacco control, and Robert Meister (UC-Santa Cruz), who now advocates an academic activism that responds to the "financialization" of capital with financialized resistance (Meister 2013). No academic today, in whatever field, can afford to be ignorant of the historical, economic and political circumstances of his or her work, and every department and program should offer courses on these subjects so that our students are also appropriately informed.

Para-academic reflection, research, and activism—and I am arguing for *enhancing their interconnections*—include creativity, as even a cursory glance at the BABEL Working Group's website will demonstrate.[28] Many new means of getting academic are now appearing, provoking fresh wonder (in me, at least) at the resourcefulness of the truth drive and the minds/brains that further it.[29] I chose to publish *Staying Alive* with punctum books because open-access publishing is a brilliant way around the failure of academic and trade publishers to fend off corporatization and the consequent loss of quality (such as the ever-intensifying limits on page-length and reference apparatus) and even corruption (see Fan 2012). Open-access publishing also helps us to resist growing administrative and corporate attempts to interfere with academic intellectual property rights (as Meister puts it, academics, unlike journalists, *do not "work for hire,"* and therefore legally *retain the right to publish their own material as they choose*)—unless, as so many scientists have done, we sign away said rights on behalf of the corporations funding

---

[28] See BABEL Working Group, http://www.babelworkinggroup. org.

[29] See Joy and Neufeld (2007). Also see De Paulo et al. (2003) on the sufferings of liars, who "tell less compelling tales" than truth-tellers, and "make a more negative impression and are more tense" (74); and Grotstein (2004) on "The Implications of a Truth-Drive in Bion's Theory of 'O'."

our research.[30] When taxpayer money is also used in such projects, the "public" university becomes yet another covert means of transferring wealth from taxpayers to private corporations.

Openness cannot guarantee fairness (only because nothing can), but in these days of plummeting transparency, it seems both strategic and joyous to embrace it. *Share what you know.* When you go to a committee meeting and hear something interesting, tell someone else. The confidentiality requirements with respect to university business, including and especially the unspoken, habitual requirements, are absurd. The vast majority of university "secrets" have nothing to do with national security or protecting the privacy of particular persons. Don't keep secrets when there's no good reason to do so. The pleasure of being in the know, of being thought a good citizen, is an indulgence we can no longer afford. I once asked the Chair of UC-Santa Barbara's Academic Senate Committee on finance and budget for some information and was told it was confidential, *on no basis whatsoever*; I had to get the Senate President to tell her she had no business keeping Senate business from a member of the Senate. Everyone has hundreds of stories like this. None of us can afford to be like that committee chair. *Unless something is stamped "confidential" and there are FBI agents hovering in the hallways, we must always tell what we know.*

I opened *Staying Alive* to companion essays by earlier-career colleagues partly because rank and status barriers interfere too much with the connectivity academic communities need to build new strengths and new ways of living and knowledge-making in our benighted times. We inspire one another across boundaries of age and privilege, and now we can publish in ways consistent with the principles and communitarian pleasures of our research. The memes and models in my own work grow

---

[30] The Public Library of Science (PLoS) is a welcome development in this regard (http://www.plos.org/).

and change in the hands, minds, and brains of those who are remaking the discipline(s). The hybridity of *Staying Alive* (part monograph, part anthology) is meant to give form, in Suzanne Langer's sense (1977), to the undead dynamism that John Milton ascribed to books, ideas and writers in *Areopagitica* (1644): "For Books are not absolutely dead things, but doe contain a potencie of life in them, to be as active as that soule whose progeny they are." *Staying Alive* means to further as well as give form to intertextual relationality and friendship. And many new academic forms far more innovative than this are appearing every day, as happened in the 1970s with Derrida's *Glas* (1990).

Both creative and critical thinking must begin at home. Academics are prone to self-righteousness—a vanity we share with the religious right—and if we do not keep ourselves honest, no one will. God is not on the side of locationalism (specific brain functions are located in specific areas of the brain), nor does Satan sponsor work on neuroplasticity (wherein different areas of the brain can be recruited to perform new functions). At least, there is no evidence for supernatural intervention on these scores. Academic truths require evidence, logic, dissent and the forging of new working hypotheses. Faith is something else: it means *the willingness to believe in the unseen and unverifiable, in what we cannot directly know.* The Academy is not cultic, even if plenty of us are religious. But we are always tempted to mistake the knowledge we make for the last word on, say, cognition, or the laws of physics, and then along comes a Heisenberg, or an Antonio Damasio.

We are as unconscious as any body or any thing of the forces that have formed us, of the lives of our own cells, of ancient, embodied memories and the transpersonal transmissions of our neighbors. But we should at least be aware that we do not know ourselves fully, and I say this not to lay claim to the privilege of enlightenment, but rather to gesture to the responsibility we have to keep our knowledge disciplines open and unsettled. As Geoffrey Bennington has written about Derrida's "university without condition,"

> The University (and, more especially . . . the 'Humanities') have a responsibility to foster events of thought that cannot fail to unsettle the University in its Idea of itself. For this to happen, the special institution that the University is must open itself up to the possibility of unpredictable events . . . in a way that always might seem to threaten the very institution that it is. On this account, the University is in principle the institution that 'lives' the precarious chance and ruin of the institution as its very institutionality. (Bennington 2010, 28)

Our awareness of the limits of our awareness guides our research, at least when we are at our best. We know that ongoing analyses of our reasons for asking the questions we ask and answering as we do helps us learn more about the research topics we pursue. But this does not make us popular, even amongst ourselves. We require critical thinking because we assert that, as mortal creatures, we have our limits—we can't remake the world according to our wishes, though we can certainly change some of its courses. We intervene in Reality in significant ways, but it always exceeds our ability to grasp and manage it, and we can only flout its obduracies up to a point. This is one reason why, at least from Pythagoras onward, knowledge-communities have so often had an ascetic, a "disciplinary" aspect—one that we tend, unfortunately, to idealize. We need endlessly to undo this idealization, which is one reason for my own concern with discipline as a mode of *enjoyment*, and my sympathy with current attempts to emphasize the ludic, experimental, experiential aspects of study. I hope we can further our understanding of critical thinking as a *form of play*, and vice-versa; our lives are the richer when perceiving, thinking and feeling, along with stillness, playing and working, are fully interconnected.

Our habitual skepticism, however, coupled with the narrowness of our training, has a down side: exacerbation of the feeling of *not-mattering* that seems now to afflict creaturely subjectivity all over the world. All life matters, *because* of its rarity, variety, and uniqueness; I share the materials, experiential and otherwise, that make me what I am with a multitude of things and creatures, but "I" am an unrepeatable combination thereof; "I" am something that will never come again, at least in this universe. I love the idea that I am made and remade by astonishing flurries of cooperative multicellular activity. I would not trade my brilliantly complex, loyal and hardworking immune system for surgical knowledge (if I had to, which thankfully I don't), nor my amazing brain, which I love just because it is a brain, and because I am so lucky to have one, for a computer, nor my nervous system, not even the soles of my feet, nor my pheromonal receptivity, for anything at all; prosthetics are brilliant achievements, but we should not allow their value to eclipse the really quite unbelievable achievement that is the human brain/mind/body. *Take the measure of, take pleasure and pride in, what an astonishing being you are.* However much education or money you do or don't have, however well or badly treated, you are a finely-wrought, irreplaceable, brilliant achievement of eons and eons of transformations in "vibrant matter"—Jane Bennett's felicitous phrase (2010).

The recognition that we do not know ourselves fully is not incompatible with an appreciation of our brilliant complexity. Rather, the two go together: both are acknowledgments of the Real, of that which exceeds signification. In my view, the Real trenches on complexity, insofar as the latter designates a truly unmanageable, nontotalizable potential for change.[31] Complexity is a concept

---

[31] Complexity theory developed out of chaos theory; it models the dynamism of complex or "open" systems, wherein new de-

whose social implications technocracy can only try to manage; and it is the complexity of knowledge-production, and of the universities that shelter it, that will always exceed whatever the technocrats have planned for us. (Take over our universities? If it comes to that, we will start—and accredit—our own schools; indeed this process has already begun.[32]) While there are always "top-down" directives at work in complexity, they are also always buffeted and constrained by contingencies, copying "errors," and strange attractors at a distance. Impulses to manage and quantify this effervescence are doomed to failure, though capable of doing very costly damage along the way. What makes non-denominational universities so important—and some denominational ones too—is the diversity and complexity of their values, goals, and expertise. (The Right complains that we don't teach creationism or intelligent design; but that is because the scientific evidence does not point in that direction. Religious faith does. And anyway, for their part, right wing "Christian" schools don't teach much evolutionary theory either. "Fair and balanced" always means that it's the *other* people who should be fair and balanced.) Universities bring together hundreds of very different, sophisticated, ever-evolving methodologies, working environments, and research topics, in the hope that interdisciplinary relations will (as studies of creativity suggest they will) spark previously unimaginable insights. Real knowledge is "emergent," because, as noted, it is artifactual; it is made by living creatures working together and against one another—playing, exploring and critiquing each other's work across as well as within disciplines. Academic (inter)disciplines produce new understandings in the way all open (self-evolving)

velopments "emerge" from interactions across and between networks of forces and events. See Waldrop 1992, 17.

[32] See, for example, The Brooklyn Institute of Social Research (http://thebrooklyninstitute.com/), The Saxifrage School (http://saxifrageschool.org/), and the Urmadic University (http://www.theodessey.org/).

systems do, as evidenced by current rapproche-ments between the sciences and the humanities. However entrenched we are in our ways of doing things, we cross-
inspire each other, sometimes when we least expect it.
*Without the arts and humanities, our potential for scien-
tific and technological invention will be significantly compromised* (and vice-versa); what must be evaluated is not
simply what happens in one discipline or "division," but
what all disciplines accomplish together and against each
other.

That complexity, of course, links us in a thousand
million ways to our environs, and vice versa. Given what
we know now about the biology of communication and
social connection, about the simultaneity of proprioception and inter/exterioception,[33] we should, more than ever, understand that *everything* becomes part of our work,
one way or another, and therefore *it must always be a deliberate part of our work not simply to think critically
about the workings of our own (embodied) minds, but also
to reflect upon, and engage, our connectedness to wider
communities, because they are always in our work.* Political and ethical engagements do not divert us from our
work, as the right wing "reports" we have been considering would like us to believe. They are an inevitable and
necessary part of it. And here lies more of the self-defeating
(self-)destructivity, the death drive, that impels contemporary "management" of universities and the interests those
managers serve. It is a fact, not a piety, that exclusivity
profits no one, not even those who most enjoy it. So the
Academy needs to educate, not just the "public," but the
powerful, much more directly. *It is essential that we combat the policies that keep faculty away from trustees, regents, donors, and alumni, as if we were bearers of infec-
tion. After all, we were once their professors.* Western po-

---

[33] "Proprioception" refers to our ability to perceive the moving
parts of bodies, especially our own, as unified and purposive.
Interoception and exteroception refer to perceptions of interior
events and of the outside world, respectively.

litical writing has long made efforts to remind the wealthy and powerful (or those who would become so at any cost) of the laws of change and death—the very topic of Hans Holbein's well-known anamorphic painting *The Ambassadors* (1533). These reminders of the Real remain the responsibility (one of them, anyway) of any thinking person.

The fact is that the wealthy are mad as hatters, just like the rest of us, and we are almost as out of touch with what goes on in their heads (and their shadow governments, foundations, and banks) as the people who love being screwed by them.[34] What they have most in common, or hope they do, is the immunity that Esposito points out is the obverse of "community." When Karen Rothmeyer, then of the *Wall Street Journal,* asked Richard Scaife why he gave so much money to the religious right, his response was "you fucking Communist cunt, get out of here"— they were outdoors at the time (Rothmeyer 1982; see also Rothmeyer 1998). For "The Family," Hitler, Lenin and Jesus are all illustrious examples of the kind of power it wants for itself—"the power of a small core of people" (Sharlett 2008, 3). Sharlett reminds us, however, that despite the Family's "theological oddities"—"its concentric rings of secrecy, its fascination with megalomaniacs from Mao to Hitler, its conviction that being one of God's chosen provides diplomatic immunity"—the Family "is anything but separate from the world" (Sharlett 2008, 57). Never mind the strange bedfellows problem; political or religious differences can always be overcome by reserving anew, by further esotericizing, core bonds, resources, and convictions, in the name of advancing, with other groups, ideas about "control" and how to maintain it. (There may be limits, however, after all: Mormons are forbidden to become Masons, lest, according to my native informants,

---

[34] On corporations and psychopathy, see Babiak and Hare (2007, 94–97); for a nuanced discussion of leadership and mental illness, see Ghaemi (2011).

they discover the non-revelatory origins of so many of their practices, like the symbols on their underwear.)

The weird commonalities thus produced are a specialty of the Heritage Foundation. Even before Cribb, Cheney and their ilk began the "counter-offensive" against "college" in the 1980s, there were some strange days indeed. In the mid-1970s, Scaife's choice for head of the Heritage Foundation, Edwin Feulner, imported Stuart Butler, a member of the British Fabian Society, and a number of other like-minded subjects of the Queen. In its early days, the Fabian Society, enchanted by the enlightenment and enterprise of Renaissance England (Henry VIII was quite the union-buster), advocated a "gradualist" socialism (i.e. social "reconstruction," not revolution). Its Australian chapter was behind the "Half-Caste Act" that "saved" a generation of aboriginal children by taking them away from their parents (Robertson 2008).[35] The Fabians advocated slum clearances, eugenics (sterilization of the weak), and health services that would assist in the formation of an "Imperial race," one that would be more productive, disciplined and militant than the "stunted, anemic, demoralised denizens . . . of our great cities" (Semmel 1968, 85–90). Of course, they also wanted a national education system to help cultivate this new race, because *"it is in the classrooms . . . that the future battles of the Empire for commercial prosperity are already being lost"* (Semmel 1968, 63; my emphasis). The British Labour Party was founded by the Fabians to serve as its executive arm, so to speak. Ba'athism was its offshoot in the Middle East. It's a funny old world.

Edward Spannaus, a longtime Scaife antagonist, thinks the Heritage Foundation's socialist-conservative connection was based on a mutual "hatred of industrial capitalism" and its resistance to the charms of international financial and social engineering schemes. The subjection of industry to said schemes does seem to have been a feature of

---

[35] See also Robertson 2006, 36, for discussion of Australia's emphasis on "assimilation."

life in the U.S. at least since the mid-1970s, but the connection goes back to the 1930s, when Friedrich von Hayek moved his "feudal, aristocratic," monetarist "Austrian School" to the London School of Economics. Subsequently, von Hayek founded and headed the neo-liberal Mont Pelerin Society, of which Milton Friedman is a member. Scaife has also been funding Mont Pelerin's spinoff think tanks in the U.S. (see Spannaus 1997). Seen from this perspective, there's nothing particularly surprising about the religious Right's embrace of Mitt Romney in the last presidential election, as he is a prominent member of yet another secretive power-net-work devoted to the "building-up of Zion" (and Zion's architectural correlate, the Tabernacle), led by a President who receives the "continuing revelation" of Jesus Christ.

Not too long ago, *Newsweek* likened the Church of Latter Day Saints to "a sanctified multinational corporation—the General Electric of American religion, with global ambitions and an estimated net worth of $30 billion" (Kirn 2011). The net worth has to be "estimated" because the Church has not released a full financial statement since 1959. Romney's refusal, during his 2012 presidential bid, to release in full his own financial statements and tax returns is, like Scaife's entitled enjoyment of obscenity and lamentable lack of chivalry, a claim to immunity that mimes the practices of his cult. This is sovereignty in the mode of what Bataille calls *heterogeneity*—power's pursuit of *jouissance* and the fascinating effects thereof on all us neighbors (see Fradenburg 2002, 84, 270n9; Bersani 2008). Likewise, the core of Dick Cheney's appeal has always been his refusal of accountability, not his respectability. Think of his remarkable contention that the Vice-President is not part of the executive branch of the U.S. government, and therefore is not bound by the same orders governing the release of classified information as the White House (Rood 2007). Or his cool explanation for why he didn't serve in the armed forces during the Vietnam War: "I had other priorities." Or the way he was protected by his Texas friends from any legal consequences that might have flowed from unaccountably unloading his shotgun into a fellow quail hunter's face. No lame excuses like Bill Clinton's "I didn't inhale" for Cheney; he knows how to recover from embarrassment: never abandon the image of arbitrary and unstoppable power. It isn't true that the cover-up is always worse than the crime; sometimes the cover-up is the very thing that the most disenfranchised most admire. As Lynyrd Skynyrd famously and confusedly put it in their song "Sweet Home Alabama": "Watergate does not bother me; does your conscience bother you?"

I once met (in 1996) a Dartmouth alum, an arbitrageur who was also a Catharist. He showed me his very thick Cathar bible, but would not allow me to look in it, despite my credentials as a medievalist who had at one time studied the Albigensian Crusade. He explained that he had been drawn to Catharism partly because, to its way of thinking, it didn't matter what you did on earth; earth is just the realm of matter and evil, and no one is responsible in it or to it. Again we find the same love of secrecy and immunity—the same claims to exceptionalism and esotericism. And the same distaste for transparency, connectivity, exoteric knowledge, and community. The Mormon Church has a ritual in which its members must agree to be disemboweled if they reveal their secret names to the wrong people. It is a death cult, which worships a certain style of power: the power to hold in reserve, to deprive, keep secret, and control, rather than develop some healthy respect for the Real. We are indeed speaking of fantasies of omnipotence, which always fail to appreciate the force of the Øther (of the non-totalizable symbolic order); of megalomania, whose ambitions, as Freud noted, become vast in proportion to traumatic narcissistic injury (Freud 1958). How can we help to deprogram the rich? *Withdraw taxpayer assistance from all colleges and universities that continue to permit fraternities, sororities, dining clubs and secret societies to flourish on*

their campuses. Exclusionary societies on college and university campuses culture the think tanks and CEOs of the
future. They are in no way entitled to associate themselves with those colleges and universities, and no public
monies should be devoted to their well-being, directly or
indirectly. Never mind substance abuse or rape; boards of
trustees protect the student right to party because exclusionary societies are the petri dishes of occult political
and economic power. *Let's party in the open instead.*

Insofar as we para-academics are committed to the
production of knowledge and to the impossibility of fin-
alizing it, our moment demands that we "learn to think
the present, the now that we inhabit . . . as irreducibly
not-one" (Chakrabarty 2000, 249).[36] This call is urgent
because our moment is characterized by a simultaneous
overvaluation of modernity in the form of technology's
promise of immunity, and hatred of modernity's democratizing and demystifying tendencies (which hatred we
are then asked to project onto Islam). Medievalists are all
too familiar with these melancholic cults and cultivations
of power: Scaife's pride in being able to trace his family
back to medieval England (so could most of the Brewsters
of the world, with DNA testing); Catharism for capitalists; the eponymous "Fabian the Delayer"; Freemason-
ry's preoccupation with Solomon's Temple, Jerusalem,
the Crusades and the Templars; nearly everybody's des-
cent from one of the Twelve Tribes of Israel. It's all back
to the future. Is it a symptom of this melancholic ambivalence that contemporary threats to academic freedom are spearheaded by Israeli antagonism toward Middle Eastern scholars and open campus discussions of the
Palestinian "question"? (see Kurwa 2012).

This intense libidinal cathexis of the Old Testament
by Christian sectarians, audible everywhere on talk radio

---

[36]Postcolonial theory and Medieval Studies have been engaged
for a while now in a rich dialogue about "modernity"; see, for
example, Cohen (2000, 2008), Davis (2008), and Davis and Altschul (2009).

and in the Holy Land itself, is familiar to medievalists for having accompanied nearly every militant, persecuting turn of events in the European Middle Ages. The Family's seminars on "Biblical Capitalism" are another example; so is John Brown, of Dallas, Texas, who founded Zion Oil because he was persuaded by God, by certain verses in Genesis and Deuteronomy, and by the evangelist Jim Spillman's "treasure map" of the Jews' ancient tribal territories, to begin drilling on Maanit, an inland plain northeast of Tel Aviv. His geologist, Stephen Pierce, also a born-again Christian, said "there is science to support their faith in this project"; according to *USA Today*, an article of his in the "leading industry publication *Oil and Gas Journal*" notes Maanit's three geological reefs, formations "whose cavities and pockets can be [*sic*] full of oil" (Krauss 2005). At about the same time that Brown gained notoriety, thousands of evangelical Christians marched on the West Bank in celebration of Israel's capture of east Jerusalem in the 1967 war; they were described by the *Seattle Post-Intelligencer* as "fervent Zionists who believe [that the] return [of the Jews] to the biblical land of Israel will speed the Second Coming of Christ" (Copans 2005). This notion of the conversion of the Jews as necessary if not sufficient to the Apocalypse is an Augustinian position (as is the doctrine of "correction" as a form of love), and it is also a Mormon position: now, in the "last moment of the world," comes the prophesied one (Mitt Romney), who, had he won the election, might have redeemed America (for Mormons, of course). It was hoped that Romney's fulfillment of messianic prophecy would start off the final millennium, during which the Jews would finally bow down to Jesus and confess their errors. This is why Romney wants Jerusalem to be the capital of Israel; Israel has to be supported in every way, *no matter what it does (immunity again)*, because the Jews are also the Mormons' ancestors, the first chosen people (it's a Twelve Tribes thing); the Jews are just currently *mistaken* chosen people, who will be given the opportunity to bow the knee, and confess their errors. For some reason (see below), Israel thinks it wise policy to ally with such people; if they knew anything about medieval history, they might more wisely hesitate to do so.

A reasonable humility might suggest the dangers of trying to speed up God's providence—certainly Fabian the Delayer might not have approved. But never mind; militant theology has for centuries told us otherwise. The past is revivified to force God's hand in the name of a future that will *really* propel the "purified remnant" towards the New Jerusalem (Weber 1999, 52–53, 77). Being one of the elect means having immunity. These days the elect are so impatient that they can hardly wait to bypass death; they want to get it over with, they want the "living beyond" death that delivers the biggest all-time rush of aliveness (see Rickels 1991, 73). They're dying to frack the planet in order to fuel the future. Their solution to the energy crisis? Keep drilling, because what is buried in the earth is sublime; it is ready to be alive again, to be fire, after matter is destroyed. Again, the death cult: this is one reason why so much Mormon ritual involves tracing genealogies and baptizing the dead; both Hitler and Mussolini have, by such means, been invited to Mormon heaven (which is the *only* heaven). There are even proxy wedding ceremonies for the newly baptized dead; maybe Eva Braun and Hitler are finally living in undead wedded bliss. We are speaking both of forwardness and of controlling *reserves*, of propulsion *and* security technology; for capital today, these are the most significant defenses against vulnerability and the uncertainty that lies ahead. The exceptionalism and esotericism associated with the premodern past by our own day's death-cults of power— the dark side, you could say, of contemporary medievalism—is being acted out, rather than analyzed, everywhere we look.

We have to put a stop to megalomaniacal capitalism, by funding projects that enhance the present experience of living in preference (if we are forced to choose) to those meant to prepare invulnerable (immune) bodies for the day when the sun goes nova. To do this, academics have to dig, not for oil and gas, but for the crazies who are planning liftoff in the shadows. *We need scholarly hacking.* Again, I am not arguing conspiracy, but the reverse. While alliances are constantly being forged among the death cults of contemporary capitalism—as noted, said cults share a certain understanding of control and exclusivity—none of them really thinks the adherents to any cult other than their own have the slightest chance of gaining control of the world or getting into heaven. This is a major weakness. However much any one cult may think it can control the world, none knows that it is *in* a world whose realities—including rival cults—far outstrip it. *Transparency is not a political solution in and of itself, and we must remember that shadows nurture beautiful dreams as well as nightmares; but in the early 21st century, it is necessary thereto. Transparency is one of the most important effects of the truth-drive, and should therefore be fought for and practiced by every scholar, scientist, thinker, physician and artist inside the academy and out.*

REFERENCES

Adams, J. (1850-1856). "Letter to John Jebb, London, 10 September 1785." In *The Works of John Adams, Second President of the United States.* 10 vols., 9:538–543. Boston: Little, Brown.

Agamben, G. (2005). *The State of Exception*, trans. Kevin Attell. Chicago: University of Chicago Press.

Ames, M. (2011). "How UC Davis Chancellor Linda Katehi Brought Oppression Back to Greece's Universities." *naked capitalism*, November 23: http://www.nakedcapitalism.com /2011/11/mark-ames-how-uc-davis-chancellor-linda-katehi-brought-oppression-back-to-greece%E2%80%99s-universities. html.

Babiak, P. and R. Hare (2007). *Snakes in Suits: When Psychopaths Go to Work.* New York: Harper.

Bennett, J. (2010). *Vibrant Matter: A Political Ecology of Things.* Durham, NC: Duke University Press.

Bennington, G. (2010). "Foundations." In *Not Half No End: Militantly Melancholic Essays in Honor of Jacques Derrida*, 19–34. Edinburgh: Edinburgh University Press.

Bersani, L. (2008). "The Power of Evil and the Power of Love." In L. Bersani and A. Phillips, *Intimacies*, 57–88. Chicago: University of Chicago Press.

Butler, J. (2004). *Precarious Life: The Powers of Mourning and Violence.* London: Verso.

Califano, J.A., Jr. (1970). *The Student Revolution: A Global Confrontation.* New York: W. W. Norton.

Carrel, P. (2010). *The Handbook of Risk Management: Implementing a Post-Crisis Corporate Culture.* Chichester: John Wiley & Sons.

Chakrabarty, D. (2000). *Provincializing Europe: Postcolonial Thought and Historical Difference.* Princeton University Press.

Cheney, L. (1992). *Telling the Truth.* Washington, DC: National Endowment for the Humanities.

Cohen, J.J., ed. (2000). *The Postcolonial Middle Ages.* New York: Palgrave Macmillan.

Cohen, J.J., ed. (2008). *Cultural Diversity in the British Middle Ages: Archipelago, Island, England.* New York: Palgrave Macmillan.

Coley, R. and D. Lockwood (2012). *Cloud Time: The Inception of the Future.* Winchester, UK: Zero Books.

Copans, L. (2005). "Evangelicals, Jews Are Kindred Spirits." *Associated Press News Archive,* 24 October; http://www.ap newsarchive.com/2005/Evangelicals-Jews-Are-Kindred-Spirits/id-72402c2a0269dc23c92d7b0f1a56c23b.

Copulus, M.R. (1984). "The LaRouche Network." The Heritage Foundation, July 19: http://www.heritage.org/research/reports/1984/07/the-larouche-network.

de Certeau, M. (1988). *The Writing of History*, trans. Tom Conley. New York: Columbia University Press.

Davis, K. (2008). *Periodization and Sovereignty: How Ideas of Feudalism and Secularization Govern the Politics of Time.* Philadelphia: University of Pennsylvania Press.

Davis, K. and N. Altschul, eds. (2009). *Medievalisms in the Postcolonial World: The Idea of the "Middle Ages" Outside Europe.* Baltimore: Johns Hopkins University Press.

De Paulo, B., et al. (2003). "Cues to Deception." *Psychological Bulletin* 129: 74–118.

Derrida, J. (1990). *Glas*, trans. J.P. Leavey and R. Rand. Lincoln: University of Nebraska Press.

Engell, J. and A. Dangerfield (1998). "The Market-Model University: Humanities in the Age of Money." *Harvard Magazine* (May-June): 48–55, 111.

Engell, J. (1999). *The Committed Word: Literature and Public Values*. University Park: Pennsylvania State University Press.

Engell, J. and A. Dangerfield (2005). *Saving Higher Education in the Age of Money*. Charlottesville: University of Virginia Press.

Esposito, R. (2011). *Immunitas*, trans. Zakiya Hanafi. Cambridge, UK: Polity.

European Ministers of Education (1999). "The Bologna Declaration of 19 June 1999," http://www.bologna-berlin2003.de/pdf/bologna_declaration.pdf.

Fan, X (2012). "University Publishers Fined Over Bribery Scandal." *Cherwell*, July 8: http://www.cherwell.org/news/top stories/2012/07/08/university-publishers-fined-over-bribery-scandal.

Fradenburg, L.O. (1991). *City, Marriage, Tournament: Arts of Rule in Late Medieval Scotland*. Madison: University of Wisconsin Press.

Fradenburg, L.O.A. (2002). *Sacrifice Your Love: Psychoanalysis, Historicism, Chaucer*. Minneapolis: University of Minnesota Press.

Freud, S. (1958). "Psychoanalytic Notes on an Autobiographical Account of a Case of Paranoia (Dementia Paranoides)." In *The Standard Edition of the Psychological Works of Sigmund Freud,* ed. James Strachey, Vol. 12, 33–82. London: Hogarth Press.

Galloway, A. (2006). *Protocol: How Control Exists After Decentralization*. Cambridge, MA: MIT Press.

Galloway, A. and E. Thacker (2007). *The Exploit: A Theory of Networks*. Minneapolis: University of Minnesota Press.

Ghaemi, N. (2011). *A First-Rate Madness: Uncovering the Links Between Leadership and Mental Illness*. New York: Penguin.

Grotstein, J. (2004). "The Seventh Servant: The Implications of a Truth Drive in Bion's Theory of 'O'." *International Journal of Psychoanalysis* 85: 1081–1101.

Hedges, C. (2012). "Criminalizing Dissent." *truthdig: drilling beneath the headlines,* August 13: http://www.truthdig.com/report/item/criminalizing_dissent_20120813/.

Hoffmeyer, J. (2008). *Biosemiotics: An Examination into the Signs of Life and the Life of Signs.* Scranton: University of Scranton Press.

Howard-Jones, P. (2010). *Introducing Neuroeducational Research: Neuroscience, Education and the Brain from Contexts to Practice.* New York: Routledge.

Hundley, K. (2011). "Billionaire's Role in Hiring Decisions at Florida State University Raises Questions." *Tampa Bay Times,* May 10: http://www.tampabay.com/news/business/billionaires-role-in-hiring-decisions-at-florida-state-university-raises/1168680.

International Commission on Higher Education in Greece (2011). "Report of the International Commission on Higher Education in Greece," February; available at: *Not the Majority Opinion* [weblog of J. Panaretos]: http://notthemajority opinion.blogspot.com/2011/04/report-of-international-advisory.html.

Jacobs, J. (1985). *Cities and the Wealth of Nations.* New York: Vintage.

Johnson, D. (2003). "Who's Behind the Attack on Liberal Professors?" *History News Network,* February 10; http://hnn.us/articles/1244.html.

Joy, E.A. and C.M. Neufeld (2007). "A Confession of Faith: Notes Toward a New Humanism." *Journal of Narrative Theory* 37: 161–190.

Kirn, W. (2011). "Mormons Rock!" *Newsweek,* June 5: http://www.thedailybeast.com/newsweek/2011/06/05/mormons-rock.print.html.

Kozlowski, K. and M. Hicks (2012). "Wayne State's Tenure Proposal Stirs Controversy." *The Detroit News,* July 23: http://www.detroitnews.com/apps/pbcs.dll/article?AID=/201207230100/METRO/207230390.

Krauss, L. (2005). "His Mission: Seek and Ye Shall Find Oil." *USA Today,* May 18: http://usatoday30.usatoday.com/news/world/2005-05-18-israel-oil_x.htm.

Kurwa, R. (2012). "How the UC Administration Censors Students and Faculty Who Stand Up for Student Rights." *Mondoweiss: The War of Ideas in the Middle East,* August 23: http://mondoweiss.net/2012/08/timeline-how-the-uc-ad

ministration-censors-students-and-faculty-who-stand-up-for-human-rights.html.

Larouche, L. and D. Goldman (1980). *The Ugly Truth About Milton Friedman*. New York: New Benjamin Franklin House.

Langer, S. (1977). *Feeling and Form*. New York: Longman.

Lee, H.K. and K. Fagan (2012). "Pepper-sprayed UC Davis Protesters Won't Be Charged." *San Francisco Chronicle*, January 23: http://www.sfgate.com/default/article/Pepper-sprayed-UC-Davis-activists-won-t-be-charged-2664257.php.

Lipton, S. (1999). *Images of Intolerance: The Representation of Jews and Judaism in the Bible Moralisée*. Berkeley: University of California Press.

Margulis, L. (1998). *Symbiotic Planet: A New Look at Evolution*. New York: Basic Books.

Meister, R. (2013). "Liquidity." Unpublished paper, presented at the "Futures of Finance" Summer Institute, June 11, New York City, New York, and at the "Cultures of Finance" Conference, August 15, Stockholm, Sweden.

Mesiter, R. (2012). "Brown and Yudof Bail on the Master Plan." *Keep California's Promise*, July 1: http://keepcaliforniaspromise.org/2628/brown-and-yudof-bail-on-the-master-plan.

Messer-Davidow, E. (1993). "Manufacturing the Attack on Liberalized Higher Education." *Social Text* 36: 40–80.

Milton, J. (1644). *Areopagitica*. *Project Gutenberg*: http://www.gutenberg.org/files/608/608-h/608-h.htm.

Nash, G.B., C. Crabtree, and R.E. Dunn (2000). *History on Trial: Culture Wars and the Teaching of the Past*. New York: Vintage.

Newfield, C. (2011). *Unmaking the Public University: The Forty-Year Assault on the Middle Class*. Cambridge, MA: Harvard University Press.

Nussbaum, M. (2010). *Not for Profit: Why Democracy Needs the Humanities*. Princeton: Princeton University Press.

Pape, R. (2005) *Dying to Win: The Strategic Logic of Suicide Terrorism*. New York: Random House.

Pritscher, C.F. (2010). *Einstein and Zen: Learning to Learn (Counterpoints: Studies in the Postmodern Theory of Education)*. New York: Peter Lang.

PRWEB (2011). "Kroll Announces Top Ten Cyber Security Trends for 2012." *PRWeb.com*, December 14: http:// www.com/releases/TopCyberSecurityTrends/2012/prweb9039507.htm.

Readings, B. (1997). *The University in Ruins*. Cambridge, MA: Harvard University Press.

Reuter, C. (2004). *My Life is a Weapon: A Modern History of Suicide Bombing*, trans. Helena Ragg-Kirby. Princeton: Princeton University Press.

Rickels, L. (1991). *The Case of California*. Baltimore: Johns Hopkins University Press.

Robertson, G. (2008). "We should say sorry, too." *The Guardian*, February 13: http://www.guardian.co.uk/commentisfree/2008/feb/14/australia.

Rood, J. (2007). "Cheney Power Grab: Says White House Rules Don't Apply to Him," *ABC News Blogs*, June 21: http://abc news.go.com/blogs/headlines/2007/06/cheney -power-gr/.

Rothmeyer, K. (1982). "Citizen Scaife." *Harvard Square Library*: http://www.harvardsquarelibrary.org/speakout/scaife.html. Abridged from H.F. Vetter, *Speak Out Against the New Right* (Boston: Beacon Press).

Rothmeyer, K. (1998). "The Man Behind the Mask." *Salon*, April 7: http://www.salon.com/news/1998/04/07news.html.

Samuels, R. (2013). *Why Public Higher Education Should Be Free: How To Decrease Cost and Increase Quality at American Universities*. New Brunswick: Rutgers University Press.

Savage, J.E. (n.d.). "The Role of Tenure in Higher Education." Brown University, Computer Science Dept.: http://cs.brown.edu/~jes/papers/tenure.html.

Schwartz, Amy E. (1992). "Some Politics at the NEH." *The Washington Post*, September 8, A 21.

Scott, D.L. (2012). "How the American University Was Killed, In Five Easy Steps." *The Homeless Adjunct* [weblog] August 12: http://junctrebellion.wordpress.com/2012/08/12/how-the-american-university-was-killed-in-five-easy-steps/.

Semmel, B. (1968). *Imperialism and Social Reform: English Social-Imperial Thought 1895-1914*. New York: Anchor.

Sharlett, J. (2008). *The Family: The Secret Fundamentalism at the Heart of American Power*. New York: Harper-Collins.

Sizemore, B. (2012). "Ex-Blackwater Faces Lawsuit Over New Name, Academi." *The Virginian Pilot*, July 7; http://hampton roads.com/2012/07/exblackwater-faces-lawsuit-over-new -name-academi.

Spannaus, E. (1997). "Richard Mellon Scaife: Who Is He Really?" *The Executive Intelligence Review*, March 21: http://american _almanac.tripod.com/scaife.htm.

Strauss, V. (2011). "Did FSU Let Billionaire Buy Professorships?" *The Washington Post*, May 16; http://www.washingtonpost.com/blogs/answer-sheet/post/did-fsu-let-billionaire-buy-professorships/2011/05/15/AFwzdR4G_blog.html.

Thacker, E. (2004). *Biomedia*. Minneapolis: University of Minnesota Press.

Virilio, P. (2006). *The Information Bomb*. London: Verso.

Waldrop, M.M. (1992). *Complexity: The Emerging Science at the Edge of Order and Chaos*. New York: Simon and Schuster.

Weber, E. (1999). *Apocalypses: Prophecies, Cults, and Millennial Beliefs Through the Ages*. Cambridge, MA: Harvard University Press.

Xu, D. and S. Jaggers (2013a). "Adaptability to Online Learning: Differences Across Types of Students and Academic Subject Areas" [CCRC Working Paper], Columbia University: Academic Commons: http://academiccommons.columbia.edu/item/ac:157286.

Xu, D. and S. Jaggers (2013b). "The Impact of Online Learning on Students' Course Outcomes: Evidence from a Large Community and Technical College System." *Economics of Education Review*, August 25: http://dx.doi.org/10.1016/j.econedurev.2013.08.001.

An Army of Lovers

Julie Orlemanski

AN ARMY OF LOVERS CAN BE BEATEN. These things appear on the walls of the Red district in the course of the night. Nobody can track down the author or painter for any of them, leading you to suspect they're one and the same. Enough to make you believe in a folk consciousness. They are not slogans so much as texts, revealed in order to be thought about, expanded on, translated into action by the people . . . .

Thomas Pynchon, *Gravity's Rainbow*

Late in the first part of Thomas Pynchon's *Gravity's Rainbow*, Leni Pökler stands at the window in the damp Berlin night. She's left her husband and is on the run with her daughter, who sleeps in a corner of the safe-house on a heap of old communist magazines. The city's stale, fungal vitality seeps into the room, across its stained walls, into the clammy chunk of bread passed from hand to hand. It seems simultaneously to smother any revolutionary spark in the Red district and to enfold its potential, to nestle and shelter it. The ambivalence of the mood—suspended between the futility and the tender possibility of revolutionary resistance—vibrates in the single snatch of graffiti glimpsed on the walls: AN ARMY OF LOVERS CAN BE BEATEN.

I was reminded of this passage, and of Pynchon's 1973 novel more generally, in reading Aranye Fradenburg's urgent, thoughtful essay "Driving Education." 1973 was the year, incidentally, as Fradenburg reminds us, when the tanks rolled in to Athens Polytechnic, suppressing campus protests against the Greek military junta. The biography of Linda Katehi, the Greek-American chancellor of the University of California, Davis since 2009, links one violent suppression to another: namely, the Greek tanks Katehi witnessed, but did not oppose, in 1973 and the point-blank pepper-spraying of UC-Davis student activists in 2011, under Katehi's leadership. Fradenburg describes how the chancellor's career links "securitization" and neoliberal educational reforms in Greece and California, forty years ago and today. The task of picturing such connections—networks of share-holder profits, of "risk" and "risk management," paranoia, emergency, fascism, violence, and precarity—is assumed both by Pynchon's novel and Fradenburg's essay. "I am not speaking of conspiracy; I am speaking of an 'emergent' phenomenon," Fradenburg writes. The "emergent" situation "certainly has concentrations of forces, but no single center point from which domination radiates." Likewise, Pynchon's novel inscribes paranoia but withholds the singular conspiracy that would justify it: "But I tell you there is no such message, no such home" (Pynchon 1973, 148–149).

Pynchon's novel remains one of the great documents for imagining the capitalism we continue to inhabit: the decentralized omnipresence of corporations, the "creative destruction" by which this infrastructure extends itself, and the aping of the web of globalized connections in (as Fradenburg writes) the "exceptionalism and esotericism associated with the premodern past by our own day's death-cults of power—the dark side, you could say, of contemporary medievalism—[that] is being acted out, rather than analyzed, everywhere we look." But *Gravity's Rainbow* also resonates with Fradenburg's larger corpus insofar as it is a vast anatomy of play, and the play of desire, within frameworks of coercion. In Pynchon's novel, playfulness is a catalyst for narrative action as well as the electric charge in the text's aesthetic plasma. Fradenburg's brilliant accounts of medieval literature and courtly culture have been exemplary in their ability to think eros within the matrices of constraint—and to explore how "restraint, sacrifice, duty, 'containment,' *are* forms taken by desire" (Fradenburg 2002, 7). Play is increasingly central to Fradenburg's conceptions of cultural and scholarly practice. "I hope we can further understand critical thinking as a *form of play*, and vice versa," Fradenburg writes. "Innovation always takes the form of manifest enjoyment of the signifier's powers" (Fradenburg 2009, 93). In joining systemicity to play and imperative to pleasure, Pynchon's novel and Fradenburg's scholarly corpus converge.

The epigraph on the first page of *Gravity's Rainbow* comes from the Nazi-turned-NASA-scientist Wernher von Braun, shortly before the 1969 Apollo moon launch: "Nature does not know extinction; all it knows is transformation. Everything science has taught me, and continues to teach me, strengthens my belief in the continuity of our spiritual existence after death." Attach-ed to von Braun's name, the novel's inaugural words (its epigraph) stage the queasy homologies of natural trans-formation, mystical consolation, and the technocratic "flex-ibility" that repurposes a Nazi weapons expert to put a man on the moon. How might we insist on the distinction between late-captialist *flexibility* and the potentially *liberatory* capacities for transformation? This is among the questions that the essays in *Staying Alive* implicitly pose as they explore the ability to change that Fradenburg elsewhere calls "plasticity" and "resilience" (Fradenburg 2011b).

While much of Fradenburg's recent work has focused on the adaptations that art and play foster, "Driving Education" performs what may be a necessary accompaniment to aesthetic imagination: a critical investigation of the social world that makes those practices possible or impossible, allows them to thrive or renders them precarious. Aside from carrying out such a critical investigation, "Driving Education" presents the claim that such self-awareness is integral to scholarly research. The irreducible and finally inexhaustible complexity out of which our knowledge emerges should appear as a dimension of that knowledge:

> *everything* becomes part of our work, one way or another, and therefore it must *always* be a *deliberate* part of our work not simply to think critically about the workings of our own (embodied) minds, but also to reflect on, and engage, our connectedness to wider communities, *because they are in our work.*

Since we can never get to the bottom of the "the forces that have formed us," as Fradenburg writes, we have a "responsibility . . . to keep our knowledge disciplines opened and unsettled." In "Driving Education," this responsibility entails mapping and describing that "edge of a knife" on which the future of the humanities teeters. The endeavor continues, after a fashion, the psychoanalytic project Fradenburg carried out so well in *Sacrifice Your Love: Psychoanalysis, Historicism, Chaucer*, insofar as it follows the premise that "the un/conscious desire of the observer changes the object of observation, and *analysis of this desire can produce knowledge about the object*" (Fradenburg 2002, 47). Such epistemic inextricability of subject and object resonates with Stefan Collini's recent account of knowledge in the humanities: "no starting-point is beyond reconsideration, because no assumptions (about how societies change or how people act or how meanings mean) are beyond challenge, because no vocabulary has an exclusive monopoly" (Collini 2012, 66). Insofar as our knowledge-production is intricated with malleable identities, communities, and historical understandings, its premises remain radically open to re-making.

Viewed from another perspective, a book like *Staying Alive* could appear to be *extra-* or *meta-*disciplinary, stan-ding over and apart from the standard production of aca-demic knowledge. For instance, Stanley Fish argues that disciplinary self-understanding is necessarily extrinsic to scholarship:

> [C]an you simultaneously operate within a practice and be self-consciously in touch with the conditions that enable it? The answer could be yes only if you could achieve a reflective distance from those conditions while still engaging in the prac-tice; but once the conditions enabling a practice become the object of analytic attention . . . , you are engaging in another practice (the practice of reflecting on the conditions of a practice you are not now practicing) . . . . Once you turn, for exam-ple, from actually performing literary criticism to examining the 'network of forces and factors' that underlie the performance, literary criticism is no longer what you are performing. (Fish 1994, 240)

What Fish does not allow for is that a scholarly text, or a body of writings, may encode a *process* for incorporating "practice" and "reflection." It is not the work of a mo-ment, a flash of comprehending both oneself and one's object. Instead, as Fradenburg avers, such a process is "about signifiying and thereby about becoming. It isn't so much about finishing." The movements of this knowledge-production are "counter-traumatic," insofar as they "permit change, tolerate the frustrations of process, and therefore address anxiety" (Fradenburg 2011a, 57). Fradenburg's whole body of work, and *Staying Alive* in particular, provide a practical rejoinder to Fish's claim that only an abrupt coincidence of scholarly practice and self-reflection will do. Issues that may well seem outside of disciplinary inquiry turn out to be right at the heart of academic knowledge, "*in our work.*"

The present essay responds to Fradenburg's "Driving Education"—tracing an echo, identifying a genre, and giving a report. The *echo* is the one shared with Pynchon's "army of lovers," a phrase that vibrates with the same chords of resistance, vulnerability, playfulness, and eros as do the pages of *Staying Alive.* An "army of lovers," after all, is one way (a sentimental, but perhaps energizing, way) of naming those who would defend and support the humanities and fine arts, or fight for speculative thought and the study of the past. The *genre* in which I locate "Driving Education" is what I am going to call "academic-activist reflexivity." Finally, I offer a *report* on three of the "publics" addressed, and in part constructed, by academic-activist writings: those of *citizens*, of *workers*, and of *amateurs.*

"Academic-activist reflexivity" is admittedly a clunky name, and I would welcome other terms to categorize the critical accounts of higher education currently being articulated in blogs, books, articles, tweets, talks, and other formats, including direct action. While there have always been "activist" texts concerning the state of higher education, the ascendance of digital media has transformed the scale and scope of the conversation. A broader range of those involved in post-secondary education can participate in the discussion and publish—*make public*—their perspectives and analyses. While "genre" may be too narrow and delimited a category for what I'm describing, and "discourse" too broad, the important point is that a set of commonalities are shared across the texts of "academic-activist reflexivity." I'll draw attention to a few. First, while these numerous accounts of higher education differ widely, they tend to express dissatisfaction with neoliberal changes to academic life—that is, with the ways in which higher education has been rendered increasingly amenable to (if not indistinguishable from) commercial and financial markets. Second, academic-activist writings produce dialogic coherence by cross-linking, or (to use a more medieval term) *compiling*, sources: by retweeting, collating links in a blog, and selecting and organizing points of knowledge from the frenetic information landscape. These practices give rise to the sense of a shared project. Fradenburg's "Driving Education" is an example of this compilatory generosity; it draws on an especially broad selection of sources—journalistic, scholarly, theoretical, documentary, electronic, print, traditionally authoritative, seemingly ephemeral . . . .

Third, these writings are *activist* insofar as they seek, explicitly or implicitly, to mobilize collective change in higher education. They pursue this end largely through *critique*: by giving an account of the kind of thing that higher education is right now—what configurations of persons, practices, moneys, attitudes, affects, and technologies it mobilizes—and identifying the consequences and the meanings of these situations. I would suggest that activist-academic writings offer counter-evidence to the rebuke of scholarly critique recently made by, among others, Bruno Latour[1] and Sharon Marcus and Stephen Best.[2] Such anti-critical polemics tend to discount the

---

[1] For instance: "*what performs a critique cannot also compose*. It is really a mundane question of having the right tools for the right job. With a hammer (or a sledgehammer) in hand you can do a lot of things: break down walls, destroy idols, ridicule prejudices, but you cannot repair, take care, assemble, reassemble, stitch together. It is no more possible to compose with the paraphernalia of critique than it is to cook with a seesaw" (Latour 2010). See also Latour 2004.

[2] Best and Marcus offer tendentious caricatures of critique's

political efficacy of knowledge about knowledge claims. However, this dismissal tends to pay attention only to the informational content of academic-activist writings, not to their rhetorical dimensions. They also communicate *to* someone. They rely on their ability to call upon and affect an audience—a potentially politicized collective. The wide range of formats, vocabularies, and modes of address characteristic of academic-activist reflexivity suggest that the effect of the genre is to pluralize and expand who we talk to when we talk about higher ed. In other words, these writings help construct new, and collective, *subjects of address.* The rhetorical work of "constructing publics" provides one means of answering Eve Kosofsky Sedgwick's call for the *tactical* analysis of critique, of whether it empowers or merely diverts us: "What does knowledge *do*—the pursuit of it, the having and exposing of it, the receiving again of knowledge one already knows? *How*, in short, is knowledge performative, and how best does one move among its causes and effects?" (Sedgwick 2002, 124). The value of academic-activist writings depends upon their performative force. Who do they mobilize, to do what? Thus, below I consider some of the audiences convoked by the blogs, essays, journalism, and social media of academic activism. Compiling a few of the powerful voices and ideas that I've come across in my own reading is one of the essay's aims; another is to take preliminary steps toward tactical evaluation.

Like Pynchon's Red district graffiti, the commun-

---

delusions of grandeur; for instance, "Where it had become common for literary scholars to equate their work with political activism, the disasters and triumphs of the last decade have shown that literary criticism alone is not sufficient to effect change" (Best and Marcus 2009, 2). They attribute to these "suspicious" readers "the untenable claim that we are always more free than those who produce the texts we study and that our insights and methods therefore have the power to confer freedom" (2009, 18).

ications of activist-academic reflexivity constitute an archive that is both monumental and ephemeral, that feels alternately neighborly and anonymous. They help form the malleable architecture of our intellectual and professional habitus. These texts link together collectives that may be irreducibly vulnerable because their unity derives not from military discipline, not from pursuit of "profit" or "security," but from something closer to caritas and eros. "AN ARMY OF LOVERS CAN BE BEATEN"—but will it be? If defeat is possible—or is *likely*, or snapping at our heels—then we have a responsibility to evaluate how best to help stave it off, cheat death, shift the tactics, transform the terrain. "Driving Education" is concerned to assemble some of the crucial facts about precisely how the liberal arts and the resources of the past are being valued and devalued, funded and defunded, desired and manipulated in the present. I offer below a partial account of the audiences to which academic-activist writings address themselves beyond any narrow definition of the university. My comments might be thought of as a gloss on the graffiti that appears on the decaying walls of Pynchon's Berlin—"not slogans so much as texts, revealed in order to be thought about, expanded on, translated into action by the people . . . ."

* * *

In his important essay "History as a Challenge to the Idea of the University," Jeffrey J. Williams points out many of the blind spots characteristic of laments over the fate of U.S. universities. One is the failure to imagine alternative futures. "We resort to nostalgia […] rather than imagine new possibilities," Williams writes (Williams 2005, 69). Such a "politics of nostalgia" tends to idealize the university lost as a "*refugium* or *humanistic enclave*," which, Williams argues, does not accurately describe past institutions nor present us with a more democratic future (Williams 2005, 59). Similarly Aaron Bady notes how our envisioning of the future tends to rely on memories of the past, especially when imagining the fate of public universities:

> . . . in practice, the "other world" we work for tends to look a lot like the world we know was possible—and can show by pointing to the past—because we can recall it through glowing accounts of the postwar boom, and because in an age of austerity, it seems more possible, more practical to recover what we used to have than to try to create something new. . . . In defending ourselves from the worsening future, we can gloss over the flaws of the past. (Bady 2013)

Williams and Bady encourage us to think carefully about the resources we have for orienting academic-activist writings toward the future. Since more than idealizations of the past are needed, mobilizing new "publics" to imagine alternatives and help construct them is essential. In calling on new collectivities to lay claim to higher education, the voices of activist-academic reflexivity are seeding futures that depart from the neoliberal horizons of austerity and crisis.

The first subject of address that I'll discuss here is the *citizenry*, or the "public" of public education. A web of political and civic ties connects people to particular schools and the broader system of higher ed. Taxes, state budgets, sports fandom, alumni networks, shared history, and civic pride already consitute a web of connections that give tensility and social reality to this group. The University of California system perhaps best exemplifies the strengths and the vulnerabilities of the attempt to mobilize the *citizenry* on behalf of higher education. In "Driving Education," Fradenburg, a professor at UC-Santa Barbara, discusses Governor Jerry Brown's disregard for the state's groundbreaking "Master Plan for Higher Education," as the 1960 Donahue Act is widely known.

The Master Plan was "a blanket commitment from the state to educate all the California students who wanted an education and, in doing so, to facilitate the kind of class mobility that has placed public education at the center of American civic life" (Bady and Konczal 2012). Governor Brown's contempt for the Master Plan, writes Fradenburg, effects an "autocratic end-run around the legislature, the thousands of Californians who have petitioned to preserve the Master Plan," and the UC faculty who ensured their institutions' compliance with the Plan. The perception of Brown's presumptiveness also indicates the grounds for resistance to it: communities of political, civic, and institutional actors are already mobilized on behalf of public higher education.

Gina Patnaik's online essay, "Breaking Trust: The Past and Future of the University of California," describes the legal history of the concept of "public trust," the phrase that defined California's protection of its universities in the state's 1879 constitution. The concept of public trust, Patnaik documents, is not reducible to a claim on land or property. In the context of legal history, "public trust" rather "reconfigures the terms of university space [...] as the area necessary for undertaking the enterprises of public education." Patnaik explicitly casts the history she tells in terms of the alternative futures it might give rise to. Faced with "the vanishing sense of public accountability for higher education," she argues, "public trust doctrine in California provides an alternate history: what *might* have shaped the terms of public education in our present moment?" If the University of California "had remained a site of embattled interests and active public dissent, would we have acquired new language to discuss the state's responsibility to protect public education? Can we imagine our way to such claims today?" Patnaik's essay is an example of critical, activist historiography, one that offers the legal concept of "public trust" as a tactical and imaginative tool for laying claim to the university system. It reveals the basis for Californians' claim on the state universities as a public good.

From the perspective of tactical analysis, how effective have academic-activist appeals to the citizenry been? Despite the democratic breadth and historical depth of appeals to California residents, the UC system remains under attack. State-specific obstacles are part of the problem—for instance, the political immunity of the UC Board of Regents. More broadly, however, U.S. politics is so saturated with the neoliberal vocabulary of austerity, and so beholden to the corporate power brokers who deliver it, that it turns out to be almost Sisyphian to advance legislation that expands state spending on education. The "public" character of higher education is being eroded nationally, as out-of-state tuition and corporate partnerships make up more and more of state-school budgets. It remains unclear what a mobilized citizenry can effectively do against today's ironclad truism that public welfare is best served by bolstering private profit-making enterprises. In many cases, for-profit companies devour whatever public funds there are. For-profit schools, for instance, while only educating about ten percent of post-secondary students, "receive around a quarter of the Pell Grants and student loans. A recent Senate study found that 'the 15 publicly traded for-profit education companies received 86 percent of revenues from taxpayers'" (Bady and Konczal 2012). Given the current system of political priorities and influence, legislators appear unlikely to recommit to massive funding for higher education. Academic-activism needs to look for effective points of leverage.

One group that does have a stronger claim to power in higher education is "laborers at the point of production"—that is, instructors, both tenure-stream and adjunct or temporary. These are the second subject of address for academic-activist writing that I will discuss. Without instructors' labor, the daily business of higher education would grind to a halt. Right now it would seem that the crucial problem facing academic-labor organizing is how to build solidarity across the hierarchies of the profession. How do shared—but not *equally* shared—conditions of precarity provide the grounds for organizing and for coordinated action?

Thus far, the advantages of concerted action have been almost entirely on the side of financial markets and their administrative yes-men. When Moody's Investors Service downgraded its financial outlook for colleges and universities as a whole in January 2013, the bond-credit-rating company advised "bolder actions by university leaders to reduce costs and increase operational efficiency," especially through "strong governance and management leadership" (Martin 2013). It is hard to miss the uniformity with such investor demands have been implemented. The "bolder" administrative measures have been concerned to reduce instructors' labor power—i.e., to decrease the value of instructors' work and thereby the leverage they have in controlling their labor. Examples of this devaluing of academic labor include investment in automatized software to grade student writing (Markoff 2013), Harvard's recruitment of alumni to act as unpaid teaching staff for online courses (Pérez-Peña 2013), the enthusiasm for massive open online courses (or MOOCs), and the current all-time high in the proportion of university faculty who are adjuncts (76 percent) (Lewin 2013). Paul Boshears notes the extreme devaluation actually realized by MOOCs: "today, the value of some of the most gifted lecturers has approached zero. Their talent at communicating their knowledge is given away for free" (Boshears 2012; also see Rees 2013).

The vulnerability of adjuncts has long been noted and lamented, but whatever good intentions tenure-stream faculty have had regarding this issue, their sentiments have been inadequate to stem the "adjunctification" of higher education. Nor have good intentions done much to change adjuncts' working conditions, including low pay, temporary contracts, lack of health insurance, and exclusion from institutional resources. The unfortunate fact is that precarity is currently being *universalized* in academic labor. A recent dispute at Wayne State well illustrates the point. In July of 2012, the Wayne State administration proposed measures to eliminate tenure protections, enabling dismissal of tenured faculty on account of a "financially based reduction in [work] force" or actions construed as disruptive to the functioning of the university (presumably including political and labor protests) (Jaschik 2012). In other words, tenure would be no defense against austerity or administrative oversight. While the faculty union eventually reached an agreement that preserved tenure protections, the case offers a pointed lesson. If each member of our profession atomistically pursues the goal of tenure, the few who achieve it may find it utterly transformed. Though perhaps still officially on the books (as it was slated to be at Wayne State), "tenure" may not offer job security or protection for unpopular opinions and actions.

Sarah Kendzior, now a journalist but formerly an academic job seeker, recently chastised tenure-stream faculty for luxuriating in their exceptionality: "Success is meaningless when the system that sustained it—the higher education system—is no longer sustainable. When it falls, everyone falls" (Kendzior 2013). While I agree with Kendzior's point, the urgent task would seem to be figuring out *how* to build labor solidarity when so many factors conspire against it, such as adjuncts' often mandated absence from institutional decision-making, their *de facto* exclusion from spaces of academic collegiality, "two-tiered unionism," and the professional demands that keep almost all faculty very, very busy. To make the collective clout of instructors a reality, academic-activist reflexivity needs both to address inequalities within academic labor and to search out the ways in which neoliberal institutions are vulnerable to labor organizing. *Mutual aid* provides the only solid foundation for such organizing: it is clear that only together can tenure-stream faculty and adjuncts insist upon the real value of academic labor. The current system relies on each group undermining the claims of the other as precarity spreads. The ethos of mutual aid is well articulated by the indigenous activist Lilla Watson: "If you have come to help me, you are wasting your time; but if you are here because your liberation is bound up with mine, then let us work together." "Success is not a pathway out of social responsibility," Kendzior writes of the academic job market (Kendzior 2013). This is not only because escaping collective responsibility is immoral; it is also poor strategy, leading to a situation in which "academic freedom" comes to mean very little.

The third of the three possibilities for rhetorical address that I'd like to outline here is that to *amateurs*, or "academics" considered not so much as institutional actors but as lovers of learning. While such a constituency may sound ideal rather than real, the experiments in teaching and publication currently being conducted under the rubric of "para-academia" provide one arena for observing such amateurism in action. Para-academia denotes a collection of grassroots, not-for-profit alternatives to accredited and accrediting institutions of higher education and "continuing" education. These alternatives stand in a contiguous, contingent relation to academia's institutional forms. The relation is, on the one hand, "parasitic," insofar as para-academia takes advantage of both "surpluses and insufficiencies" of formal institutions (Allen et al. 2012, 145). On the other hand, para-academia is "complementary or supplementary, drawing on the other meaning of 'para-,' which suggests *being alongside*" (Boshears 2012). Many of these para-academic knowledge producers (such as the editors of *continent.* and *Speculations* journals, which include Jamie Allen, Paul Boshears, Paul Ennis, and Robert Jackson, all cited here in this essay[3])

---

[3] See *continent.* journal: http://www.continentcontinent.com/index.php/continent, and *Speculations* journal: http://www.speculations-journal.org/

are students in PhD programs and also graduates of those programs who have been unable to secure regular tenure-stream appointments. In this sense, "amateur" does not necessarily mean lacking in professional training, but it does denote some sort of intellectual existence outside of the University proper.

The groups and programs that could be called para-academic are numerous. A few recent examples include The Public School New York (TPSNY), The Art School in the Art School, The Brooklyn Institute for Social Research, Mozilla Open Badges, the BABEL Working Group, a Freeskool, and the pedagogical initiatives asso-ciated with the Occupy movement, like the Free School University and the Howard Zinn Memorial Lecture Series at Occupy Boston.[4] The website of a Freeskool, based in Victoria, British Columbia, describes it as

> a space to (un)learn, rewind, share skills, dream up the sort of community we want to live in and make it a reality through our practice. A Freeskool is YOU. You are the facilitator, you are the parti-cipant, you are our community.[5]

The Public School New York defines itself as "a frame-work that supports autodidactic activities."[6] Open Badges is a non-proprietary system for recognizing learning that takes place outside of traditional avenues of accreditation. The Brooklyn Institute was founded by post-grads in New

---

[4] See The Public School New York (http://thepublicschool.org/nyc), The Art School in the Art School (http://theasintheas.org/), The Brooklyn Institute for Social Research (http://the brooklyninstitute.com/), Mozilla's Open Badges program (http://openbadges.org/), BABEL Working Group (http://www.babel workinggroup.org), a freeskool [weblog] (http://afreeskool.word press.com/), and Occupy Boston (http://www.occupy boston.org/).
[5] See a freeskool [weblog]: http://afreeskool.wordpress.com/.
[6] See The Public School New York: http://thepublicschool.org/nyc.

York City without university teaching appointments in order to provide "material and intellectual support and space for young scholars to teach, write, research, publish and, put simply, work."[7] As such examples suggest, para-academic organizations tend to challenge pedagogical hierarchies, to advocate a DIY ethos, to reject norms of accreditation, and to emphasize the creative labor of building knowledge communities.

Perhaps the most important effect of para-academia is to cast critical light on contemporary higher education, in order to corrode the stability of its forms and the assumptions they rest on. "Essentially the para-academic has a chance to reveal that which the academic 'proper' has given up, and what the price of academic 'freedom' really is," Paul Ennis remarks (Allen et al. 2012, 146). Para-academia can exert a transformative "pressure" on traditional academia, claims Jamie Allen, with the "progressive potential to evolve the ways that knowledge is accessed and thought about at pedagogic, societal and political scales," and this "pressure" encourages "continuously rethinking the nature of scholarship and teaching" (Allen et al. 2012, 140, 144). The interminable task of reconsidering what scholarship *is* returns us to Fradenburg's call "to keep our knowledge disciplines opened and unsettled." In some sense, para-academia accomplishes more directly what I have claimed is achieved by the rhetorical addresses of all academic-activist writing: it calls upon new collectivities of knowledge and thereby helps to foster alternative futures.

One way to gain purchase on the "outstitutional" models that para-academia offers is to analytically separate the "university" from "academia." "I take academia to be the culture of knowledge-communication, while the university happens to be the most notable site of such

---

[7] "About," The Brooklyn Institute for Social Research, http://the brooklyninstitute.com/the-institute/about-2/. See also Andrew Marantz, "Night School," *The New Yorker*, August 6, 2012, 23.

communication at present," remarks Michael Austin (Allen et al. 2012, 137). Boshears articulates the distinction at greater length:

> Both Academia and the University are imagined communities, to borrow Benedict Anderson's phrase. However, the University is an institution that accredits, controls, and stamps the passports of those that would enter its territory. It is a striated space as opposed to Academia's fluid space. I would suggest that an academic is someone that can identify on two levels: first, with those slighted and pressured in the [university's] above cited political and economic circumstances; second, they enjoy reading/writing footnotes/end-notes/marginalia/figures/tables, etc. (Allen et al. 2012, 139)

Boshears's account gives two criteria for the "academic," one negative and one positive: the true academic is necessarily discomfited by the current marketization of universities, and, secondly, she takes pleasure in the forms and labors of knowledge-production. Boshears describes, then, what I would call an *insurgent amateurism*, which has both constructive and critical aspects. Insurgent amateurism creates and relishes knowledge, it dissents from "the University," and (bringing the constructive and critical aspects together) it builds alternative pedagogical communities and organizations.

The prospects for para-academia are not, of course, all sweetness and light. It is important to juxtapose the growth in non-accrediting "amateur" institutions with the much more statistically significant explosion in enrollment in for-profit schools, which grew by 235 percent between 2000 and 2010. From 2005 to 2010, over 75 percent of newly accredited colleges and universities were for-profit (Bady and Korczal 2012). Given that many who enroll in the University of Phoenix and the like want to improve their options for employment (however inadequately for-profit schools deliver this), hard questions persist about how to unite the para-academic resources for playing and inventing with techniques of economic survival and the pursuit of upward mobility.

Moreover, as I mentioned above, massive open online courses (MOOC's) have in most cases dovetailed smoothly with universities' wishes to reduce costs and control educators' intellectual property. Indeed, MOOC's, along with their older cousin the "TED talk," might be thought of as the neoliberal vector of para-academia, beaming out, as it were, from Silicon Valley. The more than one thousand TED talks, distributed online by the private non-profit Sapling Foundation under a Creative Commons license, have been watched more than a billion times. TED's prevalence—and the corresponding influence of its "techno-humanitarian mentality," which re-casts essentially *political* conflicts as "problems of inadequate connectivity or an insufficiency of gadgets"—suggest the drawbacks of a globally networked and distributed academia (Morozov 2012). A few select distribution platforms will tend to increase access but homogenize content in such a way that they always (surprise!) promote the economies of scale that make their own operation possible. In the future, Robert Jackson predicts, "Everyone can produce for the collective, but only a few select collectives will organise decentralised academic practice into a manageable service, often pushing journals and authors they see 'fit' for mass appeal and attention" (Allen et al. 2012, 145).

Even in light of these developments, it is essential to find hope in the broadly shared desire for post-secondary education. People's evident hunger to learn should be a spur to our collective imagination and to our active care in shaping the futures of colleges and universities. Aaron Bady, one of the most articulate and outspoken critics of MOOC's, nonetheless draws attention to the utopian dimension that attends even the most flawed and cynical of free-education initiatives:

> If the MOOC-ification of higher ed is likely to be a dead-end, . . . MOOC's do enable us to ask a question that we've been too defensively crouched to think about: what should or could "higher education" look like, if it were stripped of its credentializing and profit-making functions? If it were free, and if it wasn't about determining who gets jobs and who doesn't, what would it look like? (Bady 2013)

Para-academia, it seems to me, is a series of practical investigations of just this question. Para-academia and "insurgent amateurism" appear to convert into a principle of action Fradenburg's acute formulation of scholarship's social immanence: "Group desire makes what we call knowledge. *There is no other kind of knowledge than this; this is what knowledge is, and we make it.*" "Group desire" and "our connectedness to wider communities" open the rhetorical dimension of critique. Academic-activist writings not only deliver dispatches from the numerous battlegrounds of higher education. They also call upon those who care to read them—those who might defend the institutional homes of speculation, imagination, and historical understanding. These writings are the communiqués that circulate within the "army of lovers" and also pass beyond them, to unpresupposed outposts and new readers. *Staying Alive* is a profound, long-meditated, and unique contribution to this circulation of mobilizing reflections about learning in the present. Taking a stand in our vulnerability, in our desire, does not mean the battle is lost. An army of lovers can be beaten, but will it be?

REFERENCES

Allen, J., P. Ennis, M. Austin, R. Jackson, T. Gokey, and P. Boshears (2012). "Discussions Before an Encounter." *conti-*

nent. 2.2: 136–147; http://www.continentcontinent.com/index. php/continent/article/download/92/pdf.

Bady, A. (2013). "A Moment of Dreaming about Higher Education." *The New Inquiry,* January 2: http://thenew inquiry.com/blogs/zunguzungu/a-moment-of-dreaming-about-higher-education/.

Bady, A. and M. Konczal (2012). "From Master Plan to No Plan: The Slow Death of Public Higher Education." *Dissent: A Quarterly of Politics and Culture,* Fall: http://www.dissent magazine.org/article/from-master-plan-to-no-plan-the-slow-death-of-public-higher-education.

Best, S. and S. Marcus. (2009). "Surface Reading: An Intro-duction." *Representations* 108: 1–21.

Boshears, P. (2012) "Open Access and Para-Aacademic Prac-tice." *continent.,* November 12: http://continentcontinent. cc/blog/2012/11/open-access-and-para-academic-practice/.

Collini, S. (2012). *What Are Universities For?* New York: Penguin.

Fish, S. (1994). "Being Interdisciplinary Is So Very Hard to Do." In S. Fish, *There's No Such Thing as Free Speech and It's a Good Thing, Too,* 231–242. Oxford: Oxford University Press.

Fradenburg, L. O. A. (2002). *Sacrifice Your Love: Psychoanalysis, Historicism, Chaucer.* Minneapolis: University of Minnesota Press.

Fradenburg, A. (2009). "(Dis)Continuity: A History of Dream-ing." In *The Post-Historical Middle Ages,* eds. E. Scala and S. Frederico, 87–115. New York: Palgrave Mac-millan.

Fradenburg, L.O.A. (2011a). "Living Chaucer." *Studies in the Age of Chaucer* 33: 41–64.

Fradenburg, A. (2011b). "The Liberal Arts of Psychoanalysis." *Journal of the American Academy of Psychoanalysis and Dy-namic Psychiatry* 39: 589–610.

Jaschik, S. (2012). "Tenure on the Line at Wayne State." *Inside Higher Ed,* July 23: http://www.insidehighered.com/news/ 2012/07/23/faculty-accuse-wayne-state-trying-kill-tenure-rights.

Kendzior, S. (2013). "Academia's Indentured Servants." *Al Jaz-eera,* April 11: http://www.aljazeera.com/indepth/opinion/2013/ 04/20134119156459616.html.

Latour, B. (2004). "Why Has Critique Run out of Steam? From Matters of Fact to Matters of Concern" *Critical Inquiry* 30:

225–248.

Latour, B. (2010). "An Attempt at a 'Compositionist Manifesto'." *New Literary History* 41: 471–490.

Lewin, T. (2013). "Gap Widens for Faculty at Colleges, Report Finds." *New York Times*, April 8: http://www.nytimes.com/2013/04/08/education/gap-in-university-faculty-pay-contin ues-to-grow-report-finds.html.

Markoff, J. (2013). "Essay-Grading Software Offers Professors a Break." *New York Times*, April 4: http://www.nytimes.com/2013/04/05/science/new-test-for-computers-grading-essays-at-college-level.html.

Martin, A. (2013). "Moody's Gives Colleges a Negative Grade." *New York Times*, January 16: www.nytimes.com/2013/01/17/business/moodys-outlook-on-higher-education-turns-negative.html.

Morozov, E. (2012). "The Naked and the TED." *The New Republic*, August 2: http://www.newrepublic.com/article/books-and-arts/magazine/105703/the-naked-and-the-ted-khanna#.

Patnaik, G. (2011). "Breaking Trust: The Past and Future of the University of California." *zunguzungu*, December 8: http://zunguzungu.wordpress.com/2011/12/08/breaking-trust-the -past-and-future-of-the-university-of-california/.

Pérez-Peña, R. (2013). "Harvard Asks Graduates to Donate Time to Free Online Humanities Class." *New York Times*, March 25: http://www.nytimes.com/2013/03/26/ education/harvard-asks-alumni-to-donate-time-to-free-online-course.html.

Pynchon, T. (1973). *Gravity's Rainbow*. New York: Penguin.

Rees, J. (2013). "Half the Professoriate Will Kill the Other Half for Free." *More or Less Bunk*, March 27: http://moreorless bunk.wordpress.com/2013/03/27/they-can-hire-one-half-the-professoriate/.

Sedgwick, E.K. (2002). "Paranoid Reading and Reparative Reading, Or, You're So Paranoid, You Probably Think This Essay Is About You." In *Touching Feeling: Affect, Pedagogy, Performativity*, 123–151. Durham: Duke University Press.

Williams, J.J. (2005). "History as a Challenge to the Idea of the University." *Journal of Advanced Composition* 25: 55–74.

continent. maps a
topology of unstable
confluences and
ranges across new
thinking, traversing
interstices and
alternate directions
in culture, theory,
biopolitics and art.

Past

Present

Future

Issue 2.2 / 2012:

Discussions Before an Encounter

The Editors of Speculations & continent.

DOWNLOAD PDF

continent. 2.2 (2012): 136–147

This introductory text is being written on a laptop on a summer Saturday in a cafe in Copenhagen by *continent.* Co-Editor Jamie Allen. It is here in order to contextualise a discussion document that was created using an unpaid version of Google's Docs service, authored collaboratively by editors from both this journal, continent. and the online journal *Speculations* in Canada, the U.S. and Europe. The outlined discussion is part of recent energies and networks actively rethinking and practically redefining the natures and practices of academic discourse. Other related activities include the Public School New York's recent Panel Discussion on Para-Academic Publishing, co-organised by punctum books and the Hollow Earth Society, as well as the upcoming interdisciplinarity-focused 2nd Biennial Meeting of the BABEL Working Group.

Robert Jackson (*Speculations*):

Whatever academia is (or whatever form of scholarship its supposed to support), it's in a crisis. Crises aren't necessarily bad, but they are unpredictable states of transition into unseen forms of production. I'm generalising, but it used to be the case that with the humanities and the arts, there were two options for a stable income; enter job markets which required individual creative talent or enter academia to teach, possibly research. These two areas are now largely defunct for the majority of students graduating from the so-called "vocational" courses. In the former, the distribution of creative entertainment now feeds off communicative user-generated creativity (everyone can be creative and must distribute their work for free to attract attention); in the latter humanities research is forced into a functional malaise which benefits statistics rather than society. What academia and academics are will emerge from these new modes of production and in turn how they navigate these constraints and affects. Everything was always-already precarious, we've only just realised it.

2: Living the Liberal Arts

An Argument for Embodied Learning Communities

Individual (co)adaptability is not only of the greatest
significance as a factor of evolution . . . but is itself perhaps the chief object of selection.
  Sewall Wright, "Evolution in Mendelian Populations"

The ability of individual organisms to respond creatively
to the creative forces in their environments is one of the
chief engines of evolutionary process (Calvin 1996). Post-
genome biology has put genetic determinism all in doubt.
Increasingly, for evolutionary theorists, the history of
living matter now derives from complex interactions between genotype, phenotype, and environmental affordances (Gibson 1977; Hoffmeyer 2008, 72–75). As a consequence of Lynn Margulis's work on the evolutionary significance of symbiosis, many different kinds of conjunctions—
not just internal experimentation and natural selection—

now appear to have forceful effects on the histories of living tissue (Margulis 1998). Genetic inheritance is no longer imagined as a digital "program" for the unfolding of a life without significant variation. Instead, we now think of the vicissitudes of genetic expression—whether, how, and under what conditions a gene will be activated or "expressed"—as the result of interactions with environmental influences. Neuronal connectivity is both "experience-dependent" and capable, over time, of altering the functional architecture of the brain (Singer 2008, 102 –105, 108). In fact, by contrast with the atomism of so much 20th-century science, holistic approaches have made us aware of the transformative power of all kinds of connectivity—neuronal, psychoendo-crinological, anthropheromonal, bacteriological—and the term "ecology" now applies widely to all open-ended assemblages of living systems and territories, in which environmental factors help to write the histories of specific organisms, and vice-versa. The causality involved is that of complexity, of self-organized systems and epigenesis, not the causality of scripts that determine all performances thereof. The organism is, simply put, no longer a "dead end" (Hoffmeyer 2008, 72). It constantly co-processes its boundaries in tandem with all the life-forms and forces to which it is connected, from which the biological meaningfulness of its life- and self-experience emerges, in a new key.

We are in the midst of a paradigm-shift whose consequences for our understanding and appreciation of the arts and humanities are profound. The latest research in contemporary study of the mind does not support the employment-oriented policies and dismissal of the arts and humanities articulated in the Bologna Process documents and their ilk.[1] Instead it asserts in powerful old and new ways the life-saving and life-enhancing opportunities afforded by liberal arts education. True, this knowledge is

---

[1] On the Bologna Process, discussed in Chapter 1 of this book, see Labi (2009).

still quite unthinkable in those cultural concentrations that still hold to scientistic or providential models of living process, and is only intermittently thinkable for the rest of us.[2] When it does capture mainstream attention, it appears in relatively neutralized forms, like studies of innovation. Venture capitalists almost by definition respect the difficulty of prediction and the productivity of broadcast investment; there is a reason why they have been so important to the knowledge industries specifically. But they also seem to misunderstand completely how minds work, if their current fixation on online education is any indication (see Bady 2013; Heller 2013), and they appear to be ignorant of the highly uneven history of scientific discovery (see Serres 1995, 2). The new paradigm keeps very uneasy company with intelligent design, top-down management, and the apocalyptic fantasy of (the O/other's) accountability—for example, the rage to quantify educational outcomes. Instead, it affirms the creativity inherent in matter, for which chaos, drift, causal parity and contingency are just as significant as codes, templates, and five-year plans. It affirms the existence of realities that far exceed us; but at the same time it acknowledges that our knowledge of those realities is artifactual—something we make together, and no less powerful for that. It encourages (the study of) real-time process, experimentation, and "becoming," and recognizes the role of the observer to be an integral (neither intrusive nor obstructive) part of discovery. In short, scientism is in flight (see Gallagher and Zahavi 2008, 29, 40–41), and plasticity and complexity may well be the biggest challenge fundamentalisms of all kinds—including invariant code worship—have ever faced.[3]

---

[2] "Automatisms of attitude have a durability, a slow temporality, which does not match the sometimes rapid change of conceptual mutation": Davidson 1987, 276.

[3] A caveat is in order here: progressive thinkers have also warned us many times against the overvaluation of flexibility and spontaneity (Malabou 2008). I deeply appreciate Malabou's

The un-thinking that always accompanies paradigm shift breaks down reason even in the academy, which organizationally has barely begun remaking itself in accordance with its own new wisdoms.[4] The effects of social learning are almost as conservative in the academy as they are elsewhere; as noted in Chapter 1, all disciplines, including the humanities, follow the "law of the group" as well as the "law of the science" (cf. de Certeau 1988, 61). Unsurprisingly, the institutional implementation of interdisciplinarity lags far behind the praise bestowed upon such by university administrators. In the humanities, the conservatism of funding institutions, calcified accounting methods, and increasingly top-heavy administrative structures make collaborative teaching and research projects exceedingly difficult to arrange, and the very narrow specialization characteristic of American science yields much the same result, despite its more collaborative working styles. It remains the case that interdisciplinarity usually depends on faculty willing to take on extra workload with little apparent support or reward in sight. (Please, colleagues: let us not, like the schmoos of L'il Abner, jump at every opportunity to suffer a thousand cuts for the sake of the new normal. This behavior is not sustainable.)[5]

---

attempt to distinguish plasticity from the neo-liberal discourse of flexibility, because so many critiques of neo-liberal discourse do not underscore the extent to which it is an *appropriation* of poststructuralist thought. Just because "flexibility" and "diversity" have become standard management-speak, does not mean that these terms have been forever detached from semantic neighbors like "social justice" and "freedom." Words are in no one's possession, even if some arrangements of them are under copyright or trademarked (see also p. 122, in this chapter).

[4] The term "unthinking" derives from the title of Christopher Bollas's book *The Shadow of the Object: Psychoanalysis of the Unthought Known* (1987).

[5] Studies conducted during the 1970s and 1980s showed that faculty across disciplines worked over 60 hours per week; all indications are that our workload has increased considerably since then, and the University of California is now hoping for

Disciplines are modes of enjoyment that unquestionably overlap, but they are also "turf"—psychical realities, so to speak—and their practitioners are increasingly encouraged by administrators to compete for, rather than share (and thus maximize), the much-diminished resources now available to faculty. Even humanists appeal at times to an antique social-Darwinist hyper-valorizing of competition as a means of securing "excellence" (i.e., as much funding for their own particular pursuits as possible).[6] Despite humanist identifications with their oppressors, however—or perhaps because of them—splitting between the humanities and the sciences rages on in many quarters and guises. Post-romantic humanists can still be antagonistic to "Western" science and "left-brain thinking," while idealizing imaginative activity and affective experience. In the sciences it is still too easy to bump up against post-Enlightenment idealization of logical positivism, and contempt for "fuzzy thinking."[7]

Disciplines are easily caught up in the imaginary register.[8] They generate all sorts of invidious mirrorings, misrecognitions, and misattributions. When post-structuralist theory argued for the plasticities of self, subjectivity, and meaning, they upset a lot of scientists; but biologists also argue that semiosis and self/non-self representation (e.g., the Major Histocompatibility Complex, or MHC[9]) are fundamental to living process. Too many his-

---

more (see UCOP 2013).

[6] There is a vast literature on the importance of cooperation amongst the great apes. For a primer, see Dugatkin (1997).

[7] The psychologist Stanton Peele responded to a call by Ellen Langer for psychologists to "open their minds to possibility" by "urging psychologists to protect their discipline as 'a beacon for a commitment to empiricism and reasoning'" (Ruark 2010).

[8] Lacan 2002, 75–81. Lacan's conception of the imaginary register of subjective experience contrasts fascination with the image of the Other with awareness of the open systematicity (multiplicities, arbitrariness) of social signification.

[9] For non-specialists, a helpful introduction to the MHC is

torians (and historicists) are still naïve empiricists who look down on "soft" cultural analysis, hoping that statistics and devotion to the archives will give their work the *élan* of science. The same misguided hope fuels the gadget-loving proponents of digital humanism who argue that the humanities can only be saved by jettisoning critical readings and embracing in their stead the computation of style and the steady production of databases.[10] Yet now, in the early 21st century, neuroscientists like Edelman are trying to restore value to (the study of) *qualia*, the felt quality of experience—the deep green of a New England summer, the wideness of the sky (Edelman 2004); computational models of mind have largely given way to complex neuroplastic ones; and phenomenology is once again giving analytical philosophy a run for its money.

It remains as noted some years ago by Engell and Dangerfield: in the age of money, things that cost a lot of money—like new technology—get much more respect and support than the new ideas that lead to their creation (Engell and Dangerfield 1998, 52). Arts departments invest heavily in alliances in the sciences and engineering, but reap little effective support therefrom for K-12 arts education—despite, in the case of music, for example, its possible contributions to the development of reading skills and

---

Phelps (2002).

[10] This characterization does not represent all who work in the Digital Humanities, of course, many of whom do not seek to eschew critical reading for data gathering, but rather, embrace both. But there are also digital humanists who do perversely insist that the primary way forward for the humanities is mainly through computing; for an overview of the debates, see Gold (2012). On gadget-love, see Rickels (1995): "Evolution provided the context for imagining that thought can or must go on without the body and that means beyond the repro-bonds between the sexes. What thus moves away from interpersonal relations of sex difference comes at us, growing stronger, as fetishism, a gadget-love that's all about getting into machines while . . . fulfilling . . . our commitment to reproduction as still the only way to keep the species and the technology going."

spatial and mathematical ability.[11] Like music departments, classics departments are regularly shut down despite the
fact that a background in classics is one of the most reliable
predictors of success in law school (Engell and Dangerfield 1998, 50). In American psychoanalytic education,
the prestige of the medical model remains strong; in
many states licensing for "lay" analysts is not available
despite their importance to the history of psychoanalysis
(think, for example, of Klein, Erikson, and Kristeva). But
while psychoanalysis grows, in some ways, more scientific
(through, for example, the contributions of developmental psychology and neuropsychoanalysis), it also grows
more and more relational, more and more aware of the
unpredictability and artfulness of psychoanalytic process.

Because of our failure to recognize that scientific
method and humanist styles of interpretation and research enhance one another (in practical as well as theoretical ways),
our ships pass in the night, bearing fantastic images of the
O/other disciplines—oblivious to the fact that the improvisational, artful nature of real-time knowing is not a
failed attempt at empiricism, but rather adaptation (and
creativity) in action. The humanities specialize in training
students in the arts of managing the uncertainties of experience—learning to see and hear better, to read quickly
but with care, to write and speak persuasively. Studies
indicate that as quickly as two hours after a learning experience, there are changes in the fibrous white matter of
the brain, the part of the brain largely responsible for
connectivity (Blumenfeld-Katzir et al. 2011).[12] If—and

[11] See Doidge 2007, 289, for a clear, accessible description of
what music can do for your brain. See also Frances Rauscher
(2008) for a summary of recent research on music education
and its influence on a variety of cognitive abilities, including
mathematics and spatial intelligence, and Anvari (2002) on
relationships between music, phoneme discrimination and
reading.
[12] See Tokuhama-Espinosa (2011) on the "human survival and
life skills" basic to learning and social situations (143).

only if—accompanied by regular practice, these gains can be real and lasting. (If I make my students read four pages of Lacan fourteen times so they can have the experience of something obscure becoming clearer, they will be much more capable of following *The New York Times*. Education enables simple pleasures and quotidian achievements as well as extraordinary ones.) Our knowledge of neuroplasticity has helped us to appreciate anew not only the importance of real-time exercise of performative and interpretive skills but also the breadth, depth, and sociality offered by immersive on-site liberal arts education. How better—where better—to acquire, maintain and develop a wide variety of cognitive and affective skills, from mathematics to music, to curating and computer engineering, to trust and teamwork, than in an environment designed to support and challenge the learning mind? Where else will students find the friends and lovers who want to meet at the library to study, work together in the lab until midnight, ease the anxieties of student life by going for pizza and gossip? Their fellow chemistry majors and violinists and future industry contacts, or (with respect) the family dog?

What most distinguishes the intelligence of humans from that of other great apes is social cognition (Herrmann et al. 2007). The cultivation of such in real-time contexts is an indispensable support to the exercise of other kinds of intelligence. Capitalist-technocratic interests want to persuade us otherwise; replacing face-to-face, embodied learning environments with online education isn't a problem because the real-time interactivity of social life has, in their view, no significance for learning or innovation. Yet so much depends—but so much has *always* depended—on developing a ready, responsive, responsible, creative and worldly brain: catholic in its pursuits but capable of focus, fascination and wonder, of enjoying the challenge of difference rather than running away in fear, of getting help rather than fighting or flying, of appreciating the brilliance of mathematical, Miltonic and Derridean signifiers (after which, reading legal briefs will feel like a walk in the park); capable of spatial thinking, of sensitivity to group psychology and the importance of ambience; and achieving all of this with the real-time, all-the-time support of other students, teaching assistants, lab assistants, librarians, professors, artists-in-residence, and visiting lecturers in an ecology and dwelling-place (the university) that mixes together all kinds of learning and states of mind, including the kind of (shared) downtime necessary for creativity. Biola University knows very well the importance of face-to-face communities, despite its online offerings, just as Dartmouth College, which grooms so many future captains of industry, still (for now) sponsors the arts and humanities education increasingly out of reach to less advantaged students.

The hard truth is that it is very far from being a good idea to subordinate one's education to one's "life," as so much online university advertising encourages us to do, unless (for psychological, familial or economic reasons), *there really is no other way.* Young, single high-school graduates are not being dashing individualists when they opt for online higher education; they have plenty of company both past and present. Diploma mills, correspondence courses, and night and extension programs have been around for a long time—they just relied on other technologies (books, snail mail, television and radio programming, etc.) to provide the same services. The captains of the online education industry—including some of the Regents of the University of California—don't want to improve the delivery of traditional or alternative educational opportunities; they want to replace face-to-face, bricks-and-mortar education outright, luring students and educational institutions with the promise of easy savings while watching their gold pile up in the sub-dungeon. But online education is in fact expensive, for individuals as well as institutions (Newfield 2013a, 2013b), and the only reason it is ever competitive with public university tuition costs is because the same investors have lobbied so successfully to raise the latter. In his May 2011 summary of the University of California Faculty Senate's report on Mark Yudof's "Online Education Project Plan," Daniel Simmons noted that "several divisions and committees pointed to research on the high rates of noncompletion of online courses. . . . The literature also demonstrates that less well-prepared students will require significant additional resources for support services" (Simmons 2011, 4). There is no good evidence to support the claim that online education does a better job overall than face-to-face education. Studies indicate that online resources can be very effective *in the context of* embodied, face-to-face education, less so on their own; the latest, best, most independent research also indicates that male students of all kinds, and the economically disadvantaged, are *least* likely to benefit from online education.[13] (Of course it mat-

---

[13] See the U.S. Department of Education's 2010 "Review of Online Learning Studies": "When used by itself, online learning appears to be as effective as conventional classroom instruction, *but not more so* . . . . Despite what appears to be strong support for blended applications [mixtures of online and face-to-face learning], the studies . . . *do not demonstrate that online learning is superior as a medium.* . . . the online and classroom conditions differed in terms of time spent, curriculum and pedagogy," and "the combination of elements in the treatment conditions . . . produced the observed learning advantages" (xviii). Further, the same DOE report found that "many of the studies suffered from weaknesses such as small sample sizes; failure to report retention rates for students in the conditions being contrasted; and, in many cases, potential bias stemming from the authors' dual roles as experimenters and instructors." A new study of 500,000 online courses in the state of Washington found that, "[o]verall, the online format had a significantly negative relationship with both course persistence and course grade, indicating that the typical student had difficulty adapting to online courses. [Moreover,] males, Black students, and students with lower levels of academic preparation experienced significantly stronger negative coefficients for online learning compared with their coun-

ters a great deal how we understand the "job" education is supposed to do. Not simply the retention of "information," but the encouragement and development of thinking *about* information, is crucial; so is finishing one's coursework.) My point is not that rugged individuals, or even just earnest individuals, or even entire communities, can't benefit from such offerings; many do, and go far. There is no question that alternative educational opportunities have been a crucial means for women, minorities, and the economically disadvantaged to embark on careers and enterprises of all kinds. But there is also no question that learning benefits enormously from full and flexible relationality, chance encounters and spontaneity—getting coffee after class, sitting down on a bench to chat with your TA, running into your professors in the bookstore, experimenting with new subjects and methods in an immersive environment that appreciates wonder and provides a little time for rumination. The relational context is, after all, how we first learned everything—in moments of "proto-conversation" with our caregivers, through the development of joint attention and the sustained negotiations of rapprochement (Tomasello 1995; Mahler 1972). Living well depends on good education (the more embodied and interactive, the better), and good education should be available to everyone.

Academic psychology has unfortunately provided an assist to the technocratic narrowing of cultural experience by trophying the limitations of the human brain rather than its uniquely marvelous abilities. I am, of course, in favor of anything that helps us think better, but I am not in favor of the condescending rhetoric (e.g., "folk psychology") adopted by many scientists and philosophers

terparts, in terms of both course persistence and course grade. . . . These patterns also suggest that performance gaps between key demographic groups already observed in face-to-face classrooms . . . are exacerbated in online courses. This is troubling from an equity perspective" (Xu and Jaggers 2013a, 23; see also Xu and Jaggers 2013b).

when discussing evolution's most astonishing achievements. In his review of Damasio's *Descartes' Error*, Daniel Dennett writes:

> The legacy of René Descartes' notorious dualism of mind and body extends far beyond academia . . . . Even among those of us who have battled Descartes' vision, there has been a powerful tendency to treat the mind (that is to say, the brain) as the body's boss, the pilot of the ship. Falling in with this standard way of thinking, we ignore an important alternative: viewing the brain (and hence the mind) as one organ among many, a relatively recent usurper of control, whose functions cannot properly be understood until we see it not as the boss, but as just one more somewhat fractious servant, working to further the interests of the body that shelters and fuels it, and gives its activities meaning. (Dennett 1995, 3)

I know of no well-respected scholars in the humanities or social sciences who, in 1995, thought of the mind or brain as the "boss" of anybody.

Note that Dennett's rhetoric mixed old and new workplace terms—and hierarchical ones at that ("servant," "boss")—with the language of political subordination and domination ("usurper of control"). Dennett's rhetoric was, arguably, democratizing to an extent; but why did someone still have to be the boss and someone else the servant? Why couldn't the brain just be an important part of the open systematicity of the body? Or part of a cooperative community? Would we have lost anything by conceptualizing it in this way? And whose folly, whose fantasy of control, did he mean to unmask?[14]

---

[14] The pleasure of unmasking folly was, of course, a big part of the affective fuel of (Enlightenment) empiricism and its scientistic heirs and commentators (Zilsel 2000). But it has a long history in iconoclastic thought, and I acknowledge its role in this

All crypto-Cartesians? Presumably, at the time of writing, Dennett was unaware of the ongoing humanist critique of the mind's independence from and superiority to the body. But Lakoff and Johnson's *Metaphors We Live By*, an extraordinarily influential argument for the grounding of figuration in bodily experience, had been published fifteen years previously (Lakoff and Johnson, 1980).

Also writing at the time when academic humanists and social scientists were busily deconstructing "common sense" as an ideological formation, Patricia Churchland offered her own critique, arguing that the "tools" of common sense were not "up to the task" of building an adequate theory of "the cognitive dynamics of intelligent beings" (Churchland 1980, 153).[15] The mind, that is to say, is largely incapable of understanding itself, unless it is a very special mind that has very special training in studying itself as an object of scientific interest. Dennett's distinction between first- and third-person knowledge makes a similar point, though it confers some value on subjective experience as a way of knowing; but the critique of common sense in the context of arguments for special mental training in fact goes back to Descartes (1996, e.g., 22, 59). It is therefore a bit surprising to learn that so many post-Enlightenment scientists thought "common sense" up to the task of theorizing cognitive dynamics, though no doubt Churchland is correct in claiming that some psychologists have mistaken its nature and purposes. Early in the history of the term "common sense," and for some centuries thereafter, it designated the mind's ability to combine many different kinds of sensory perception into intelligible assemblages—and thus, I might add, to construct interpretations vital to survival. Scientific circles no longer

book. I favor the unmasking of folly; but with Erasmus, I also praise it.

[15] For an example of recent social science critiques of "common sense," see Darder and Torres 1999, 174 ff. Gramsci analyzed "common sense" as an aspect of ideology in *The Prison Notebooks* (2003, 22, 58).

locate common sense in the pineal gland, nor do they use the term "common sense" to refer to mind/brain connectivity, but the science of neuroplasticity has affirmed the importance of "cross-modal" perception to the project of thinking about anything at all. The evident pleasure Churchland's rhetoric, like Dennett's, takes in the unmasking of folly is, I propose, a symptom of the melancholia that undergirds scientistic fantasies of omnipotence.[16]

Mental training is a concern for the humanities as well as the sciences. But scientific methods and humanist arts of interpretation, while drawing on each other in many important ways, do not on the whole mean to accomplish the same things. Humanists are interested in training the everyday functions of the brain, functions that respond to real-time, ever-changing conditions. Despite advances in algorithmic complexity and ecologically-sensitive conceptualizations of phenomena, scientists still rely largely on specially-constructed laboratory conditions and equipment, as well as manipulations of data, that screen out the higgledy-piggledy circumstances in which we normally think. Statistical analysis reduces phenomena to countable units analyzed retroactively and only then projected into the future. It deserves our interest because it is indeed capable of revealing uncanny truths about group behaviors we rarely experience consciously. But even though we can carry statistical knowledge around in our heads, we do not conduct statistical analyses in those heads while crossing the street, when we are trying to calculate our chances of survival. Nor can we, at that moment, set up a laboratory simulation of the circumstances in real time. Despite the appreciation of real-time decision-making, and even "guessing," in studies of the evolution and neurobiology of intelligence (Calvin 2001),

---

[16] I discuss this melancholic formation further below. I do not, by the way, intend these remarks as a critique of expertise, but we should remember that it is fallible, and reflect on the regularity with which scientific method fails to give the basic brain functions on which it depends their due.

many 20th-century scientists and analytical philosophers regard these activities not as "best practices" in the domain of surviving and thriving, but as woefully imprecise by comparison with knowledge generated by means of traditional scientific methods.

Consider the following email exchange between two professors living in faculty housing in Santa Barbara:

> Professor 1: I'm worried that if the county fixes those little roads, people will drive faster on them. The potholes are kind of like natural speed-bumps. Maybe we should keep them.

> Professor 2: It seems to me that if we want to know whether and when people's speed slows down or picks up, we would have to collect data on that after the roads are paved. Let's not speculate wildly.

We might well wonder why we would wait till after the roads are re-paved; why not begin data-collection before, to enable comparison? But that is a minor concern for the purposes of the present argument. Not only is data analysis invariably retrospective, it rarely decides for us. It can't settle questions like, "is it worth our while to wait until the county agrees to pave the roads and then install the roadside detectors needed to record traffic speed on a little out-of-the-way dead-end road?" And we would still have to find a solution to competing interests: some drivers will be concerned, above all else, about their wheel alignment and suspension, or disappearing into sinkholes, and others will be concerned, above all else, with the safety of children, pets, and meadow creatures, and/or maintaining a serene atmosphere in our seaside *locus amoenus*. Data cannot deliberate for us; it can only help. And "speculation" is not the only alternative to measurement. There's also making the best possible decision you can. Respect your first impulses (the non-conscious mind is trying to tell you something); but inform yourself, and consult with others before you decide on a point of view, and do this within a reasonable time-frame, or your paralysis will make the decision for you (as it did in the above case; but note that indecision is occasionally the best prelude to good policy). When, at the age of six, I was looking into the eyes of my little classmate Toril Johnson, who was trying to convince me to push the fire-alarm button, I could not call a time-out to measure her levels of arousal, or observe her in the wild sufficiently to acquire reliable knowledge about her capacity for and styles of deception. Again, we forget to praise our everyday knowledge of how to do things, how to evaluate what stands before us in real time and relatively uncontrolled conditions. Of course we do a lot of things badly, but we do many things very well indeed—and measurement is also perfectly capable of contributing to bungling and even disastrous outcomes.

Scientific method is one of many ways of organizing intelligence, *all* of which are important to the study and practice of living process. I am not a Luddite, and I am well aware that the day is coming when our brains will be equipped with computers that can escort us across the street the way Boy Scouts used to do, just as smart cars now wake us up when we're getting sleepy, and calibrate the distance between my fender and that of the car in front of me. Computers are already an important part of our experience of embodiment. Nor am I arguing against the creation of special liminal circumstances to shelter experimentation; play is exactly that, and we need to recognize (without conflating) the affinities between laboratory experimentation and the ludic practices of the arts and humanities. My point is rather that life comes at us fast, and the plasticity needed to respond (with curiosity and/or suspicion, generosity and/or rejection, action and/or deliberation, etc.) to that rush of information and experience is lost when we insist that our brains confine themselves to a few highly specific context-dependent standards of accuracy. Furthermore, if the historians of our own time are to be believed, life now comes at us even more quickly than it did before ("it is as if the desire for personal speed, granted as the gift of a prosthetic technology, is so intense that we are content to ruin our planet to experience it": Duffy 2009, 264). If this is true, we are even more vulnerable to trauma (toxins, climate change, superbugs, and all their psychical equivalents) than we used to be, and we need, all the more, brains that can respond to the unexpected. But we need not rely altogether on this argument. Contemporary life has no monopoly on trauma, even though its stylizations of such are distinctive enough to warrant close scrutiny. The brain's resilience and capacity for approximation are among its most outstanding achievements, and this fact itself testifies to our species' longstanding need to respond to changing circumstances and uncertain outcomes.

There is no fixed difference between ordinary and extraordinary thinking, of course. Knowledge of dark matter or Pythagorean politics does and will contribute to everyday thinking, and the pursuits of higher math and human-computer interactions will refine the way our brains work over time. Everyday thinking is also an essential part of extraordinary thinking—even philosophers who scorn language, like the aforementioned (and, in fact, very chatty) Patricia Churchland, use it constantly (Churchland 1980, 164). Everyday thinking includes most non-conscious and conscious mental activity, and the inextricably intertwined activities of the body, including imagination, memory, executive functions, perception, sensation, proprioception, kinesis, and affect. In Charles Peirce's terms, everyday thinking requires facility in the interpretation of iconic and indexical signs, not just symbols; in fact it is the product of the interdependent workings of all three (Hoffmeyer 2008, 284–290).

The importance of culture to evolution is now widely accepted (Doidge 2007, 287–312), and culture depends to a large extent on language. Paraverbal and verbal language do not always get the respect they should in Anglo-

American philosophical circles; but there is nothing ordinary about them. For one thing, verbal language has digital as well as analog aspects (Hoffmeyer 2008, 78–80), insofar as it consists of interconnected and systematic assemblages of discrete, abstract elements that are switched on and off (vocal cord vibration, yes or no; stoppage of airflow, yes or no). Most importantly, ordinary language is an open, complex, combinatorial system, and therein lies, not a lamentable slipperiness, but a creative resource capable of responding improvisationally to unforeseen developments, and of communicating to others affects and sensations that would otherwise be limited to non-linguistic coding and replication. The arts of living are *necessarily* open to experience; they must cope with, and ideally make creative use of, both constant change and causal parity (overdetermination).

The humanities are important not only for the content that they convey but even more so for the techniques of living—the "life-skills"—they teach. There are no good knowledge-based reasons to abandon the cultivation of everyday thinking, and very good reasons to continue teaching students how to use language fluently and persuasively, how to perceive the world as richly and informatively as possible, and how to extend memory to pasts that have largely disappeared. The most important purpose of the humanities and fine arts is to refine the brain's ability to do innumerable real-time things necessary for surviving and thriving: to perceive color keenly; hypothesize about the intentions and direction of moving shapes; listen with sharp ears for changes in tone, or the slightest rustle in the bushes; read faces and para-language; model fictions and possible futures; and understand, in however limited a fashion (the miracle is that we can do it at all), the wishes and intentions of other beings (see Gallese 2007). These are priceless abilities, and we need to refine them (now more than ever—but when have we not?), owing to the vulnerability of the lives of mortal creatures—a vulnerability that is the special target of the contemporary globetrotting Ubermensch's attempts at immunity (on immunity, see Esposito 2011, and Chapter 1 in this volume).

Neuroscience is now establishing, however (at times) unintentionally, the importance of artistic and humanist training to mental functioning. But, as noted, these discoveries have sadly done little to protect the academic disciplines of the arts and humanities from budget cuts and closings. If contemporary boosters of employment-related technical and scientific education have any interest in the new knowledge of the brain that scientists are actually producing, they're keeping it close. We need to reverse this unthinking, to speak for the lifesaving powers of the liberal arts, and for the inextricability of thriving and surviving. Surely the brain (such an astonishing creation, the product of millions of years of internal experimentation, capable of infinite jest and most excellent fancy) deserves more respect, especially from the people whose work has done so much to establish its wondrous qualities—its neurochemical resilience, its perceptual outreach, the lavish redundancies, multiple pathways and "degeneracies" that enable its creative connectivity (Edelman 2004, 154).

The academy participates all too often in the unthinking of the import and potential of the humanities, and if we are to change the course of our current off-world death-drive, we need to be very well acquainted with the forces that feed our own creaturely melancholy and crises of enjoyment. As noted, disciplinary tensions are easily assimilated to the rivalrous, zero-sum phantasies of the imaginary register; the positivist-empiricist automaton and the radical relativist snob function as imaginary figures designed to reduce a much more complicated picture to fighting form. Splitting of this sort does not, however, function simply to divide the sciences from the humanities (and thus conquer both—in the case of the sciences, by subordinating them altogether to the research agendas of capitalism: Press and Washburn 2000). Splitting is repeated inside nearly every contemporary academic discipline. Turf wars break out between humanist sociologists and their statistically-minded colleagues. Experimental physicists think theoretical physicists look down on them. Neither linguists nor those who profess "communication" are to be found in language departments; analytic philosophers warn their graduate students away from Nietzsche (and other philosophers foolish enough to traffic in "big ideas") with all the fervor of the pastors of the Church of the Militant Lamb. The near-ubiquity of this kind of splitting of potential disciplinary affinities demands that we consider its psychological and social meanings. Something is at stake here that is as yet poorly understood; and perhaps that something is what Timothy Gilmore has called "biophobia" (Gilmore n.d., 11). Contemporary de-valuation of the mind's ability to size up new situations, and its corollary idealization of technological prosthesis, is a melancholic denial of creaturely inventiveness *and* precariousness.

In the disciplinary imaginary of contemporary discourse on the academy, the sciences are self-evidently utilitarian, and the humanities somehow lofty and lovely and loveable, but useless and impossible to evaluate. Stanley Fish, in a thought-piece published in *The New York Times*, asserts that the humanities don't pay for themselves: "indeed, if your criteria are productivity, efficiency and consumer satisfaction, it makes perfect sense to withdraw funds and material support from the humanities—which do not earn their keep" (Fish 2010). But if "consumer satisfaction" means anything like "student interest," the humanities are in reasonably good form, despite the drops in enrollment that typically accompany hard times. Cuts to the humanities are not inspired by that kind of market force. Enrollment in language courses has even been climbing, at some universities at least, while language departments are being closed down or "consolidated"; sometimes faculty are whittled away on the grounds of small numbers of language majors, without consideration of overall enrollment numbers. The (now former) President of the University of California,

Mark Yudof, remarked in 2009 that "[w]e roughly have a $20-billion budget; $3 billion comes from the state. That's the English department, the Spanish department, economics—that have difficulty generating the big outside grants. I love the humanities . . . . But the engineering colleges are going to bring in more external research support, and that money's crucial" (Morrison 2011). This is a disingenuous and misleading statement. Engineering colleges are expensive; the humanities, not so much. Yudof knows perfectly well that the tuition dollar brought in by popular undergraduate majors in the humanities and social sciences is essential to the financial solvency of the UC system; humanities professors typically teach twice as many classes a year as do scientists, make smaller salaries, and publish just as much research, if not more. So: what desires are served by "love" for the lovely humanities? What kind of "love" is it that can so easily be brushed aside (as Yudof does in his statement)?

"The big outside grants" to which Yudof refers—from NIH, NSF, and so on—only contribute a portion of the costs of research. Certain percentages of extramural grants are appropriated by host institutions to support the indirect costs of managing and housing such research—construction, dismantling of disused labs and equipment, custodial upkeep, waste disposal, administrative services (payroll, human resources, accounting, student and faculty housing, student services, library collections, and much much more.) As a consequence, scientists have come to believe—it is like an article of faith—that their grants help to support the rest of the university. But there is no evidence for that conviction; there isn't even any evidence that research in the sciences and engineering is self-sustaining. An American Association of Universities (AAU) report on "Facilities and Administrative Cost Reimbursement" found that "universities contribute more than $8 billion of their own funds each year to support their R&D activities, or nearly 20 percent of their total research and development expenditures" (AAU 2007). A more recent AAU report on "Regulatory and Financial Reform of Federal Research Policy" concludes that the pressure on universities to share the costs of funding external grants has worsened considerably since 2007:

> [T]he current regulatory climate has become dysfunctional—regulations do not align closely with true risk, and new regulatory mandates are unfunded due to the 26-percent cap on reimbursement of administrative costs. It is a growing fiscal challenge for universities to manage unfunded mandates as institutional budgets are being reduced, administrative cost reimbursements are being suppressed, and cost-sharing requirements are increasing. (AAU 2011)

Under the pressure of recent budget cuts, universities are working more closely with major granting institutions on the problem of indirect costs, and taking more from extramural grants to cover the losses they think are engendered thereby. One result of this belated prudence is likely to be even more pressure on scientists to spend their time writing grants instead of doing science and teaching students, thus driving them ever more into the arms of the defense, security and pharmaceutical industries. The evaluation of indirect costs is an area of academic finance that requires considerably more transparency than is characteristic of current practice. But the best available estimates do *not* point in the direction of the profitability of scientific and technological research to the universities that support it.

So why do these facts have so little purchase on the self-proclaimed pragmatists amongst us? Questions about "indirect costs" are not new; they have been raised for decades. Most reasonable scientists will readily acknowledge (to colleagues and friends, if not to funding agencies) the enormous role played by "luck" and "accident" in scientific discovery, as well as the near-certainty that current means of modeling reality will be superseded by new ones. It is, furthermore, still the case that many scientific patents do *not* create wealth or portend social "impact." They are far from useless—often they are small parts of larger efforts that, in time, may well lead in exciting and even monetizable directions. The connection between scientific research and utility is notoriously indirect and unpredictable, but many studies have shown that there are real payoffs in supporting research regardless of the difficulty of predicting outcomes.

Current funding conditions favor scientific work that can, one way or another, be commodified, but the "accountability" drive ironically costs a great deal (one of the reasons administrative costs have burgeoned) and appears to do a poorer job in the long run of producing important innovations. "Pure" science is arguably more likely to generate transformative knowledge and technology than is research directed at specific interventions and applications guided by commercial or political interests.[17] Investment in knowledge, of whatever sort, requires a spirit of adventure—because, no matter how mathematical we are being, we cannot say with absolute certainty where we will end up, or even to what we will have contributed, when it is all over, which it never is. Obfuscation of the risks and costliness of scientific research is an ideological symptom, fueled more by ambition and fear of dispossession than by reason and data.

Both the UK and Canada have mandated that academic research should be funded only if it has "impact" on business or social goods like health and welfare. In those countries, "impact" is the favored alibi for the de-

---

[17] See Greenberg [1967] 1999, *passim,* but especially 29 and 290–291 as a starting point. Greenberg is friendlier to the value of policy involvement than I am, but his book is an invaluable introduction to this complex issue, especially with respect to the theoretical and historical difficulties of maintaining a hard-and-fast distinction between pure and applied science. See Lövbrand (2006) for a case study that queries the distinction.

funding not only of the humanities, but also of scientific and economic studies that do not further the agendas of global capital. "Scientific discovery is not valuable unless it has commercial value," according to John Macdougal, President of the National Research Council of Canada (cited by Tobis 2013). For Macdougal, science has no more inherent value than do the humanities. The criterion that trumps all evaluations of all knowledge disciplines, humanist or scientific, is commercial value. The effect of "imaginary" differences between the sciences and the humanities is legible here: the obscuring of our common vulnerability to capital. A 1997 survey of 2,167 university scientists showed that nearly one in five had delayed publication of corporate-funded research results for more than six months "to protect proprietary information—and this was the number that admitted to delay"; a few years later, the *Journal of the American Medical Association* published an analysis showing that nonprofit studies of cancer drugs were eight times as likely to reach unfavorable conclusions as those funded by pharmaceutical companies (Press and Washburn 2000; see also Washburn 2011). The culture of secrecy that pervades the "academic-industrial complex" not only destroys academic freedom—which includes the right to share one's research results with other investigators and the public—but also undermines the spirit of community that has done so much to *advance* knowledge in the age of liberal arts education.[18]

The accountability drive scorns pleasure, passion, leisure, and luxury (except for the wealthy) in order to convince us that none of these things have anything to do with "necessity," usefulness or practicality. (Never mind that the mind and body both really need downtime in order to work well.) One of the problems with this view-

---

[18] See also Washburn 2005, 85 ff., on the impact of this culture of secrecy on graduate student work. Her book is a must-read for anyone seeking to understand the corporatization of contemporary science.

point is that the terms "necessity" and "luxury" do not designate stable essences, but highly variable and relative qualities. One is thirsty, but what, and in what circumstances, does one drink? As Bataille puts it, "there is nothing that permits us to define what is useful to man" (Bataille 1985, 166)—as the futility of Christianity's longstanding attempts to define what is needful to man might have suggested to us long before now. Utility depends on context. It is a function of the organism's (co)-adaptation with its environment; one creature's utility is another's impossible luxury, and the dividing lines between them have been drawn variously at different times in different cultures (see Fradenburg 1999; Fradenburg 2002, 68, 68n59, 297n3; Sternberg 1997). The fact that the notion of the "useful" has so often been used to attack imaginative work (and pure science) does not mean that it should not be reclaimed, and I believe it should be reclaimed now.[19]

The *Oxford English Dictionary* (*OED*) defines "utility" as "fitness for some desirable purpose or valuable end" (s.v. "utility"); but desirable in what way, and for whom? Arguably, some of the most useful items around would include condoms, energy drinks and smartphones, but no politician is promising to make these things universally available, and all have ties to important forms of enjoyment. Philosophical utilitarianism concerns "the ability, capacity, or power of a person, action or thing to satisfy the needs or gratify the desires of the majority, or of the human race as a whole" (*OED*). But in our own day, this definition sounds more like communism than a funding rationale, and it would almost certainly rule out ascriptions of utility to gated communities. In short, which majority? It is, moreover, impossible to divorce the satisfaction of a need from the enjoyment attendant on that satisfaction. It is always *some* kind of joy to satisfy needs,

---

[19] See Barbara Johnson's *Persons and Things* for a brilliant and highly influential discussion of the ethics of "use" (2008, 63, 97); Gibson's concept of "affordances" is also relevant (1977).

even if the process of satisfying them is neverending. It can even be a joy to feel need; as noted, failure to thrive in infants can be caused by hyper-attention to their needs, not just by neglect thereof. A lot of U.S. social and economic policy depends on the belief that we can and should distinguish states of need from other states like withdrawal, obsession, compulsiveness, and urgency, but this is no easy matter; we can read neurochemical markers, so to speak, but even if there were no significant overlap between these states of feeling, how would we estimate the significance of such differences?

Desire trumps "need" all the time. History is rife with examples of those who choose passion over survival: revengers, berserkers, Young Werthers, militia members, suicide bombers, freedom fighters, addicts, self-immolators, revolutionaries, hunger-strikers, lovers—the list goes on. This is by no means confined either to humans or to violent enactments; recall the well-known study that showed that little monkeys preferred clutching fuzzy blankets to eating from mechanical food dispensers even if they were starving. The political and economic implications of the relationship between need and desire are as wide-ranging now as they were in the days when medieval Christendom was fighting over the meaning of poverty, property, and charity. U.S. welfare policy rests on the assumption that we can easily differentiate the basic needs of others (which we will *perhaps* agree to pay for) from caring for states of mind (which we really don't like to pay for). Welfare policy similarly assumes that we have more right to interfere in the lives of those who are "needy" than we do in the lives of the powerful, despite the fact that the children of the wealthy notoriously show just as many signs of emotional deprivation as the children of the poor.

But psychological pain is often far more difficult to resolve and forget than physical pain, and in any case it is now settled knowledge that the feedback loop between psyche and soma is both intense and ongoing. Insofar as the distinction between need and desire rests on the belief that the former is somehow a somatic condition and the latter a psychical one, it cannot hold. We can spend an entire life dying psychically, or fending off that death, or becoming ill, feeling tortured or killing ourselves, because of psychical pain (see Freud 1900, 613). Both physical and psychological pain threaten our survival and self-extension. Pain makes us want to curl up, sleep, die; but expressing pain, and feeling that our pain is understood, at least begins to undo pain's terrible work of isolation (Scarry 1985, 4). For both kinds of pain, we need techniques of living that extend us into the world—or help us act creatively along with it—and that also help us to forge links with other minds by means of receptivity and expressivity. This is one of the many reasons why online education should be a helpful supplement to face-to-face education, not a replacement for it. The opportunity afforded by the live and lively classroom to inspire and integrate affect, sensation and thought, is priceless and contributes to the richness of life.

Accountability rests on the phantasy of the "thief of enjoyment": "I am not happy—though I would never mention this to anyone, I find that my money can't buy everything, and I never feel as though I have enough, and I have to keep finding more, and more, and more, in order to feel like a 'winner,' blah blah blah—and the reason is that someone has stolen it from me, by being lazy, or overly rational and well-informed. It's not because perfect enjoyment is simply impossible for all mortal creatures, regardless of their circumstances."[20] However, it *is* because perfect enjoyment is impossible for mortal creatures, however elect and immune some imagine themselves to be. So the sciences are not suffering because hu-

---

[20] See Žižek 1990, especially 55n7, on the fantasy of the "theft of enjoyment," a kind of splitting that attributes to the Other behavior that "steals" enjoyment from "my" group—for example, by not working hard enough, or working too much, or expecting pensions as compensation for low public-service salaries.

manists are teaching too many small classes (we are not); neither are humanists suffering because extramural funding agencies give more money to the sciences than they do to the humanities. Humanists are not, on the whole, more lovable than scientists, nor do they need more love, though they might have an easier time acknowledging love's crucial role in evolution. I personally think rotifers are as beautiful as an illuminated capital. Well, almost as beautiful. So, again, let us avoid polarization; all disciplines are currently suffering more from recent trends and hype trails in management theory than they are from the other disciplines' imagined luxuries.

The real question is whether or not humanists can or should justify their work on the grounds that they (and their texts, images, music) provide moral, spiritual or psychological uplift. These justifications, however, were abandoned by most humanists long ago. We have been criticizing our claims to moral and aesthetic authority at least since World War II suggested that lovers of opera and Germanic folklore are not invariably good people. In fact, critiques of humanist idealizations of the greatness, profundity, and coherence of the self and its (self)-knowledge appear in Montaigne's *Essais*, and continue in contemporary writing on post-humanism (Derrida 2008, Hayles 2008, Wolfe 2010), as well as in affect theory (Terada 2003). We have perhaps been *too* hard on ourselves; the "ethical turn" in theory has produced wonderful, inspiring work (Davis and Womack 2001), and Raymond Mar's research (2008) shows that reading fiction may enhance our capacities for empathy, mentalization, and social intelligence. The activations involved in the experience of aesthetic enjoyment are also central to many other important brain functions (cf. Zeki 2008, 2009). We can't draw compelling conclusions from these findings, but neuroplastic connectivity does invite us to re-evaluate all activities of the brain from the standpoint of complexity. Still, for the most part, post-WWII humanist literary study has focused on renewing the study and practice of rhetoric, including critique of the ways rhetoric some-times likes to masquerade as unassailable truth or "gut feelings."

However—there are many twists and turns in this history—where humanists might once have been consid-ered arrogant for presuming to pronounce on the cultural and moral value of all human productions, they are now considered godless hedonists for disposing of their own pretensions. Those who think the arts are worthwhile only if they imply loyalty to the values of the Confederacy have been upset by humanist questioning of cultural au-thority and discourses of power, and for decades have been calling for the defunding of the National Endow-ment for the Humanities, partly on the grounds that its pitifully tiny budget is a threat to the national fisc. For somewhat different reasons, many scientists have also been offended by humanist critiques of objective stand-ards of value; the term "radical relativist" is a slur with more than one derivation. It does no justice to the hu-manities' passionate interest in the validity of interpreta-tion—in *why* three people can hear or read the same words and interpret them differently, and what this plas-ticity is *for*, evolutionarily speaking or otherwise. Human-ists do also know, with Jacques Derrida (1973, 134), that none of us speaks or interprets without appealing in some way to truth, however contextualized and contingent that truth (and truth-telling process) may appear, or be. But truth is no less truthful because it is context-dependent (see Latour 1999). Mathematics remains as elegant as ever, but consider how much, and how, mathematics changed in the course of the development of systems theory. From the standpoint of complexity, truth has new modalities, al-most new flavors. All shifts in thought bring curses as well as blessings; systems theory is not a gift from the angels. Centers of power, wealth and influence have good reasons to herald any and all concepts that promise to diffuse responsibility. But complexity also promises an emancipatory shift. We may no longer have to devalue the world, or ourselves, as rife with error, delusion, and fancy; instead, we can live in a world of artfulness, possibility, and plenty.

In rethinking what's left of the Enlightenment opposition between Truth and Fancy, we should also remember that the humanities learned to be wary of absolute certainty partly from post-Newtonian scientific critiques of certainty. Humanities disciplines have also, throughout their history, welcomed insights from philosophy, philology, linguistics, statistics, anthropology, sociology, psychology, cognitive science, and evolutionary biology. Many humanists respect the sciences and like thinking with them, and vice-versa; hence the new fields of quantitative literary studies, neurohumanism, cognitive religious studies, neuropsychoanalysis, neuroaesthetics, and affect theory. Scientists, in turn, are increasingly interested in holistic and ecological analyses of mentation; cognitive psychologists leaven their reliance on flashcards with study of real-time reading process, and environmental theory investigates the interdependence of perception of inner and outer worlds (an oversimplistic description of Gibson 1997). Complexity theory's claim that novelty "emerges" out of the play of open systems undoes the antinomy between variation and repeatability on which so many past distinctions between the sciences and the humanities have depended.

One of the central claims of this book is that poststructuralist science embraces many values and insights more usually attributed to (post)humanism. Today's scientists came of age in the days when Michel Foucault and Joan Kelly were dismantling *les grands récits narratifs* of European history, and Derrida was unfolding the philosophical implications of the linguistic sign. For scientists now, "it's all about plasticity," as a biologist colleague of mine said to me not long ago. Even the multiculturalism once criticized by scientists because of its apparent disrespect for universals has become a highly beneficial part of experimental method. Indeed, the charges have been re-

versed; when the subjects of our psychological observation are diverse in age, ethnicity, gender, and so forth,
we are less likely to claim universality for findings that are
true only for certain (sub)cultures, and more likely to
map the influence of experience on relatively stable features of the mind/brain. Comparative research is as likely
to clarify the latter as it is the former (see, for example,
Lee Sui Wan's [2000] nuanced thesis on the "possibly
universal aspects of 'motherese'"). We have also learned
that cognition is not "opposed" to affect; affect, rather,
helps us think, by encouraging us to pay attention, try out
new things, and form memories.

The interdisciplinarity of liberal arts education works
in many different ways on many different levels, only one
of which is professional collaboration in academic research projects. Thankfully, for the time being, at least,
the liberal arts are still alive in K-12 education, even
though so many language and arts programs have been
foolishly cut. I was a member of my high school Science
Club; in eighth grade, I elected to join a group of students
who went spelunking with one of our teachers. We all
know that affect is very powerful in determining the importance we give to different subjects. Many of today's
scientists also studied arts and humanities in high school
and college, even if they didn't major in them. Long before the specialization that takes place in the course of
higher education, interdisciplinary awareness prepares
the ground for the new hybridities and collaborations of
the future. And, as noted, embodied communities provide the best possible support for this cross-disciplinary
creativity. It's under these circumstances that we're most
likely to attend lectures in other departments and talk
about them afterwards with colleagues, perhaps bringing
with us a copy of Michel Serres' *Biogeia*, or stopping by—
even if one is a humanist—to 'ooh' and 'ah' over interesting new developments in somebody's slime mold. Research
thrives when researchers live and work together. It also thrives
when we can work with far-away colleagues; virtual reality

is not deprived of reality, but it is also only one version thereof. We need not scorn the simulacrum for its lack of vitality and veracity; we can still respect the signifier's powers of transmission and social linkage without denying the virtues of living presence. We are beings with a long history of exploring the power of prosthesis; language itself is a distance medium. But we invest as heavily in prosthetics as we do to a significant degree because of our anxieties about the fragility of our enjoyment, bodies, lives, and loves.

The knowledge and technology we make is a consequence of the kind of creature we are (and vice-versa)— vulnerable, curious, affect-laden. We fall for the melancholic lures of prosthesis and genetic engineering—the promise of a better, cleaner, invulnerable, endlessly gratified body—while the "creature" is in fact a more and more endangered species. In the academy, the newest biophobic symptom is the devaluation of "life" as a tiny dead-end anomaly in a brutal universe that is indifferent to us. Why not rather celebrate its rarity? Why not rather appreciate the astonishing phenomena that emerge from possibility? While admiring the superintelligent cyborgs we already expect to become, we forget how amazing our brains and bodies already are, and how many remarkable things they allow us to do. We can support and extend sentience without pretending to ourselves that we have escaped from a world of change. The biggest problem our world faces today is not humanist overvaluation of subjectivity or scientific empiricism; it is melancholic scorn for the everyday lives of mortal creatures, and the wanton discarding of lives that goes on daily (see, for example, Bauman 2003). Neither gadget-love nor rhinocerous horn will eliminate the vicissitudes of our enjoyment.[21]

---

[21] I caution my colleagues to consider what the devaluing of self and subjectivity might mean in a time of drone warfare, technocratic biophobia, and human trafficking (see Butler 2004; Chakravorty and Neti 2009; Waldby 2004). For work on reconfiguring the ethics and discourses of biopolitics in light of posthu-

In the sciences, self, culture, even the life experiences of creatures still hover somewhere "over" the real action, apparently towards the top of the disciplinary heap but in fact epiphenomenal. Despite Dennett's elegant, nuanced critique of his own influential distinction between "subjective" or "first-person" knowing and objective or "third-person" knowing (Dennett 2007, 252), the distinction still makes a difference, and the privilege goes to third-person knowledge. Edward Wilson's (1999) call for "consilience" between the humanities and the sciences has not gotten us much further, because the former are subsumed into a larger explanatory framework, leaving behind all of their messy and valuable complexity. Ted Slingerland's arboreal schema posits scientific "ground" for the treehouses of culture, thus bearing an uncanny and no doubt unintended resemblance to Marx's much-criticized distinction between economic structure and cultural superstructure (2009).[22] But encoding and decoding, pattern-recognition and construction, are fundamental to living process, sentient or otherwise. Sentience itself is highly varied, consisting of very "early" functions and forms working cheek by jowl with "later" ones. If, as Barbieri (2009) contends, symbolic semiosis emerges from the code semiotics of early organic life, ideas like consilience relegate semiosis to much too narrow a band of material activity. Similarly, the privileging of third- over first-person knowledge downplays both the extent of their interdependence and the enormous pragmatic value of the latter.

But self has also been acquiring new significance all across the sciences and philosophy. Biologists speak of recognition of "self/non-self" as basic to the workings of

---

man developments and philosophies, see Zylinska (2009), MacCormack (2012), and Chen (2012).

[22] Slingerland (2008) seems determined to make the humanities responsible for, instead of critical of, "mind-body dualism"— but despite its unwarranted polarizations, his book is a challenging discussion of current claims that the sciences can help the humanities "progress."

immune systems (the Major Histocompatibility Complex,
again). Does this install a primitive binary at the heart of
organismic experience? Perhaps. But what if that binary
were an element in an open network of signifying chains
constructed out of familiarity and unfamiliarity? Could
the digital be partly responsible for the multicellular pro-
pensities of living matter? Can self be thus distinguished
from its idealist forebear, the "soul"? Self-experience is a
neural phenomenon, embodied and always-unfolding (Ledoux
2010). Self is not the ultimate arbiter of reality, even of its
own psychical reality. Arguably, however, neither is it
merely a befuddled, delusional witness nor an aggressive
display of false coherence. Hood (2012) argues that self is
an unfolding narrative; it is, so to speak, what episodic
memory is *for*. Self is critic and storyteller, inventor and
historian (Boyd 2009). Many contemporary psychoana-
lysts understand self to mean a succession of self-states
often unaware of their discontinuity (see Lachmann and
Beebe 1997). Above all, self-process is generated by neuronal and neurochemical activity in the service of organismic attempts to shape and evaluate lived experience.
Thus the self can also be imagined as a moving point in
an open, self-organized, living system (see Bersani and
Dutoit 2008, Bersani 2010); if not globally coherent and
stable, that is to say, it most certainly has elements thereof.[23] We do not need to jettison subjectivity and self-
process; instead we need to redescribe them, so as to include the self-constitutive activity of the semi-permeable
sac whose formation arises from non-sentient activity,
but is at the same time necessary to life.

Didier Anzieu's "skin-ego" (1989, 1993) and Hoffmeyer's notion of skin as self (2008, 25–36) both illustrate
the conceptual relocation of self to the activity of the
membrane. Damasio argues for a "proto-self" that doesn't
simply await neo-cortical developments but rather sha-

---

[23] As Doidge (2007) points out, plasticity and entrenchment are
two sides of the same coin.

pes, and is shaped by, very ancient brain-stem functions (Damasio 2010, 31–62). This is a neural platform whose plasticity eventuates in the complexity and historicity of "personal" selfhood. Self-process plays a crucial role in directing attention and concern, thereby shaping the brain and its ability to (co)adapt to inner and outer environmental change. It is one of the chief shapers of the "appetitive motivational system" Panksepp calls SEEKING (Panksepp 1998, 24–27, 51). Organisms, it seems, always seek enrichment, not just "bare life"; as J.Z. Young puts it in *The Study of Man*, art is biologically significant because it insists "that life be worthwhile, which, after all, is the final guarantee of its continuance" (Young 1971, 360). However fallible, the sophistication of sentience is an aspect of, and enables, living process.

Dissanayake's suggestion that "making special" is one of the core functions of art helps to explain why we have such difficulty appreciating the artistry of everyday life (Dissanayake 1988, 74–106). Art does in fact capture attention by, say, making us see or feel the creamy or gleaming character of rock rather than its overfamiliar immobile lumpiness. What is of importance in this process is not simply the separation of self from non-self, but the work done on the boundary between the two, where we can make the familiar unfamiliar just as readily as the other way round. (Indeed it is embellishment, not necessity, that is the mother of invention.) Jane Jacobs notes that the ludic and ornamental applications of our most important technologies (such as ceramics, metallurgy, plastics) preceded their practical applications; our oldest known examples of wheels are from toy wagons (Jacobs 1988, 221). The placard, the territorial marker, the beautiful or forbidding entryway, are all forms of display, and hence instruments of living process. Avian and simian performance displays (e.g., in courting) must vary from "tradition" if they are going to attract attention to this specially plumageous or architecturally creative bird, or that small but exceptionally boisterous and noisy chimpanzee. The crafting of insult and satire marks emergence or expulsion from the crowd, as in the scene of Homeric single combat, or the horripilation and posturing of little pussycats intent on territorial defense or combat (see Fradenburg 1991). These are stylizations of the gaze—the being looked at—fundamental to the co-constructions of creatures and territories (Lacan 1998, 75; Caillois 2003, 89–106). My point is not to reduce the arts to "survival" practices, but rather to expand our understanding of survival practices themselves as including and being included by the arts of thriving and enjoyment.

Because female sexual choice is practiced by a wide variety of species, including primates, many evolutionary theorists have considered the possibility that female "taste" or aesthetic judgment may be the most important factor in evolutionary change (for discussion see Rothenberg 2005, 34–39). Hoffmeyer's critique of Dawkins suggests that aesthetic judgment does not simply serve the "selfish gene" but rather points to the agency of phenotypal experience in general (Hoffmeyer 2008, 75–78, 96–98). Arts of any kind depend and elaborate on signaling and its interpretation; all benefit from play, practice and sophistication; all depend on the construction and deconstruction of meaningful patterns, among which are the "vitality affects" Daniel Stern (2010) writes about: intensity, stillness, exaggeration, subtlety. The arts foreground expression and interpretation—they heighten sentient experience, and in this way sustain the attention that can lead to neuroplastic change (Mahoney 1991, 69ff, 95–100). Art is what a behavioral ethologist would call a "costly," but therefore noticeable, signal (Reader 2003, 5.). Animals "exaggerate" signals because exaggeration is part of living process: little siamangs and chimpanzees try regularly to avoid the responsibilities of adult life by means of exaggerated distress calls and temper tantrums; when ready to mate, female chimps will moan theatrically to attract the attention of the males that interest them; we all perfume the air when we want love, or give each other the evil eye, often in order to *avoid* injury—war by other means, i.e. politics (Byrne 2003). These are the masks of love and war—when I unfurl my best feathers, or costume my destrier to enhance the appearance of my monstrous, chivalric oneness with him.

Classical and medieval animal lore is full of examples of beasts' love of the arts. John of Trevisa writes that oxherders know to "please their oxen with whistling and song to make them bear the yoke better"; "deer love melody by kynde, as Avicenna says"; they marvel at "the noise of pipes," and enjoy "accord of melody" (Seymour [1975] 1988, XVIII.xv, XVIII.xxx).[24] Horses are "glad of the noise of symphony," and are "comforted with the noise of a trumpet to battle and to fighting" (XVIII. xxxix). In distinguishing between beasts that have voices and those that do not, John of Trevisa notes that the former "make tunes and melody . . . namely in time of engendering," when they "pray for love." Darwin, in effect, agrees: "[T]he power of intercommunication between members of the same community—and . . . between members of the opposite sexes . . . is of the highest importance to [social animals]" (Darwin 1872, 60). Antonio Damasio's work on emotions recalls Darwin's by defining emotions as expressive and embodied social activity (Damasio 2003, 46). The grimace does not simply "represent" pain, fear or anger; like tears, it relieves pain by means of projection, ex-pression in both senses of the term. Emotions are extimate, part of the inherent expressivity of affective process. The mask hides the face and its emotional displays, but also calls attention to the presence of disguise. Hiding and making appearances—camouflage and display—are functions crucial to life, and both are ways of shaping sentient awareness.

---

[24] All citations to Trevisa are taken from Seymour's edition ([1975] 1988), cited by book and section number. On John of Trevisa and his "auctour" Bartholomaeus Anglicus, see Keen (2007) and Fowler (1995). My remarks on Trevisa draw on Fradenburg (2012).

Steen (2009) argues that consciousness is for the purpose of responsiveness to novelty, in the same way that the plasticity of memory does not simply lead to "distortions," but creates new narratives and understandings of our lives in accordance with changing realities. The kind of representational accuracy admired by empiricists, that is to say, may not be as high a priority for episodic memory as the social and psychological renegotiability of life-stories.[25] We need to model reality in malleable fashion if we are to live and learn; even the evidence of our senses is based on interpretation (what you might call the outreach capacities of the optic nerve: Mahoney 1991, 106–108). Relationality, intellectual stimulation, and the arts are not fripperies, but activities for life. What is "mentalization" if not awareness, via signification, of the sentience of others—of minds "like our own" (or not) (see Fonagy 1998)? We know that our lab rat brothers and sisters will run mazes out of curiosity, sans reward; fish will swim mazes for the same reason, because they enjoy SEEKING (Panskepp 1998, 24–27). So, at the Santa Barbara Zoo, the zookeepers dig and reshape the soil in the meerkat habitat so that the meerkats will follow them around and then dig and reshape it all over again. Thriving and surviving are fully intricated with each other; cultural activity is neither epiphenomenal, nor dispensable, but essential to our ways of living.

Culture is what Elaine Scarry, in her unsurpassable book on *The Body in Pain*, calls "self-extension" (Scarry 1985, 33). We might call it the caring side of prosthesis, because it tends to the body's vulnerabilities, rather than denying that they exist. By comparison with the humble proximity of lightbulb to eye, or bed to aching legs, she writes,

elaborate forms of self-extension occur at a . . . dis-

---

[25] Schacter 1996, 98–133, discusses the "troubling" plasticity of memory.

tance from the body; the telephone or the airplane is a more emphatic instance of overcoming the limitation of the human body than is the cart. Yet even as here when most exhilaratingly defiant of the body, civilization always has embedded within it a profound allegiance to the body. (Scarry 1985, 57)

The sciences study patterns in matter and physical forces (among other things); the humanities teach human organisms how best to move, and keep on moving, with maximum power and grace. If the humanities are "fuzzy" and their processes and outcomes difficult to quantify, that is because living is "fuzzy." It demands artfulness, experimentation, and hypothesis.

Athletes and musical prodigies benefit from training, mental as well as physical; to suggest that training in rhetorical, critical, and scholarly abilities accomplishes nothing is as foolish as suggesting that actors and dancers should be exclusively self-taught. It only makes sense that we would train ourselves and our young how best to interpret and address the world, as sentient entities living in complex ecologies. The idea that life is artful and requires creativity, technique, and practice, is of course an ancient one; indeed there is no culture, no group, without stylized and distinctive arts of living. In Volume 3 of *The History of Sexuality*, Foucault studies the classical regimens that taught the arts of living to Western antiquity (one of his chapters is on Artemidorus's *Oneirocriticon*, the treatise on the interpretation of dreams discussed by Freud at the beginning of his own tome by that name) (see Foucault 1988; Fradenburg 2009). Within and beyond the regimens of antiquity, formalized arts of living included "consolations" and "inspirations" (for example, how to endure awaiting execution in a Roman prison, with both sons already dead).[26] We cannot jettison the arts and hu-

---

[26] The most famous example of the consolation is *De Consola-*

manities without also jettisoning counsel and healing. (This argument will not, of course, sway anybody who wants to jettison teaching, healing, and helping, despite the fact that *all* lives demonstrably depend on such arts.) Freud wrote, in *Civilization and Its Discontents*, that life was too hard for us. But we had, he thought, developed "techniques of living" to help us manage—such as remaking the world according to our wishes (courageous, but probably futile), and love (most likely to succeed) (Freud 1961b, 62ff.). Jung formulated the ideal outcome of psychoanalysis as "creative living": "as a living phenomenon," he wrote, "[the psychological fact] is always indissolubly bound up with the continuity of the vital process, so that it is not only something evolved but also continually evolving and creative" (Jung 1953, par. 717).

Jazz, writes Steven Knoblauch, is "a model for improvising within and flowing with the rhythms of life, for inhabiting experience in its fullness . . . and for sustaining and surviving . . . treatment relationships" (Knoblauch 1996, 324). Philip Ringstrom's discussions of improvisation see psychoanalytic technique in much the same way (Ringstrom 2001, 731). Biological processes are also improvisational, at least in the sense that no moment, no challenge to life, is ever exactly the same as another. Whether we argue, with the evolutionary psychologists, for an "improvisational intelligence" produced by selection, or with the anthropologists for the dependence of ecological (co)adaption on social learning, the (living) processes involved have much in common: pattern-recognition and interpretation, copying of motifs and errors therein, pattern change, environmental complexity, and temporality in the form of generational (and phenotypal) innovation and its miscalculations (Calvin 1996; Boyd, Richerson and Henrich 2011). The humanities are interpretive arts, whatever else they may be; they teach necessarily improvisational, real-time, and unpredictable practice, because

---

tione Philosophiae, by Boethius (ed. Moreschini 2000).

that is the lion's share of living (Aron 2006, 355). Ringstrom contends that there is no technique for improvisation; but in fact we do teach improvisation as technique,
in manners as well as in theatre—as we do in the humanities, at least in classes small enough to engage in discussion, when we are thinking on our feet, pulling words out
of nowhere, expressing new ideas and *linking* them to
familiar ones. Creativity means pattern-definition *and*
change.[27]

The vitality affects—loudness, intensity, speed of
movement, and so forth—and the "forms of vitality" that
transmit them, are crucial to the semiosis of living process, as well as to the arts (Stern 2010). We can see re-
shapings of these forms in the styles of signification that
followed the plagues of 14th-century Europe.[28] According
to the literary historian Siegfried Wenzel, the arts of 14th-
century England made scant mention of the plague, by
comparison with, for example, the ubiquity of the *danse
macabre* on the continent; English medical writing on the
plague was derived from a narrow range of authorities,
primarily Guy de Chauliac (Wenzel 1982, 150). Can we,
as Wenzel did—and rather too many medievalists after
him—conclude from this and similar evidence that the
English were less traumatized by the plague than the
French and the Italians (see, for example, Lewis 2003,
148)? I think not. For one thing, post-traumatic disorders
express themselves in many different ways (phobic and
counterphobic, melancholic and maniacal), including silence. We still know very little about how and why these

---

[27] T. Paul Cox's essay "The Slopes of Davos" is critical of the
idea that improvisation might be "a way of life" (Cox 2013, 8).
But I do believe it is the nature of all living process. The fact that
improvisation has been captured on occasion by neo-liberal
discourse, or at least by the entertainments neo-liberalism puts
on "*outside* . . . the secure perimeter" (my emphasis) that shelters the big capitalist powers from lesser ones at Davos, does not
mean we can't reclaim it for another kind of thought.

[28] On cultural epidemiology, see Trostle and Sommerfeld (1996).

different pathways are taken, by any particular person, in any historical situation. But I suggest there is plenty of evidence of trauma in the writing of the period. One of late medieval England's foremost (post)traumatic symptoms is the acceleration and expansion of preparedness: newly Englished almanacs and divination guides, astrological and medical treatises, and herbals, herbals, herbals. We see English prose, which in this period is increasingly associated with the dissemination of plain truths legible to ordinary minds, rather than with the especially difficult challenge to memory it had been in earlier periods. We see attempts to manage anxiety by means of improved foresight, and to take talismanic action against abandonment: read it yourself, do it yourself, because *cura*, 'care,' has fled the land. *Cura* shrinks to the precincts of St. Paul's; the surviving doctors and priests are all running away from the villages and towns. Have an herbal and an almanac on hand, maybe a treatise on astrology, because you are on your own. After the plague, catastrophic loss of *Heimlich* ('homely') space leads to the re-territorializing of the human mind as *Heimlich*. How can we feel companionated by other minds under these circumstances? And if we can't, what happens to the common weal? If no one cares for the commons, the commons must care for itself. The survivors make the world "home" again—they re-environ—by learning about it and the minds in which they keep it. This is familiar to us from our own time; from the 1970s onward, when Great Society initiatives were blamed by right wing opportunists for the economic crash brought on by the OPEC oil crisis of 1974, and U.S. leadership offered little or nothing in the way of intelligent and forward-looking responses, our non-fiction bestseller list has been crammed with "self-help" books.

In the 14th century, translation into the vernacular became lifesaving, restorative activity, in a way that medical humanists would understand well, to say nothing of the Franciscans (St. Francis is credited with having writ-

ten some of the earliest poems in Italian). The aforementioned John Trevisa was probably the most ambitious and
prolific of the new translators in plaguey England. His
Properties of Things, a translation of Bartholomaeus Anglicus' *De proprietatibus rerum*, contains knowledge of
plants and many other "things" of medicinal value. The
Sixth Book treats of sleep, dreams, and exercise, like an
old regimen (or, to use Foucault's term, "care of self"
treatise). The *Properties* discuss vertigo, spasms, the "things
that befall man against kynde," but also those things of the
earth that "are made to relieve . . . many kinds of infirmi-
ties" of "mannes kynde," to "comfort, help, and succour,
and keep and save [us]" (VII.i). It's not all bad out there;
lunatics can be healed by the long teeth of wolves (XVIII.i). And
why not? If, while in the middle of a psychotic break,
someone handed me a lupine incisor to bind to my cheek,
I might well feel a new spring in my step. I have a talisman.
Someone—me?—has replied to my howls. Post-trauma, popular knowledge about care upholds relationality, however
tenuously.

It is hard to ignore the affection, registered in the (pa-
ra)language of Trevisa's translation (as in Bartholomaeus's balanced, rhythmic Latin), for the beasts that move
upon the earth: sadness over the ignoble deaths of faithful
old dogs; wonder at the intelligence of spiders, evident in
their works but unknowable to us, a kind of secret, un-
translatable mental life. The expressive power of Trevisa's
translation—its transmission of affects, like curiosity and
sympathy—is at least as significant as its content, in a
plague-decimated land with no reason to celebrate the
gifts of nature. As noted above, a new vernacular audience could read or hear this science—this "natural history"—and bind its wounds accordingly. And they could
hear the "things" of nature (and beyond) described in
poetical English prose, in the "mother tongue," which has
its own healing powers, like music; it evokes attachment,

re-environs us in *chora*.[29] The earth is not simply a purgatory readying us for heavenly places; it is a *home* for all living creatures.

Trevisa transvalues earth and heaven by turning the latter into the *chora* of the earth. Heaven, though above earth (in all senses), is in a position to "influence" it fully, and thus quicken it: "[A]lthough the earth is lowest in comparison to the body of heaven, nonetheless it receives the most influence of the light of heaven and is therefore most plenteous as the mother of all, and brings forth many diverse and most contrary kinds" (XIV.ii). A *heimlich* place indeed. The text continues: "[W]hat seems lacking [in the earth] of nobleness of substance is recovered in effect and virtue, for . . . it brings forth some more noble [kyndes] than heaven does. . . . [It] brings forth creatures with life, feeling and reason" (XIV.ii). Trevisa describes all sentient life, not just reason, as "noble." Influence is glad to touch the earth, to make it heavenly, to link different entities and territories. Trevisa's prose make us feel the earth's specialness: Book XVII treats of "the fairness of the earth, touching virtues and properties of ore and of metal and stones and things that grow under the ground, and of trees, herbs, grass and weeds that *grow and spring from* the earth" (my emphasis). This is *amplificatio, enumeratio* (amplification, enumeration)—an emparadising, as Milton might have put it, of the lively mind. The rhythm first tumbles along with energy and then, paralleling two doublets, begins to enchant us. Book VIII will clarify that human beings are beasts too; Trevisa writes about "the virtues and properties of things that have life and feeling; and all that is comprehended of flesh and of spirit of life and so of body and soul is called animal 'a beast,' whether it be airy as fowl, or watery as fish that swim, or earthy as beasts that go on the ground and

---

[29] On the "semiotic chora"—the primordial "receptacle" whose rhythms precede but always undergird language and our perceptions of space—see Kristeva 1984, 25–30, and Kristeva 1980, 6–7.

in fields, as men and beasts wild and tame." This is anaphora, pleonasm, a reveling in the multitudinousness and variousness of beasts, all brought together by rhythm ("men and beasts wild and tame").

In today's world, Trevisa would have had a lot of trouble finding funding for such a project. What could England hope to gain from a translation of a 200-year-old enormous Latin tome? Territory is bound up with affect: we mark it with our memories, and vice versa, and this expressivity helps us process the vicissitudes of territory (and of the territory of the O/other—territory is always extimate), as I argue happened in 14th-century England. (It is also happening today, visible, as noted, in the deadly fantasy of immunity, but also audible in the material of those of my patients whose fears are embedded in identifications with endangered species.) Denmark's loss of Schleswig-Holstein to the Austro-Prussian army in 1864 also meant the loss of most of Denmark's non-Danish-speaking population; the monarchy "turned its eyes inward under the rationale that 'outward losses must be made up by inward gains'" (Blau and Christensen 2002). The "working through" that might otherwise have been enabled was compromised by the imperative to "make it up"; the result was the interior colonization of Jutland and the emergence of a "common Danish culture," best exemplified by the religious poet and national icon N.F.S. Gruntvig, a great promoter of the purity of the Danish language, and an anti-Semite (see Blau and Christensen 2002). Denmark's loss of its non-Danish-speaking population is redressed with one of the most venerable maneuvers of magical thinking: we didn't want them anyway. This is only one aspect of Denmark's cultural renascence; but it is a sobering one to say the least, since we all know how that sort of thing turned out in the end for the chosen people. The arts exaggerate, foreground, make spectacular, and thereby help us attend to and learn better the formal features of the more quotidian arts of living; but the rigid and rigidifying forms of stereotype and propaganda can narrow our vision down almost to nothing. The arts are at work in human predation and defense and also in the ineradicable cultural dimension of epidemic.

Interpretation and relationality depend on one another; all relationships are unending processes of interpretation and expression, listening and signifying. In turn, sentience assists relationality: we can neither thrive nor survive without minds alert to possibility. Psychoanalytic attention to somatic and paraverbal communication and to "primary" and "secondary" process (such as multiple-code theory: see Bucci 1997) attests to the many different (but interlocking) modes of sentience that constitute living process and our awareness and experience thereof. Psychoanalysis is also an art that cultivates sentience; the ear of the analyst—of the analysand too—is a highly sensitive instrument. Analysts try to listen to all the ways people signify, all at once. We try to reach all different parts of the (embodied and motoric) mind, all different modes of (un-)consciousness, all the different intensities and gradations of human sentience, all at once (cf. Kohut [1953] on empathy as a mode of knowing). And though psychoanalysis is particularly focused on real-time inter-subjective engagement, so are many other efforts to teach, heal, help and befriend, like the medical humanities (Charon 2006).

No organism lasts for long if it can't interpret signals well, or signal what it needs to communicate. Both the fine arts and the arts of living exercise therapeutic powers of expression and interpretation. Psychoanalysis is still the Talking Cure. But it is also the Listening Cure, the Seeing and Being Seen Cure, the Screaming Cure, and the Cure by means of Metaphor, Quietness, Silence, and Hospitality. The enhancement of sentience in the service of relationality is its aim, as is true also of the arts and humanities. "[H]umans are interpretations of their worlds; we are embodied tacit theories" (Mahoney, 88). Infantile fantasies are hypotheses about self and other that are tested, refined and transformed in the course of development. Our interpretations of relational experiences, and the resulting expectations about how such experiences will and should be negotiated, are stored as "procedural memories"—memories we keep, non-consciously, of techniques of living, and how to use them (Herbert 2006, 43; cf. also Brickman 2008). The quiet non-consciousness of procedural memory is one of the most important reasons why the complexity and artistry of living process is so easy for us to forget. We like to take our templates and skills for granted as much as possible. We become neurally entrenched. Once we have learned them, we never have to ponder the rules governing utterances in English, or bicycle-pedaling, until something goes wrong, and we often resent the labor it takes to give such basic assumptions fresh attention; the act of making-conscious almost always meets resistance, because it takes energy. Affect plays its role here, by attaching us to (relational) expectations we hope will always be met, and making it hard for us to (co)adapt to, and create, new circumstances. Because it is non-conscious, because we take for granted the knowledge of practice encoded by procedural memory, we do not think of it enough when we consider the work of self-transformation (see, for example, Modell 2003, 42–47). But making-conscious is another way to foster mental plasticity (resilience); it is not simply a matter of shining a light, but rather of the spreading neuroplastic change set off thereby. The complexities of living process require enormous finesse to negotiate, and it is part of the work both of psychoanalysis and the liberal arts in general to focus attention on the activities of procedural patterns, so naturalized, so in the background, so difficult to describe and explain.

Living process depends on preservation as well as innovation. The relational arts teach us how better to protect the bonds that help us thrive, while also allowing them to change and grow, and even make way for new ones. But, as Malabou notes, thriving is not a matter of infinite "flexibility," but rather of plasticity (Malabou

2008, 47). Forces do not shape us willy-nilly, which is a good thing, because plasticity means we can be profoundly influenced over time. Some "innovations," after all, are to be avoided, like most online universities, or the latest thing in mortgage-backed securities. As noted, these days we have to wrap our minds more and more around the idea that the living can be replaced, not just on the assembly-line, but in the classroom and the hospital. This accelerating devaluation of life serves domination, the antidote to which is to know that *we are all mortal creatures—immunity remains impossible.* It is only with the "sole support" of this knowledge that "we can attempt to live with others" (Kristeva 1992, 170). There are many different kinds of intelligence, and there will always be a few writers who don't need to read Shakespeare in college, or game designers who don't need economics courses to get rich. But a terrible narrowing of the mind and of mental experience is ongoing in our country, sometimes waved on by the very scientists who ought most of all to respect the mind's powers. As the philosopher Guillaume LeBlanc has argued throughout his *oeuvre*, philosophy is work performed in and on behalf of particular cultures and ecologies. This requires a new ethos of the philosopher, for whom the question of belonging to an ordinary world has become, not something to bracket or transcend, but vital. Understanding how ordinariness is produced, and critiquing self-evidence, remain crucial activities of cultural analysis. But we are also bound to deciphering the relationship of our work to the arts of thriving and surviving, and it is time to fight not just for this or that way of thinking, but for the experience of mind itself.

REFERENCES

American Association of Universities (AAU) (2007). "Facilities and Administrative Cost Reimbursement: Resources, Facts and Figures," *AAU: Policy Issues* [website], August 10:

http://www.aau.edu/policy/associations_background.aspx?id
=7366.

American Association of Universities (AAU) (2011). "Regula-
tory and Financial Reform of Federal Research Policy."
AAU: Policy Issues [website], January 23: http://www.aau.
edu/policy/associations_background.aspx?id=7366.

Anvari, S. et al. (2002). "Relations among Musical Skills, Phono-
logical Processing, and Early Reading Experience in Pre-
school Children." *Journal of Experimental Psychology* 83.2:
111–130.

Anzieu, D. (1989). *The Skin Ego*. New Haven: Yale University
Press.

Anzieu, D. (1993). "Autistic Phenomena and the Skin Ego."
Psychoanalytic Inquiry 13.1: 42–48.

Aron, L. (2006). "Analytic Impasse and the Third: Clinical Implications of Intersubjectivity Theory." *International Journal of Psychoanalysis* 87.2: 349–368.

Bady, A. (2013). "The MOOC Moment and the End of Reform."
zunguzungu [weblog], *The New Inquiry*, May 15: http://the
newinquiry.com/blogs/zunguzungu/the-mooc-moment-and
-the-end-of-reform/.

Barbieri, M. (2009). "A Short History of Biosemiotics." *Biosemiotics* 2.2: 221–245.

Bataille, G. (1985). *Visions of Excess: Selected Writings, 1927-
1939*, ed. and trans. A. Stoekl. Minneapolis: University of
Minnesota Press.

Bauman, Z. (2003). *Wasted Lives: Modernity and Its Outcasts*.
Cambridge, UK: Polity.

Bersani, L. (2010). "Psychoanalysis and the Aesthetic Subject."
In *Is The Rectum a Grave? And Other Essays*, 139–153. Chicago: University of Chicago Press.

Bersani, L. and U. Dutoit (2008). *Forms of Being: Cinema, Aesthetics, Subjectivity*. London: British Film Institute.

Blau, J. and M. Christensen (2002). "The Denmark Worth Protecting." *Humanity in Action*: http://www.humanityinaction.org/
knowledgebase/196-the-denmark-worth-protecting.

Blumenfeld-Katzir, T. et al. (2011). "Diffusion MRI of Structural
Brain Plasticity Induced by a Learning and Memory Task."
PLoS ONE 6(6): e20678: doi:10.137/journal.pone.0020678.

Bollas, C. (1987). *The Shadow of the Object: Psychoanalysis of
the Unthought Known*. London: Free Association Press.

Boyd, B. (2009). *On the Origin of Stories: Evolution, Cognition
and Fiction*. Cambridge, MA: Harvard University Press.

Brickman, H.R. (2008). "Living Within the Cellular Envelope: Subjectivity and Self from an Evolutionary Neuropsychoanalytic Perspective." *Journal of the American Academy of Psychoanalysis and Dynamic Psychiatry* 36.2: 317–341.

Bucci, W. (1997). "Patterns of Discourse In 'Good' And Troubled Hours: A Multiple Code Interpretation." *Journal of the American Psychoanalytic Association* 45.1: 155–187.

Butler, J. (2004). *Precarious Life: The Powers of Mourning and Violence.* New York: Verso.

Byrne, R. (2003). "Novelty in Deceit." In Reader and Laland, eds., *Animal Innovation*, 237–259.

Caillois, R. (2003). *The Edge of Surrealism: A Roger Caillois Reader*, ed. C. Frank. Durham: Duke University Press.

Calvin, W.H. (2001). "Pumping Up Intelligence: Abrupt Climate Jumps and the Evolution of Higher Intellectual Functions during the Ice Ages." In *The Evolution of Intelligence*, eds. R.J. Sternberg and J.C. Kaufman, 97–115. London: Taylor & Francis.

Chakravorty, M. and L. Neti (2009). "The Human Recycled: Insecurity in the Transnational Moment." *differences: A Journal of Feminist Cultural Studies* 20.2-3: 194–223.

Charon, R. (2006). *Narrative Medicine: Honoring the Stories of Illness.* New York: Oxford University Press.

Chen, M.Y. (2012). *Animacies: Biopolitics, Racial Mattering, and Queer Affect.* Durham: Duke University Press.

Churchland, P.S. (1980). "Language, Thought and Information Processing." *Noûs* 14.2: 147–170.

Colman, W. (2007). "Symbolic Conceptions: The Idea of the Third." *Journal of Analytic Psychology* 52.5: 565–583.

Cox, P.T. (2013). "The Slopes of Davos." *The New Inquiry* 16: 8–14.

Damasio, A. (2003). *Looking for Spinoza: Joy, Sorrow and the Feeling Brain.* New York: Harcourt.

Damasio, A. (2010). *Self Comes To Mind: Constructing the Conscious Brain.* New York: Pantheon.

Darder, A. and R. Torres (1999). "Shattering the Race Lens: Toward a Critical Theory of Racism." In Tai 1999, 173-192.

Darwin, C. (1872). *The Expression of Emotions in Man and Animals.* London: John Murray. Available online: http://dawin-online.org.uk/content/frameset?pageseq=1&itemID=F1142&viewtype=text.

Davidson, A.I. (1987). "How to do the History of Psychoanalysis: A Reading of Freud's *Three Essays on the Theory of Sexuality*." *Critical Inquiry* 13.2: 252–277.

Davis, T.F., and Womack, K. *Mapping the Ethical Turn: A Reader in Ethics, Culture, and Literary Theory.* Charlottesville: University of Virginia Press.

de Certeau, M. (1988). *The Writing of History*, trans. T. Conley. New York: Columbia University Press.

Dennett, D.C. (1995). Review of Antonio Damasio's *Descartes' Error. Times Literary Supplement*, August 25, 3–4.

Dennett, D.C. (2007). "Heterophenomenology Reconsidered." *Phenomenology and the Cognitive Sciences* 6.1-2: 247–270.

Derrida, J. (1973). *Speech and Phenomena: And Other Essays on Husserl's Theory of Signs*, trans. D.B. Allison. Evanston: Northwestern University Press.

Derrida, J. (2008). *The Animal That Therefore I Am*, trans. D. Wills. New York: Fordham University Press.

Descartes, R. (1996). *Meditation on First Philosophy.* Ed. J. Cottingham. Cambridge, UK: Cambridge University Press.

Dissanayake, E. (1988). *What Is Art For?* Seattle: University of Washington Press.

Doidge, N. (2007). *The Brain that Changes Itself: Stories of Personal Triumph from the Frontiers of Brain Science.* New York: Viking Penguin.

Duffy, E. (2009). *The Speed Handbook: Velocity, Pleasure, Modernism.* Durham: Duke University Press.

Dugatkin, L. (1997). *Co-operation Among Animals: An Evolutionary Perspective.* Oxford: Oxford University Press.

Edelman, G.M. (2004). *Wider than the Sky: the Phenomenal Gift of Consciousness.* New Haven: Yale University Press.

Engell, J. and A. Dangerfield (1998). "The Market-Model University: Humanities in the Age of Money." *Harvard Magazine*, May-June, 48–55, 111.

Engell, J. and A. Dangerfield (2005). *Saving the Humanities in the Age of Money.* Charlottesville: University of Virginia Press.

Esposito, R. (2011). *Immunitas: The Protection and Negation of Life*, trans. Z. Hanafi. Cambridge, UK: Polity Press.

Fish, S. (2010). "The Crisis of the Humanities Officially Arrives," *The New York Times: Opinionator* [weblog], October 11: http://opinionator.blogs.nytimes.com/2010/10/11/the-crisis-of-the-humanities-officially-arrives/.

Fonagy, P. and M. Target (1998). "Mentalization and the Changing Aims of Child Psychoanalysis." *Psychoanalytic Dialogues* 8.1: 87–114.

Foucault, M. (1988). *The History of Sexuality, Volume 3: The Care of the Self*, trans. R. Hurley. New York: Vintage.

Fowler, D.C. (1995). *The Life and Times of John of Trevisa, Medieval Scholar.* Seattle: University of Washington Press.

Fradenburg, L.O. (1991). *City, Marriage, Tournament: Arts of Rule in Late Medieval Scotland.* Madison: University of Wisconsin Press.

Fradenburg, L.O.A. (1999). "Needful Things." In *Medieval Crime and Social Control*, eds. B. Hanwalt and D. Wallace, 49–69. Minneapolis: University of Minnesota Press.

Fradenburg, L.O.A. (2009). "(Dis)continuity: A History of Dreaming." In *The Post-Historical Middle Ages*, eds. E. Scala and S. Frederico, 87–115. New York: Palgrave-Macmillan.

Fradenburg, A. (2012). "Among All Beasts: Affective Naturalism in Late Medieval England." In *Rethinking Chaucerian Beasts*, ed. C. Van Dyke, 13–32. New York: Palgrave Mac-Millan.

Freud, S. (1950). *Project for a Scientific Psychology* (1895). In *The Standard Edition of the Works of Sigmund Freud*, ed. and trans. J. Strachey, Vol. I, 281–397. London: Hogarth Press.

Freud, S. (1955). *The Interpretation of Dreams (First Part)* (1900). In *The Standard Edition of the Complete Psychological Works of Sigmund Freud*, ed. and trans. J. Strachey, Vol. 4, 1–338. London: Hogarth Press.

Freud, S. (1961a). "Letter from Sigmund Freud to Ludwig Binswanger, April 11, 1929." In *Letters of Sigmund Freud, 1873-1939*, ed. E.L. Freud, trans. T. Stern and J. Stern. London: Hogarth Press.

Freud, S. (1961b). *Civilization and Its Discontents* (1930), trans. J. Strachey. New York: W.W. Norton.

Gallagher, S. and D. Zahavi (2008). *The Phenomenological Mind: An Introduction to Philosophy of Mind and Cognitive Science.* New York: Routledge.

Gallese, V. (2007). "Before and Below 'Theory of Mind': Embodied Simulation and the Neural Correlates of Social Cognition." *Philosophical Transactions of the Royal Society* 362. 1480: 659–669.

Gallese, V. (2011). "Mirror Neurons and Art." In *Art and the Senses*, eds. F. Bacci and D. Melcher. New York: Oxford University Press.

Gazzaniga, M.S. (1998). *The Mind's Past*. Berkeley: University of California Press.

Gibson, J.J. (1977). "Theory of Affordances." In Shaw and Bransford, *Perceiving, Acting and Knowing*, 67–82.

Gilmore, T. (n.d.). "After the Apocalypse: Wildness as Preservative in a Time of Ecological Crisis." Unpublished paper.

Gold, M.K., ed. (2012). *Debates in the Digital Humanities*. Minneapolis: University of Minnesota Press.

Gramsci, A. (2007). *Prison Notebooks*, Vol. 3, ed. J. Buttigieg. New York: Columbia University Press.

Greenberg, D. ([1967] 1999). *The Politics of Pure Science*. Chicago: University of Chicago Press.

Greenberg, R. (2003). "The Role of Neophobia and Neophilia in the Development of Innovative Behavior of Birds." In Reader and Laland, *Animal Innovation*, 175–196.

Hayles, N.K. (2008). *How We Became Posthuman: Virtual Bodies in Cybernetics, Literature, and Informatics*. Chicago: University of Chicago Press.

Heller, N. (2013). "Laptop U." *The New Yorker*, May 20, 80–91.

Herbert, J. (2006). "The Analytic Pair in Action: Finding the Missing Mental Life: An Intersubjective Approach." *The Psychoanalytic Study of the Child* 61: 20–55.

Herrmann, E. et al. (2007). "Humans Have Evolved Specialized Skills of Social Cognition: the Cultural Intelligence Hypothesis." *Science* 317.5843: 1360–1366.

Hoffmeyer, J. (2009). *Biosemiotics: An Examination into the Signs of Life and the Life of Signs*. Scranton: University of Scranton Press.

Jacobs, J. (1984). *Cities and the Wealth of Nations: Principles of Economic Life*. New York: Random House.

Johnson, B. (2008). *Persons and Things*. Cambridge, MA: Harvard University Press.

Jung, C.J. (1953). *Collected Works, Volume 6: Psychological Types*, trans. H.G. Baynes. New York: Pantheon.

Kandel, E. (2007). *In Search of Memory: The Emergence of a New Science of Mind*. New York: W. W. Norton.

Keen, E.J. (2007). *The Journey of a Book: Bartholomew the Englishman and the Properties of Things*. Canberra: The Australian National University E Press.

Knoblauch, S.H. (1996). "The Play and Interplay of Passionate Experience: Multiple Organizations of Desire." *Gender and Psychoanalysis* 1.3: 323–344.

Kohut, H. (1953). "Introspection, Empathy and Psychoanalysis—An Examination of the Relationship Between Mode of Observation and Theory." *Journal of the American Psychoanalytic Association* 7.3: 459–483.

Kristeva, J. (1980). *Desire in Language: A Semiotic Approach to Literature and Art*, trans. Leon Roudiez. New York: Columbia University Press.

Kristeva, J. (1984). *Revolution in Poetic Language*, trans. M. Waller. New York: Columbia University Press.

Kristeva, J. (1992). *Strangers to Ourselves*, trans. L. Roudiez. New York: Columbia University Press.

Labi, A. (2009). "In Europe, Skeptics of New 3-Year Degrees Abound." *The Chronicle of Higher Education*, June 11: http://chronicle.com/article/In-Europe-Skeptics-of-New/44467/.

Lacan, J. (1992). *The Seminar of Jacques Lacan, Book VII: The Ethics of Psychoanalysis, 1959-1960*, ed. J.-A. Miller, trans. D. Porter. New York: W.W. Norton.

Lacan, J. (1998). *The Four Fundamental Concepts of Psychoanalysis*, trans. A. Sheridan. New York: W.W. Norton.

Lacan, J. (2002). "The Mirror Stage as Formative of the I Function as Revealed in Psychoanalytic Experience." In Lacan, *Écrits*, 75–81.

Lacan, J. (2002). *Écrits*, trans. B. Fink. New York: W.W. Norton.

Lachmann, F.M. and B. Beebe (1997). "Trauma, Interpretation and Self-State Transformations." *Psychoanalysis and Contemporary Thought* 20: 269–291.

Lakoff, G. and M. Johnson (1980). *Metaphors We Live By.* 1st edition. Chicago: University of Chicago Press.

Latour, B. (1999). *Pandora's Hope: Essays on the Reality of Science Studies.* Cambridge, MA: Harvard University Press.

Latour, B. and V.A. Lèpinay (2009). *The Science of Passionate Interests: An Introduction to Gabriel Tarde's Economic Anthropology.* Chicago: Prickly Paradigm Press.

Lee Sui Wan, S. (2000). "Acoustic Properties of Aspect Markers and Their Homonymous Lexical Counter-parts." PhD dissertation, University of Hong Kong: http://hub.hku.hk/bitstream/10722/56302/1/ft.pdf?accept=1.

Lewis, C. (2003). "Framing Fiction with Death: Chaucer's *Canterbury Tales* and the Plague." In *New Readings of Chaucer's*

Poetry, eds. R.G. Benson and S.J. Ridyard, 139–164. Woodbridge: Boydell and Brewer.

Lövbrand, E. (2007). "Pure Science or Policy Involvement? Ambiguous Boundary Work for Swedish Carbon-cycle Science." *Environmental Science and Policy* 10: 39–47.

Mahler, M.S. (1972). "Rapprochement Subphase of the Separation-Individuation Process." *Psychoanalytic Quarterly* 41.4: 487–506.

Ledoux, J. (2002). *Synaptic Self: How Our Brains Become Who We Are*. Harmondsworth: Penguin Books.

MacCormack, P. (2012). *Posthuman Ethics: Embodiment and Cultural Theory*. Surrey, UK: Ashgate.

Mahoney, M. (1991). *Human Change Processes: The Scientific Foundations of Psychotherapy*. New York: Basic Books.

Maiello, S. (1995). "The Sound Object: A Hypothesis about Prenatal Auditory Experience and Memory." *Journal of Child Psychotherapy* 21.1: 23–41.

Malabou, C. and M. Jeannerod (2008). *What Should We Do With Our Brain?*, trans. S. Rand. New York: Fordham University Press.

Mar, R.A. et al. (2009). "Effects of Reading on Knowledge, Social Abilities and Selfhood: Theory and Empirical Studies." In Zyngier et al., *Directions in Empirical Literary Studies*, 127–137.

Margulis, L. (1998). *Symbiotic Planet: A New Look at Evolution*. New York: Basic Books.

Modell, A. (2003). *Imagination and the Meaningful Brain*. Cambridge, MA: MIT Press.

Moreschini, C., ed. (2000). *Boethius: De Consolatione Philosophiae; Opusculus Theologiae*. Munich-Leipzig: Bibliotheca Teubneriana.

Metzinger, T. (2009). *The Ego Tunnel: The Science of Mind and the Myth of the Self*. New York: Basic Books.

Morrison, P. (2011). "University of California President Mark Yudof: The BMOC." *Los Angeles Times*, January 15: http://articles.latimes.com/2011/jan/15/opinion/la-oe-morrison-yudof-20110115/2.

Newfield, C. (2013a). "Waypoints in the MOOC Debates, Part III," *Remaking the University* [weblog], June 25: http://utotherescue.blogspot.co.uk/2013/06/waypoints-in-mooc-debates-part-iii.html.

Newfield, C. (2013b). "Where Are the Savings?" *Inside Higher Ed*, June 24: http://www.insidehighered.com/views/2013/06/24/essay-

sees-missing-savings-georgia-techs-much-discussed-mooc
-based-program.

Nussbaum, M.C. (2010). *Not for Profit: Why Democracy Needs the Humanities*. Princeton: Princeton University Press.

Panksepp, J. (1998). *Affective Neuroscience: The Foundations of Human and Animal Emotions*. New York: Oxford University Press.

Phelps, D.J. (2002). "Major Histocompatibility Complex (MHC)." *Encyclopedia of Life Sciences*. New York: Macmillan.

Press, E. and J. Washburn (2000). "The Kept University." *Atlantic Monthly*, March: http//www.theatlantic.com/issues/2000/03/press.htm.

Rauscher, F.H. (2009). "The Impact of Music Instruction on Other Skills." In *The Oxford Handbook of Music Psychology*, eds. S. Hallam et al., 244–252. Oxford: Oxford University Press.

Reader, S.M. and K.N. Laland, eds. (2003). *Animal Innovation*. Oxford: Oxford University Press.

Rickels, L.A. (1995). "The Show and Wear of Trauma Weaving." *XenArts* [website]: http://www.xenarts.com/art_org/raw/psyfi/rickels.html.

Ringstrom, P.A. (2001). "Cultivating the Improvisational in Psychoanalytic Treatment." *Psychoanalytic Dialogues* 11: 727–754.

Rothenberg, D. (2005). *Why Birds Sing: A Journey into the Mystery of Birdsong*. New York: Basic Books.

Ruark, J. (2010). "The Art of Living Mindfully." *The Chronicle Review*, January 3: http://chronicle.com/article/The-Art-of-Living-Mindfully/63292/.

Scarry, E. (1985). *The Body in Pain: The Making and Unmaking of the World*. New York: Oxford University Press.

Schacter, D. (1996.). *Searching for Memory: The Brain, the Mind and the Past*. New York: Basic Books.

Serres, M. (1995). *A History of Scientific Thought: Elements of a History of Science*. Cambridge: Blackwell.

Seymour, M.C., ed. ([1975] 1988). *On the Properties of Things: John of Trevisa's Translation of Bartholomaeus Anglicus's De Proprietatibus Rerum*. Oxford: Oxford University Press.

R. Shaw and J. Bransford (1977). *Perceiving, Acting and Knowing: Towards an Ecological Psychology*. Hillsdale: Lawrence Erlbaum.

Singer, W. (2008). "Epigenesis and Brain Plasticity in Education." In *The Educated Brain: Essays in Neuroeducation*, eds.

A.M. Batrow and K.W. Fischer, 97–109. Cambridge, UK: Cambridge University Press.

Slingerland, E. (2009). "Exorcising the Geist in the Machine: Taking the Humanities Beyond Dualism." Paper presented at Literature and the Mind symposium, University of California, Santa Barbara, February 20.

Slingerland, E. (2008). *What Science Offers the Humanities: Integrating Body and Culture.* Cambridge, UK: Cambridge University Press.

Steen, F. et al. (2009). "Participatory Knowledge and Transformative Understanding: Bridging Some Gaps Between the Sciences and the Humanities." Paper presented at Literature and the Mind symposium, University of California, Santa Barbara, October 19.

Stern, D. (2010). *Forms of Vitality: Exploring Dynamic Experience in Psychoanalysis, the Arts, Psychoanalysis, and Development.* New York: Oxford University Press.

Sternberg, R.J., "The Concept of Intelligence and Its Role in Lifelong Learning and Success." *American Psychologist* 52: 1030–1045.

Tai, R., *et al.* (1999). *Critical Ethnicity: Countering the Waves in Identity Politics.* Lanham: Rowman and Littlefied.

Terada, R. (2003). *Feeling in Theory: Emotion after the "Death of the Subject."* Cambridge, MA: Harvard University Press.

Tobis, M. (2013). "Canada to Abandon Pure Science Altogether?" *Planet 3.0: Beyond Sustainability*, May 13: http://planet 3.org/2013/05/13/canada-to-abandon-pure-science-altogether/.

Tokuhama-Espinosa, T. (2011). *Mind, Brain, and Education Science: A Comprehensive Guide to the New Brain-Based Teaching.* New York: W.W. Norton.

Tomasello, M. (1995). "Joint Attention as Social Cognition." In C. Moore and P.J. Dunham, eds., *Joint Attention: Its Origins and Role in Development*, 103–130. Hillsdale: Lawrence Erlbaum.

University of California Office of the President (2013). "Academic Performance Indicators at the University of California: Executive Summary": http://regents.universityofcalifornia.edu/regmeet/may13/e1.pdf.

U.S. Department of Education, Office of Planning, Evaluation and Policy Development (2010). "Evaluation of Evidence-Based Practices in Online Learning: A Meta-Analysis and Review of Online Learning Studies": http://www.ed.gov/about/offices/list/opepd/ppss/reports.html.

Waldby, C. (2004). *The Visible Human Project: Informatic Bodies and Posthuman Medicine*. London: Routledge.

Washburn, Jennifer (2005). *University Inc.: The Corporate Corruption of Higher Education*. New York: Basic Books.

Wenzel, S. (1982). "Pestilence and Middle English Literature: Father Grimestone's Poems on Death." In *The Black Death: The Impact of the Fourteenth-Century Plague*, ed. D. Williman, 131–159. Binghamton: Center for Medieval and Early Renaissance Studies.

Wilson, E.O. (1999). *Consilience: The Unity of Knowledge*. New York: Vintage Books.

Wolfe, C. (2010). *What Is Posthumanism?* Minneapolis: University of Minnesota Press.

Womersley, J. (2013). "Being Unreasonable: The Value of Pure Science." *Symmetry: Dimensions of Particle Physics*, Feb. 21: http://www.symmetrymagazine.org/article/february-2013/being-unreasonable-the-value-of-pure-science.

Wright, S. (1931). "Evolution in Mendelian Populations." *Genetics* 16: 97–126.

Xu, D. and S. Jaggars (2013a). "Adaptability to Online Learning: Differences Across Types of Students and Academic Subject Areas." CCRC Working Papers 54. New York: Community College Research Center, Teachers College, Columbia University: http://academiccommons.columbia.edu/item/ac:157286.

Xu, D. and S. Jaggers (2013b). "The Impact of Online Learning on Students' Course Outcomes: Evidence from a Large Community and Technical College System." *Economics of Education Review*, August 25: http://dx.doi.org/10.1016/j.econedurev.2013.08.001.

Young, J.Z. (1971). *An Introduction to the Study of Man*. Oxford: Clarendon Press.

Zeki, S. (2008). *Splendor and Miseries of the Brain*. London: Wiley-Blackwell.

Zeki, S. (2009). "Statement on Neuroesthetics." *Institute of Neuroesthetics* [website]: http://www.neuroesthetics.org/statement-on-neuroesthetics.php.

Zilsel, E. (2000). "The Sociological Roots of Science." *Social Studies of Science* 30.6: 935–949.

Žižek, S. (1990). "Eastern Europe's Republics of Gilead." *New Left Review* 183: 50–62.

Zylinska, J. (2009). *Bioethics in the Age of New Media*. Cambridge, MA: MIT Press.

STAYING ALIVE | 133

Zyngier, S. et al., eds. (2008). *Directions in Empirical Literary Studies: In Honor of Willie Van Peer*. Amsterdam: Benjamins.

Human-Tongued Basilisks

Daniel C. Remein

Let us tie the strings on this bit of reality
                                    Jack Spicer

I would like to begin with a short poem by Jack Spicer: [1]

---

[1] Spicer was an important contributor, along with Robin Blaser and Robert Duncan, to the "Berkeley Renaissance" in the late 1940s and early 1950s (later folded into the San Francisco Renaissance and the "New American Poetry"). Spicer only published, as a matter of policy, with very small, local, presses; and, since private and public readings constituted a major scene of the circulation of his poetry within various coteries, a number of interesting poems exist only in manuscript. Spicer died in 1965 at the age of forty from alcoholism-related complications, and is buried anonymously in San Francisco. This poem, as yet unpublished, is held among the Jack Spicer Papers, BANC MSS 2004/209, The Bancroft Library, University of California, Berkeley. See Box 6, folder 30.

> Poetry is action like a bird
> Flying around a room.
> Birds usually fly
> From window to window
> Or, on stormy nights of bad luck,
> In the door and out the other door so fast
> No one knows they are flying.

Partaking of the discourses of both lyric poetry and *poetics* (as a discursive-performative theorization of *poesis*), Spicer's little poem refuses to adopt either a defensive posture or a transparent explanatory discourse. The poem consists of only two sentences that narrow in scope as the poem progresses; the first sentence begins with a metaphor and ends with a simile modifying the second noun-phrase of that metaphor, and the second sentence is an amplification of the simile in the first sentence. The relatively colloquial diction (including the use of "fast" as an adverb instead of "quickly") and the syntax seem simple enough at first glance, and the association of (especially lyric) poetry and birds is conventional enough in English verse.

Yet the poem arrives at the conventional association of poetry and birds through an unlikely route, enunciating the association, not in terms of a similarity of poetry to a bird's *song*, but a similarity of the *action* which constitutes poetry to a particular ornithological behavior: "a bird / flying around the room." A bird flying around the room may be flying "window to window"—presumably stuck in a house and trying to break free to the outdoors. But, this flight path might also mark an attempt to get in and stay in the human shelter, ending in an all-too-brief bivouac owing to the bird's "bad luck." Both possibilities underscore the nature of the action in question as the *survival behavior* of an organism—flouting convention and focusing on a creaturely, rather than a symbolic, bird of poesy. The first line break of the poem reinforces this sense, suggesting that one first read "poetry is action like a bird" as a sentence unto itself, ahead of its participation in the syntax of the second line. In this most basic tool of de-subordinating standard syntax (the line break), the poem insinuates that the simplest kinetics involved in the survival of mortal creaturely life make for a sufficient comparison to the action of poetry: *poetry is action like the organism of a bird is action—poetry is action like the existence/survival of a bird in any given moment is action.*

The description of a bird flying all-too-briefly through a human shelter in the last three lines further associates the action that is poesy with the survival of life that is precariously *mortal*, yet paradoxically, requires *more* than the conditions of bare survival in order to survive. Drawing on his graduate study of Old English literature with philologist Arthur G. Brodeur, Spicer here introduces an allusion that most of his avant-gardist colleagues might have missed—gesturing to the account of the conversion of Northumbrian King Edwin in Bede's *Ecclesiastical History of the English People.* In a very famous passage, after Edwin has been advised by Coifi, the "chief priest," to accept the faith preached by the missionary Paulinus, one of Edwin's advisors reasons that Christianity might offer insight into human life beyond mortality:

> when we compare the present life of man on earth with that time of which we have no knowledge, it seems to me like the swift flight of a single sparrow through the banqueting-hall where you are sitting at dinner on a winter's day with your thegns and counselors. In the midst there is a comforting fire to warm the hall; outside, the storms of winter rain or snow are raging. The sparrow flies swiftly through one door of the hall, and out the other. While he is inside, he is safe from the winter storms; but after a few moments of comfort, he vanishes from sight into the wintry world from which he came. Even so, man appears on earth for a little while, but of what

went before this life or of what follows, we know
nothing . . . . (Bede 1990, 129–130)

Spicer, however, implicitly demonstrates how the example of the sparrow-flight—here deployed as a demonstra-
tion of how Christianity claims to offer more information
than paganism about the fate of the soul—might just as
easily return one's focus to creaturely life, insofar as Spicer's poem affirms the sparrow's attempt to thrive—
however briefly—in a cozy shelter, by comparing such
creaturely behavior to the action of poetry. In the process,
the poem intertwines life-processes and the desire to not
only survive, but to thrive (enjoying the love of movement, either sheltered beside a warm fire, or freed from
the confines of the windows), with the action of the poem
itself. Although the poem is grammatically "about" the
"subject" of poetry, it advances a certain experiential
claim about poetry without definitively representing poetry per se. The brevity of the poem, combined with the
opacity of the action with which it equates poetry and
then modifies it with a single subsequent sentence in relatively colloquial diction (i.e., "bad luck," "so fast"), does
not represent posited kinetics of poesy as much as it performs them. In its performance of these poetics, the poem
advances a claim on their necessity for mortal creatures
like Bede's sparrow. The poem has the capacity to leave a
reader or hearer with less a clear sense of what poetry or
this poem's "object of representation" *is*, than with a clear
experience of what poesy *does*—though it goes by so fast
as to feel like a phenomenological blur. The very brevity
of the poem is bound up with the experience of this *læne
lif* (brief, fleeting life, lit. "loaned life")—with the mortality of a human reader. But the poem is not an appeal to a
binary of experience versus cognition, nor a populist dis-
avowal of serious thought or exacting description—in fact, it
shows off its learnedness with a relatively obscure and complicated allusion, even as a very tiny poem.

This blurry sense of a bird-action passing through/ by/past one's consciousness as part of cognizing and striving after a desire, or need, for not only shelter, but also for a warm fire in order to survive, makes no excuses for its "fuzziness." In fact, the semantic and performative intertwining of organismic and poetic kinetics and mortality here enshrines something like what Maurice Merleau-Ponty would call the whole "phenomenal field" as necessary for life.[2] Such fleeting and fuzzy moments do not fail to admit a real world to thought, but neither do they fail to engage the richly rewarding problem of how consciousness and the actual intertwine. That *poesis* itself, as the experience of the actual, may pass so fleetingly and unquantifiably, is not something for which Spicer's poem seems interested in apologizing.

Too often, however, defenses of the humanities, and specifically works of poetics, are just that: defenses, apol-

---

[2] Merleau-Ponty writes: "We shall no longer hold that perception is incipient science, but conversely that classical science is a form of perception which loses sight of its origins and believes itself complete. The first philosophical act would appear to be to return to the world of actual experience which is prior to the objective world, since it is in it that we shall be able to grasp the theoretical basis no less than the limits of that objective world, restore to things their concrete physiognomy, to organisms their individual ways of dealing with the world, and to subjectivity its inherence in history . . . . This phenomenal field is not an 'inner world,' the 'phenomenon' is not a 'state of consciousness,' or a 'mental fact,' and the experience of phenomena is not an act of introspection or an intuition in Bergson's sense . . . . Thus what we discover by going beyond the prejudice of the objective world is not an occult inner world. Nor is this world of living experience complete closed to naïve consciousness, as is Bergson's inferiority" (Merleau-Ponty 2002, 66–67). Even more starkly, Merleau-Ponty famously explains that, "a philosophy becomes transcendental, or radical, not by taking its place in absolute consciousness without mentioning the ways by which this is reached, but by considering itself as a problem" (2002, 73).

ogetics.[3] This may result from the famous poieiaphobic
offensive in the Fifth Book of Plato's *Republic*, a much
earlier suspicion of the illimitable iterative capacity of
context, utterance, and inscriptions, or a later development of what Fradenburg calls (borrowing from Christopher Bollas) *unthinking.* Too often, a colleague has said to
me something to the effect of, "oh, I have no idea how to
read *poetry,* I work on prose." Certainly, in Modern English writing, ever since Sidney's *Defense of Poesy,* main-
streams of work in poetics and the humanities too often
position themselves on the defensive, framing the moralizing side-effects of poesy as excuses for its apparent an-
cillary relation to the sort of knowledge production that
can be easily valued on scales of the state, war, and value
itself. I invoke the term poetics insofar as it concerns the
artifacts made by humans and other provisional life-
processes and the interpretations, critiques, readings, com-
mentaries, editions, exhibitions, et alia, that the humanities
make of and with such artifacts. But, as Fradenburg's
work suggests, the news is out: Poetics is on the offensive,
and "the organism" constitutes a viable critical term. In
responding to Fradenburg's repositioning of thriving as a
necessary condition of life, I want to suggest some alter-

---

[3] *Poetics* itself is admittedly a weird genre—perhaps more accurately a *style* or rhetorical force—that constantly demonstrates
theory as praxis in discussing the ontology, conditions of, and
limits of making, while also on occasion attempting to direct it,
produce norms, or even catalyze new makings. The wide and
widely divergent use of the term "poetics" as a contemporary
disciplinary designation in the North American academy can be
used to refer to works as divergent as Charles Bernstein's *A
Poetics* (1992), Lyn Hejinian's *The Language of Inquiry* (2000),
and a series of what for the most part amounts to innovative
works of literary criticism published in the "Modern and Contemporary Poetics" series of Alabama University Press, including Miriam Nichols' *Radical Affections* (2010), Juliana Spahr's
Everybody's Autonomy (2001), Peter Middleton's *Distant Reading* (2005), Jerome McGann's *The Point is to Change It* (2007),
and Steve McCaffery's *The Darkness of the Present* (2012).

natives to a language of representation not adequate to the complexity of the poetics of the thriving organism. For Fradenburg, making and the critical study of such making actually constitute a basic function of organismic life that "constantly co-processes its boundaries in tandem with all the life-forms and forces to which it is connected."

This argument stands refreshingly far out from the kinds of answers instructors often give to undergraduate non-humanities majors enrolled in compulsory humanities core courses. I consistently hear two responses to the question "why should I have to take this class?" from the mouths of colleagues (for whom I generally have the utmost respect), both of which put the humanities hopelessly on the defensive: that, 1) reading Homer, Virgil, Shakespeare (unsurprisingly, such courses perennially skip over the Middle Ages), even Melville, will make one a more interesting and well-rounded person (and indeed, as Fradenburg herself points out, well-cultured Wagner fans in the Nazi party likely felt that they led very interesting lives), and that, 2) practicing creative thinking and critical reading/writing will equip one to engage in creative problem solving and to be innovative in one's professional field. Reading "great books" will make business and finance majors, for example, into more inventive capitalists. Not only is this second argument party to the same logic that would reduce English departments to centers for technical writing or a kind of innovation workshop for corporate America, but given the disastrous effects of the sub-prime mortgage crises, the idiocy of "innovations" in hedge-fund trading and similar financial instruments—not to mention the bulge of wealth-disparity to which these have indelibly contributed—*innovation* and *creative problem solving* would appear as the very last tools with which to further equip Capital and its future technocrats now. The impoverishment of both of these arguments, aside from their complicity in capitalism and state power, emanates from taking an initially defensive combative position. Again, such a position leads, like the argument consolidated by Sidney's *Defense of Poesy*, to *making excuses* for poesy by pointing to its moralizing side effects. In doing so, the defense of poesy reduces the possible radicalism of the "delight" component of "to teach and delight" to a normalizing and hopelessly mimetic discourse.

Fradenburg, however, implies (and here I borrow a phrase coined by Liza Blake) the *offense of poetry* by positively differentiating and entangling the humanities with mathematical, experimental, statistical, and observational sciences, *without ever demanding that the humanities attempt to behave like the "sciences" in order to "survive."* Fradenburg puts it this way:

> The sciences study patterns in matter and physical forces (among other things); the humanities teach human organisms how best to move and keep moving, with maximum power and grace. If the humanities are "fuzzy" and their processes and outcomes difficult to quantify, that is because *living* is "fuzzy."

At no point, therefore, in a humanistic gesture, can a chunk of scientistic data stand as self-evidentiary, for "data cannot deliberate for us, *it can only help*." The humanities fundamentally concern *making*. This means that while the tasks of the humanities can include knowledge-production (through various processes of making, which are themselves forms of knowledge), the humanities are concerned first with simply *paying attention to and caring for making/poesy in "real" time.*

Thriving, it turns out, is a prerequisite for the survival of most kinds of life processes—not the "reward" for the few who can pull themselves up by their bootstraps: "Living well *depends* on good education, and it should be available to everyone." Believing that "the biggest problem our world faces today is not humanist over-valuation of creaturely invention and experience, but melancholic scorn for the everyday lives of mortal creatures," Fradenburg asserts that "thriving and surviving are fully intricated with each other; cultural activity is neither epi-phenomenal, nor dispensable, but essential to our way of living." The basic political implications of this fact alone could be catalogued at some length in an invective against material conditions and attendant attitudes (both global and local) which continue to determine the dismantling of any whiff of (sensible, much less revolutionary) wealth re-distribution amidst the current global obsession with "austerity." Take, for example, one New York National Public Radio listener's complaint that persons receiving assistance from the Supplementary Nutrition Assistance Program (formerly Food Stamps) may use taxpayer mon-ey to purchase lobster or other "luxury" foods not strictly necessary for nutrition and "survival."[4] But the *entangle-ment* of *poetics* with the life-processes of organisms is what undergirds these flashpoints in current politics of thriving. If the organism, as Fradenburg avers, "constant-ly co-processes its boundaries in tandem with all the life-forms and forces to which it is connected, from which the biological meaningfulness of its life- and self-experience emerges, in a new key," then, as understood through the disciplines cited by Fradenburg (including contemporary psychology, neuroscience, immunology, cell-biology), the organism depends on poetics—the capacity to make its relations to, and co-make its relations with, its environ-ment in a manner that results in varying, adaptable, and *aesthetically interesting* entanglements and negotiations of everything from transport to attraction, digestion, space, use, acquiescence, sexualities, temporalities, organisms, ideas, concepts, and codes.

---

[4] The October 12, 2010 episode of the Brian Lehrer show on New York NPR station WNYC included a segment that ad-dressed an attempt to ban the use of SNAP funds to purchase soda. See, in the online discussion board for that episode, the comments of "Steve from Queens" on lobster: http://www.wnyc.org/shows/bl/2010/oct/12/food-stamp-approval/.

What sort of lexicon can more closely describe the texture of a poesy necessary for living without compromising its necessary fuzziness? William Carlos Williams' *Spring and All* similarly re-situates poetry, and its prime mover (Williams' complicated concept of the "imagination"), outside of moralizing *apologia*:

> The inevitable flux of the seeing eye toward measuring itself by the world it inhabits can only result in himself crushing humiliation unless the individual raise to some approximate co-extension with the universe. This is possible by aid of the imagination. Only through the agency of this force can a man [*sic*] feel himself moved largely with sympathetic pulses at work. (Williams 2011, 26–27)

The urgency here is unmistakable. The organism must *make* an interface, a co-extension, with the very physics of the Universe. Without an act of the imagination the organism will fail, shaken to pieces. As Robin Blaser puts it (expanding Williams' visual register into the auditory, tactile, and proprioceptive), "the body hears the world, and the power of the earth over the body, the city over the body, is in terms of rhythms, meters, phrasing, picked up—the body's own rhythms compose those or it would shake to pieces—The music of the spheres is quite real, but the sounds of the earth must meet it" (Blaser 2006, 4). With poesy as the *necessary* construction of these byways, these ports and pores of a phenomenological architecture, the organism can simultaneously differentiate *and entangle* itself with various registers, even to the point of *displacing* Structure, however locally. Such simultaneous differentiation and entanglement recalls the manner in which, as contemporary poet Lisa Robertson writes, German Romantic architect and art historian Gottfried Semper "proposed a four-part unsubordinated architectural topology, where surface was in non-hierarchical relationship with molded plasticity," and in which "the transience and non-essential [and, I would add, provisional or *mortal*] quality of the surface did not lessen its topological value" (Robertson 2003, 129).

If all of this is indeed the case, then as humanists we need to radically ramp up our practical and strategically biologizing investigations into mechanisms of entanglement, and also into intensifications of co-extensiveness. We need to better understand how entanglement and co-extensiveness are co-produced from the side of the humanities—to develop a sort of "rhyming dictionary" for certain aspects of life-processes and the forces of the physical cosmos. Take, for example, mid-twentieth-century psychologist Silvan Tomkins' theorization of the role that *interest* plays in the affect-system of an organism:

> We are arguing that this affect [interest] supports both what is necessary for life and what is possible, by virtue of linkages to sub-systems, which themselves range from concerns with the transport of energy in and out of the body, to concerns about the characteristics of formal systems such as logic and mathematics. The human being cares about many things and he does so because the general affect of interest is structurally linked to a variety of other apparatuses which activate this affect in ways which are appropriate to the specific needs of each sub-system. While excitement is sufficiently massive a motive to amplify and make a difference to such an already intense stimulation as accompanies sexual intercourse, it is nonetheless capable of sufficiently graded, flexible innervation and combination to provide a motive matched to the most subtle cognitive capacities. (Tomkins 1962, 345)

The upshot of such a system, in which interest, a most basic sort of motivation, plays such a plastic role—often feeding back to the extent that interest itself can become interesting—is a banal but too-often forgotten element of a capacious poetics of the organism: that we need to find or make interesting things, or to make things interesting, in order to survive. This is why it is not merely a trend of the neo-baroque, or a hipster-poet caginess, when Lisa Robertson writes, "ornament is the decoration of mortality," or insists that to ask "what shall our new ornaments be?" amounts to "a serious political question" (Robertson 2003, 67). Making, and its more seemingly "frivolous" possibilities, or *poetics*, are a biological necessity, and as such, one the humanities can think *with* the sciences if we first positively think the humanities as something different.

These statements of Robertson's might alert us as well to the ethical function of taking a stand for the viability of words like "organism," "living," "life," etc., as critical terms. The most orthodox practitioners of genealogical readings or of negative dialectics might scoff at such potentially "biologizing" accounts of living and its affects. Many a near-sighted reading of certain sections of Deleuze and Guattari's *One Thousand Plateaus* would bewail the administrative tyranny of the organism as arboreal organization of a Body. Object-oriented philosophers like Graham Harman vigorously renounce any concern for ethics or politics,[5] and the most interesting and productive lines of new materialist or speculative realist thought tend to ground ethics in a discourse of a monist cosmos, dispensing with the question of accessing alterity as a ruse of "correlationism," rank anthropocentricism, or a violent liberal humanism (e.g., Bennett 2009, 122). Yet, while a less ego-maniacal vision of the cosmos might lead us to say,

---

[5] Harman often addresses his sense that his politics do not pertain to his philosophy, and vice-versa, in his many public speaking appearances. However, a literary critic might be more likely to encounter this attitude in Harman's (2012) "reluctant" address to literary-critical interest in his work in his essay "The Well Wrought Broken Hammer: Object Oriented Literary Criticism."

with Whitman, that "to die is different than any one supposed," the thriving organism (the consciousness that,
however provisional, feels the intractable reality of ontological difference when faced with a feeling, a plant, a
wind, gravity, a lover, a cat, the mortality of a lover, or—
not to be too Heideggerian—its own mortality) may yet
have difficulty adding with Whitman, "and luckier"
(Whitman 1959, 30). For, following Fradenburg, "Self is
not the ultimate arbiter of reality, even of its own psychical reality; but neither is it merely a befuddled, delusional
witness or an aggressive display of false coherence."

As Fradenburg further notes, "recognition of self/
non-self" is "basic to the workings of immune systems."
However, Fradenburg suggests, not at all does this process of self/non-self recognition slip into a paranoia that
would limit the role of surrounding entities in an organism's co-production to that of "hostile pathogen." Rather,
concepts of emergence cannot be severed from questions
of differentiation, and perhaps more importantly, from
mortality. The organism may only provisionally act on
behalf of its communities of cells, but its provisionality
does not render it less important. As Fradenburg writes,

> . . . these days we have to wrap our minds more
> and more around the idea that the living can be
> *replaced,* not just on the assembly-line, but in the
> classroom and the hospital. This accelerating de-
> valuation is a threat in service of domination, the
> antidote to which is to know that *we are all mortal
> creatures—immunity remains impossible.* It is only
> with the "sole support" of this knowledge that "we
> can attempt to live with others."

Allowing critical thought to emanate from a position of
our own creaturely finitude thus assumes a place of the
highest importance. This may sound like I am advocating
in favor of continuing to pursue what object-oriented
philosophers and new materialists disparage as "the ques-

tion of access" (meaning: philosophy and thinking as conditioned by the supposed primacy of human-centered access to knowledge and being-in-the-world). But this is because the logical gymnastics required to evade the limits of the human organism in a lexicon of critical thought too easily flip into a fantasy of tyrannical, infinitely-extendable human perception and knowledge in an attempt to instrumentalize *everything* (and isn't that Capitalism, after all?). Pretending that we might ever entirely dispense with the complications of perception (without which *life* would probably not *be*) can only result in a gnostic and thus anti-human fantasy of the redemptive quality of knowledge as acquired through an infinite and homogenous extensibility of intellect—a sublimated desire for deliverance from mortal worldliness. Critic Paul A. Bové, in his book *Poetry Against Torture*, differentiates these tendencies in contrasting the projects of Bacon (and Descartes) with Italian critic Giambattista Vico:

> Bacon and Vico share the classical and liberal ideal of perfectibility, but Bacon dreams of achieving this by expanding the domain of knowledge, indeed, by producing knowledge as a necessary and sufficient domain for human aspiration and activity: "so that human wisdom may be brought to complete perfection." Vico does not share Bacon's vision of the modern for two reasons. First, its totalizing ambition is reductive in a way that leaves behind all that tradition and older forms of life might offer to imagine and fulfill the aspiration to and practices of human wisdom. Second, it is not only willfully amnesiac but also violently arrogant and uncomfortably close in kind and ambition to then new forms of imperial and authoritarian political ambition. Vico's language, always precise, rewards the sort of attention that literary readers properly learn from the study of poems . . . . (Bové 2008, 7)

To promote thriving in the face of the total domination of global Capital and the accelerating ecological cataclysm, it will be necessary to recognize a panoply of differences in something other than a purely abstracted infinite Other. To discuss the "organism" posits neither the structure of the monad as subject of consciousness (but without necessarily dispensing with everything phenomenology continues to teach) to which all else is *equally* Other and only ever an Object of representation, nor a model in which the experience of consciousness is no longer of any concern.[6] As Fradenburg writes,

> encoding and decoding, pattern-recognition and construction, are fundamental to living process, sentient or otherwise. Sentience itself is highly varied, consisting of very "early" functions and forms working cheek by jowl with "later ones." If, as Barbieri contends, symbolic semiosis *emerges* from the code semiotics of early organic life, ideas like consilience relegate semiosis to much too narrow a band of material activity.
>
> . . . We do not need to jettison subjectivity and self-process; instead we need to redescribe them, so as to include the self-constitutive activity of the semi-permeable sac whose formation arises from non-sentient activity, but is at the same time necessary to life.

Eve Sedgwick and Adam Frank point to the role of complexity in Tomkins' attempts to think the organism as a system of *incompletely* overlapping and partially redundant feedback systems. If the details of Tomkins' some-

---

[6] Derrida is not *wrong* to write that "tout autre est tout autre" (e.g., Derrida 1995, 82). We readers just tend to do the wrong sort of algebra with this equation so that its results suggest a homogenous "Other," when the whole point is that the Other/Outside is already included as a structuring principle of the supposed "One."

times laughably obsolete biological model no longer hold (due to its dependence on a hazy concept of "density of neural firing"), the flexibility of his conceptual framework remains useful. As Sedgwick and Frank write, "We discuss this pattern in the framework of Tomkins' habit of layering digital (on/off) with analog (graduated and/or multiply differentiated) representational models, and we argue for the great conceptual value of this habit" (Sedgwick and Frank 2003, 101).[7] The principle of incompletely layering digital and analog systems in complexity offers a way to conceptualize learning, change, and movement, while such finitely differentiated systems also allow for selective interface of the organism-system with its environment *at certain points*, but not in infinite contiguity.

Pointing out the usefulness of Tomkinsian thought for conceptualizing values or qualities that function or operate in terms more than two but less than infinity, Sedgwick and Frank argue that "the hygiene of current antiessentialism seemingly depends on rigorous adherence to the (erroneously machine-identified) model of digital, on/off representation: insofar as they are 'theorized,' affects must turn into 'Affect'" (Sedgwick and Frank 2003, 108, 111).[8] The work of the humanities, ironically, in its most psychologizing moments, must resist the urge to commit a certain kind of abstraction and train

---

[7] As Fradenburg points out, the biosemioticians make this same point.

[8] Sedgwick and Frank further explain: "any definitional invocation of analogically conceived, qualitative differences, in the form of *finitely many (n>2)* values, does indeed run the risk of reproducing a biologizing essentialism . . . [but] that risk is far from being obviated by even the most scrupulous practice of digitalization." Further, "[t]he essentialism that adheres to digital models is structured differently from the essentialism of the analog. . . . To see the latter [digital] as a less 'essentialist' metaphorics than the former reflects, we argue, only the habitual privileging of digital models wrongly equated with the machines over analog models wrongly equated with the biological" (Sedgwick and Frank 2003, 111).

itself not necessarily on this or that particular account of "materiality," so much as upon the *precarious particular* situated within the physics of the cosmos. Sedgwick and Frank argue, "there is no reason to believe that the necessarily analog models of the color wheel, or say, the periodic table of the elements constrain an understanding of difference, contingency, performative force, or the possibility of change" (2003, 114). To produce critical thought that does justice to sentience and the various kinds of texts and plastic artifacts that sentience (of many kinds) can produce, we will need *fuzzy*, and sometimes *necessarily questionable* models.

To support Fradenburg's theorization of the humanities as a necessary aid to thriving, I think we will further need to employ a more capacious lexicon of poetics—specifically, flexible alternatives to vocabularies oriented around poetics determined most saliently as representation, mimesis, expression, and semiosis. Such a lexicon, however, would not exclude Fradenburg's assertions that "*no organism lasts for long if it can't interpret signals well, or signal what it needs to communicate,*" and that, "both the fine arts and the arts of living further exercise *therapeutic* powers of expression and interpretation." To invoke the complexity of the organism in a discussion of systems of signal-making and signal-interpretation is to imply a truly complex concept of signaling whose performative forces still include those before, after, or to the side of signaling. In order to follow Fradenburg's argument and to do justice to the complexity of the signal-interpretation necessary for the survival of an organism, the humanities also need a more interesting vocabulary for the para-signaling capacities of organisms and artifacts. A building may "signify" a whole set of forces and depend on a set of codes to inform its inhabitants how to move through it, and a poem may "mean" something, but a building can also shelter or hold, and a poem can also *make one feel things* quite apart from what and how it signifies. That the "arts of living" and their luxurious functions are for Fradenburg so intertwined with the therapeutic powers of expression serves to suggest that these possible "extra-semiotic" functions inhere in even the most coded of displays.

Regardless of any individual critic's good or bad reasons for disliking the writings of Martin Heidegger (I assume most of us will have some of one or the other), most humanists still fail to grasp the *possibility* in shedding the correspondence theory of truth in language and trying to grasp the responsibility of realizing, as Hediegger did, that

> language is not only and not primarily an audible and written expression of what is to be communicated. It not only puts forth in words and statements what is overtly or covertly intended to be communicated; language alone brings what is, as something that is, into the Open for the first time. (Heidegger 1971a, 71)

Objections to this statement easily arise: the exclusivity with which Heidegger offers hermeneutics as the alternative to the representational and expressive force of language, the patent anthropocentrism of this remark (sure, it is arrogant and violent to think that the nominating power of language speaking the human allows things to so shine for the *first* time). But such objections can be provisionally set aside much more easily than is conventionally thought if one would listen here for the force of what is by no means a "difficult" observation:[9] that lan-

---

[9] In fact, speaking anecdotally of many conversations at academic conferences, it is by raising objections to Heidegger's anthropocentricism and related reprehensible politics that critics perennially, and lamentably, divert conversation away from the challenge of alternatives to representation contained within Heidegger's work. I have no desire to deny the risk of engaging with writing that was deeply entangled with the Nazi death ma-

guage does things other than signaling, that the particular rhetorical and paraverbal forces of language (or, more capaciously, any force of relational intimacy) are not *secondary* to language's semiotic function or construction.[10]

Thinking about poetics in terms of "poems" (what I still, perhaps rather conservatively, believe to be a privileged space in which to think about making), twentieth-century poet Charles Olson suggests in his notes that, "the poem's job is to be able to attend, and get attention to, the variety of order in creation" (Olson 2010, 15). Such a "variety of order" (to be found either in the creation of the world, the world as an auto-, but also multi-poetic creation, or the creation of the more conventionally conceived poem) would require a more *variegated* and *differentiated* lexicon (not necessarily a more precise lexicon, as we are humanists, after all—amateurs, not technocrats). Such a poem would accede to the status of a physical organism. Alluding to Alfred North Whitehead, Olson writes that "a strain is characterized by close associational qualities and definite geometric relations, and a growth of ordered physical complexity (which ought to be the poem) is dependent on the growth of ordered relationships among strains" (Olson 2010, 28).

Hans Ulrich Gumbrecht's efforts, in his *Powers of Philology: Dynamics of Textual Scholarship* (2003) and

---

chine, but the risk of not paying attention to what it may have discovered is also not one I am willing to take.

[10] Such a gravitational intimacy is exactly what Heidegger's concept of language might suggest, denuded of its anthropocentric relation to "History." If we assume, with Heidegger, that it is language and not the human who speaks, then what "language" names is less a purely semiotic system than a way to talk about intimacy and relationality itself. Heidegger writes in his essay "The Nature of Language": "Language, Saying of the world's fourfold, is no longer only such that we speaking human beings are related to it in the sense of a nexus existing between man and language. Language is, as world-moving Saying, the relation of all relations" (Heidegger 1971b, 107).

The Production of Presence: What Meaning Cannot Convey (2004), make significant strides in contributing to such a vocabulary, provisionally distinguishing between a "presence culture" and the overwhelming push of a contemporary "meaning culture" that dominates by *interpretation* and is heedless of a concept of power thought in terms of "the potential of occupying or blocking spaces with bodies" (something that Occupy-movement general assemblies world-wide understood very well in 2011) (Gumbrecht 2004, 83–84). Gumbrecht beseeches fellow critics to "try to pause for a moment before we begin to make sense . . . then let ourselves be caught by an oscillation where presence effects permeate the meaning effects [of an artifact]" (2004, 126). What I want to take from Gumbrecht here is not, however, a ban on "making sense" so much as an effort to give a little more time or ontological weight to understanding rhetorical force apart from its subordination to systems of "meaning." Fradenburg's work seems to suggest a certain push past Gumbrecht's sense of an "oscillation" between presence and meaning effects. And Gumbrecht implies that "presence" and "meaning" cannot be thought at the same time (much like the position and momentum of electrons in the Heisenberg uncertainty principle). Instead, Fradenburg posits that, even in the most over-coded moments of linguistic systems, language harbors a capacity to to carry simultaneously within itself the sort of paraverbal effects that I am discussing. If I suggest a kind of divagation from Fradenburg's commitment to thinking the symbolic and the parasymbolic *at the same time*, it is as a corrective to a humanities still obsessed with a paranoid critique of the logic of representation—a desire to give some equal time to the implications of insights like those of Olson and Heidegger mentioned above.

Medievalist Mary Carruthers attempts to correct an over-theologization of the medieval arts by exploring how these medieval arts conceived of "'making sense' of physical sensations derived from human encounters with their own crafted artifacts," arguing that "medieval art is not only explained by considerations of semiology, representation, *mimesis*—though these are of course important—but also by persuasion" (Carruthers 2013, 13, 14)—which is to say, *rhetorical* force (on a non-representational and a-semiotic level of affective and sensory aesthetic perception). Similarly, as I think the psychoanalytic spirit of "Living the Liberal Arts" would suggest, even in the most therapeutic of situations, there are makings which do not consist of an organism "expressing" in a purely emetic-coding model, but in fact need to be understood *literally* as the production of certain kinds of provisional shelters for contact with the world, of *literal* forces that repel or attract, that hook into the affects and senses of other beings, sentient and non-sentient. The inner-outer intertwining of an organism and its "Outside" suggests a model of making very different from "expression" determined as the communication of an "inside" state to an Outside. In the discourses of ethology cited by Fradenburg (for both human and non-human creatures), the concept of "expressivity" is related to "display," as performativity and persuasion.[11] In Elizabeth Grosz's Deleuzian reading of the

---

[11] For example, Fradenburg writes, "Art does in fact capture attention by, say, making us see or feel the creamy or gleaming character of rock rather than its overfamiliar immobile lumpiness. What is of importance in this process is not simply the separation of self from not-self, but the work done on the boundary between the two, where we can make the familiar unfamiliar just as readily as the other way around. (In fact embellishment, not necessity, is the mother of invention.) Jane Jacobs notes that the ludic and ornamental applications of our most important technologies (such as ceramics, metallurgy, plastics) preceded their practical applications; our oldest known examples of wheels are from toy wagons (Jacobs 1988, 221). Further, the placard, the territorial marker, the beautiful or forbidding entryway, are all forms of display, and hence instruments of living process. Avian and simian performance displays (e.g., in courting) must vary from 'tradition' if they are going to attract attention to *this* specially plumageous or architecturally

ethology of birdsong, display functions to render a "territory" provisionally perceptible: "the space in which sensations may emerge, from which a rhythm, a tone, a color-
ing, weight, texture may be extracted and moved elsewhere" (Grosz 2008, 12; cf. Grosz, 2008, 48–49, 68–69).
The ontology of such *poesis* is not exhausted as expression
of an "inside" (although signals are certainly involved),
but operates as "an arena of enchantment, a mise-en-
scène for seduction that brings together heterogeneous
and otherwise unrelated elements: melody and rhythms, a
series of gestures, bows, dips, a tree or a perch, a nest, a
clearing, an audience of rivals, an audience of desired
ones" (Grosz 2008, 28). For Grosz, following Deleuze, the
"first artist" is not the maker of symbols, but "the architect" (2008, 48). And indeed, an organism must also make
forces, skins, envelopes, sounds, textures, *loves*, and more,
in order to survive.

If we can talk about even the most seemingly theolog-
ically charged medieval literature as having non-representational and non-expressive functions (even if that
literature also inevitably succumbs to certain semiotic
and representational logics), then certainly, we can and
indeed need to think about a poetics of thriving in more
adventurous and less *abstracting* terms. This is to say, too,
that Fradenburg's commitment to thriving also convinces
me of the potential perniciousness of a "taste" (on the
part of certain schools of criticism) for evaporating pleasur-
able or even relaxed affects or sensations from the poetics of
poems or art-objects of any kind—or from critical readings and critical theorizing. Such devotedly paranoid analysis, wholly abstracted from any concrete therapeutic
function, is gnostic in its aims and can only read poesy as
purely a symptom of the Death Drive or of Capital. In
either case, one does disservice to actual therapeutic practices (and analysts and patients), to an artifact's texture,

---

creative bird, or *that* small but exceptionally boisterous and
noisy chimpanzee."

or to *actual* material labor struggles (including most especially those of adjunct and other precarious academic labor), by abstracting from the particular forces and feelings of the co-makings in question.

In a letter from Jack Spicer to his friend Robin Blaser, Spicer risks a more than sufficiently wild vocabulary in offering Blaser advice on how to proceed with the composition of an especially appealing poem. Spicer writes:

> I know you. You will have suspicions of it (CLEVER READER) and you will accuse it of lies which are only (would be only) lies because the other poems do not exist that you would refuse to write. Thus Ginsberg and Wieners pop like firecrackers while a great poet (Blake, Rimbaud, Yeats) why his whole life of writing is one immense soundless explosion.
>
> I exhort you—accept it (UNCHANGED) and hatch it as an eagle would basilisk's egg. Do not change, shift, cross out sections but let them change, shift, cross out themselves as you raise (the egg raises) a whole family of human-tongued basilisks. The court of the gods lies in the poem properly extended into poetry.[12]

Unfortunately, advice of such vitality, weirdness, or *fuzziness*, is rarely offered as instruction to either producers or critical readers of poetry in contemporary North American academic settings.[13] Spicer's exhortation proposes, however tongue-in-cheek, or self-consciously performative (in the vein of an overblown lexicon of "magic" and

---

[12] The letter is held in the Jack Spicer Papers, BANC MSS 2004/209, The Bancroft Library, University of California, Berkeley.

[13] This is especially true in the American poetry workshop system, which illegibly prizes a normalizing "craft"—determined by a pseudo-transparent language of mechanics—while also disavowing formal "Theory."

divinity), a model which demands attention to the co-production of poems with organic and inorganic forces that are nothing like a fantasy of transcendence of worldliness. He offers the poem as an emblem of a very medieval desire for a *mixture* of styles in a set of hybrid organisms. The poet as an eagle mothering mythical beasts offers an antidote to the "cleverness" (in the American English pejorative sense of the term) of the reader that would turn the possibility for radically amplifying life into a calculated joke instead of the organic thinking—nay, co-thinking—of on-the-spot *decisions* in a larger cosmos. The dance between the advice to raise the hybrid-beast snake-poems and to let the "egg" itself raise them not only suggests an organismic co-production of boundaries, but also a process that must be rigorously theorized and cannot be represented in/as quantity, tested in a controlled experiment, nor reduced to reproducible procedure: it is only had in *living* with the poems as a way of living. Moreover—the multiplication and transformation of poems into mythical deadly snakes (right out of a medieval bestiary) which perform human speech, suggests again a kind of poem whose functions, though *fuzzy*, are certainly potentially vital, or at least dangerously *interesting*, relative to one's own mortal living. Aside from their emblematic nature, or potential symbolism (and surely the tone of this passage suggests that the beasts operate as organisms and forces more so than as mere allegory), these poems bite, soothe, sing, and perhaps, even heal the clever reader too paralyzed to write more poems, or even get up in the morning.

Spicer's bird-nest of singing snakes, finally, suggests that the relation of poetics and life might be sought in what I would consider a very medieval understanding of these hybrid creatures: as *wonders, marvels*. These human-tongued basilisks are wondrous in their excess of conventional epistemological categories, yes, but also in their capacity (thanks to their varied and enigmatic appearance in language) to make us cognize the feelings of living first as feelings and not as signification. They offer to human organisms an attention to the forces of a real cosmos traversing our living, forces that can stream and snake sneakily around the abyssal logics of representation. Such poems, like living, require a kind of *reading* with one's own wits—often slowly and recursively. This is a reading whose value lies in the particularities of its experience, which cannot be replicated by data, and which cannot be reduced to decoding. For the humanities to thrive, we need to use a more variegated vocabulary for the poetics of the organism, a lexicon that is flexible and alternative to that of representational poetics, yet not amnesiac of history. Many artifacts indeed do represent, mimic, or encode—but some ornaments just decorate, an appointment for which they are no less needful in the physical wonder of sentience.[14]

REFERENCES

Bede (1990). *Ecclesiastical History of the English People*, trans. L. Shirley-Price, rev. R.E. Latham. New York: Penguin.

Bennett, J. (2008). *Vibrant Matter: A Political Ecology of Things*. Durham: Duke University Press.

Bernstein, C. (1992). *A Poetics*. Cambridge, MA: Harvard University Press.

Blaser, R. (2006). *The Fire: Collected Essays of Robin Blaser*, ed. M. Nichols. Berkeley: University of California Press.

Bové, P.A. (2008). *Poetry Against Torture: Criticism, History, and the Human*. Hong Kong: Hong Kong University Press.

Carruthers, M. (2013). *The Experience of Beauty in the Middle Ages*. Oxford: Oxford University Press.

---

[14] This is a point Fradenburg herself attends to in her commentary on John of Trevisa's Middle English translation of the Latin *Properties of Things*, which she sees as reveling in the "multitudinousness and variousness of beasts, all brought together by rhythm," and which "evokes attachment, re-environs us in *chora*."

Derrida, J. (1995). *The Gift of Death*, trans. David Wills. Chicago: University of Chicago Press.

Grosz, E. (2008). *Chaos, Territory, Art: Deleuze and the Framing of the Earth*. New York: Columbia University Press.

Gumbrecht, H. (2003). *Powers of Philology: Dynamics of Textual Scholarship*. Urbana: University of Illinois Press.

Grumbrecht, H. (2004). *Production of Presence: What Meaning Cannot Convey*. Stanford: Stanford University Press.

Harman, G. (2012). "The Well Wrought Broken Hammer: Object Oriented Literary Criticsm." *New Literary History* 43.2: 183–203.

Heidegger, M. (1971a). *Poetry, Language, Thought*, trans. A. Hofstadter. New York: Harper Perennial.

Heidegger, M. (1971b). *On The Way to Language*, trans. P.D. Hertz. New York: Harper & Row.

Hejinian, L. (2000). *The Language of Inquiry*. Berkeley: University of California Press.

McCaffery, S. (2012). *The Darkness of the Present: Poetics, Anachronism, and the Anomaly*. Tuscaloosa: University of Alabama Press.

McGann, J. (2007). *The Point is to Change It: Poetry and Criticism in the Continuing Present*. Tuscaloosa: University of Alabama Press.

Merleau-Ponty, M. (2002). *Phenomenology of Perception*, trans. C. Smith. London: Routledge.

Nichols, M. (2012). *Radical Affections: Essays on the Poetics of Outside*. Tuscaloosa: University of Alabama Press.

Olson, C. (2010). *The Principle of Measure in Composition By Field: Projective Verse II*, ed. J. Hoeynck. Tucson: Chax Press.

Robertson, L. (2003). *Occasional Work and Seven Walks from the Office for Soft Architecture*. Astoria, OR: Clear Cut Press.

Sedgwick, E.K., and A. Frank (2003). "Shame in the Cybernetic Fold: Reading Silvan Tomkins." In E.K. Sedgwick, *Touching Feeling: Affect, Pedagogy, Performativity*, 93–122. Durham: Duke University Press.

Spahr, J. (2001). *Everybody's Autonomy: Connective Reading and Collective Identity*. Tuscaloosa: University of Alabama Press.

Tomkins, S. (1962). *Affect, Imagery, Consciousness: Vol. 1, The Positive Affects*. New York: Springer.

Williams, W.C. (2011). *Spring and All*. Reproduction of 1923 edn. New York: New Directions.

Whitman, W. 1959. *Leaves of Grass: The First (1855) Edition,* ed. Malcolm Cowley. New York: Viking.

3: Breathing with Lacan's Seminar X

Expression and Emergence

[An] intimate relation . . . exists between the movements of expression and those of respiration.
Charles Darwin, *The Expression of the Emotions in Man
and Animals*

The greatest significance is ascribed to oxygen in the
pleasure-unpleasure workings of the psyche.
Sandor Ferenczi

Is a panic attack "a phenomenon of a psychological" nature? Or of a "neurobiological (or even neurochemical)
nature" (Masi 2004, 311)? Arguably, the question is not
well-formed; panic—a critical somatic as well as psychical
experience—defies rather than invites categorization. Many
practitioners have regarded the plasticity of the nonethe-

less vital and "involuntary" process of respiration to be particularly persuasive evidence for psychosomatic connectivity: if the organism can make even breathing serve its ends, the links between soma and psyche must be powerful indeed. Breathing troubles the boundary between the voluntary and the involuntary; it is visceral, but available to (un)conscious manipulation. Respiration is meaning-making, as "the first postnatal communication that we establish with our environment"; nonetheless it is "rhythmically verified under the command of an urgent need" (Wyss 1947; Chiozza 1998, 32). Breathing tells us that we are and are not captains of our fate.

Nowadays, from neuroscience to affect theory to psychoendocrinology, the "embodied" character of psychological process is nearly axiomatic, despite the continuing obscurity of "mind/brain" connectivity (cf. Fonagy and Target 2007, passim). But interest in embodiment has a long history, notably (for my present purposes) in psychoanalytic writing on disorders like neurasthenia and hysteria. Lacanian psychoanalysis—generally understood to be more disembodying than not—may *prima facie* seem more of a diversion than a contribution to the psychoanalytic thinking of embodiment. This chapter argues, however, that the Lacanian *objet a* is a striking conceptualization of the embodied mind's experience of change. Further, it is a conceptualization that trenches on the psychosomatic nature of rhetorical activity.

In the rhetoric of respiration, paramount tropes are activity and passivity, self and other, consciousness and unconsciousness. Respiration links the history of what and how the body takes in, and why, to narrative structure, comical or tragical (that is to say, man's fate). Eisler notes "profound connections" between respiration and consciousness; e.g., "inhibition in breathing is the dominating symptom that distinguishes [disturbances of consciousness, i.e. "fits,"] . . . from sleep" (Eisler 1922, 41).[1]

---

[1] If, as Francis Steen argues (in forthcoming work), conscious-

Even vital organs respond "dispositionally" to regression, i.e., to the organism's activation of its oldest modes of functioning, like those that create distinctions between *me* and *not me* (Eisler 1922, 41). We cannot choose to stop breathing, but we *can* stylize the rhythms of our "exchange of gases," as instance and anticipation of the roles played by intake and expulsion in the construction of the self (Weiszaecker 1950b; Chiozza 1998, 32). In object relations, the "'first phantasies'"—infantile "theories" that try to explain and map sensations and perceptions—are "'bound up with sensations' resulting from stimuli experienced at birth, [of intake and expulsion,] during respiration, feeding and elimination" (Mitrani 1993, 322–323; citing Isaacs 1952, 910). Breathing is the first taking in, but also invasion by, something other—something that is not exactly chosen.

Discrimination of "self" from "not-self" is a vital function at the biomolecular level. It eliminates pathogens, and, less helpfully, "rejects" transplants (Mahoney 1991, 226). The proteins at work in self-/non-self recognition (the Major Histocompatibility Complex [MHC]) seem also to be involved in judgments about relationships—of kinship, group, species, territory.[2] Display behavior marks distinctions between self/non-self, my group/yours. "Core variability" in display behavior promotes the recognition of individuals and "may be the origin of new unique display patterns for newly evolving sibling species" (Jenssen 1977, 210).[3] Modifying basic display patterns enables the

---

ness arises the better to process novelty, it could readily enlist anxiety and its respiratory features to calm or to screen (hide, but also project) trauma—trauma being, by definition, a breaking-through of boundaries, a wound, and therefore the action of a force that is not adequately *anticipated*.

[2] A lot of data indicates that "we use these to judge relatedness," on which cooperative behavior depends: Dr. Antony de Tomaso (Life Sciences, UC-Santa Barbara), personal communication. See also Havlicek and Roberts (2009).

[3] A humanist might think of "core variability" as "variations on

evaluation of different intra- and interspecific performances ("I like *his* mating dance the best"; "how do I best
get this crow to understand I want him out of here, without getting hurt"). Considering the claim made by Lakoff
and Johnson (1980), and centuries of rhetoricians before
them, that metaphors signify the mind's embodiment, we
should recall Freud's notion of the "bodily ego" and its
introjections and projections, which, he believed, found
their prototypes in exhalation and inhalation. Sighing and
yawning directly stimulate the respiratory zone: "there is
an hedonic element in breathing," in feeling the ebb and
flow of not-self into self (Forsyth 1921, 125).

The work of self-other distinction-making always leaves a
lot of things out. The creation of the *objet a*, the remainder,
is also the creation of "me." Subsequently, the *a* jogs my
memory as that part of "me" that I experience as lost (or
would like to believe I've gotten rid of), such that, if I
could only recover it (or completely rid myself of it), I
would be complete (not haunted). Its various avatars are
therefore notoriously hard to pin down. The voice and
the gaze can come at me from all sides, and of course I
can't be sure they're human. Is the sound of the *shofar*
human, or not, let alone a sound "I" make? Who or what
is it that assembles me, calls me together, alarms or or-
ganizes me, when "I" am emerging, or fading out?[4] What
gives "me" life/death? Art foregrounds this (d)estrange-
ment; since "I" am not all there when I am changing,
adapting, mutating, something must speak *for* me. The
(re)formations of the *objet a* mark the course of the organism's vital experimentations, meaning also each eclipse of
self-feeling entailed in such transformations.

Living is constrained not just by factors like gravity

---

a theme."

[4] Lacan discusses the *shofar* in *Seminar X: Anxiety* (1962/63,
XIX.171–179). All citations of Lacan's *Seminar X* are from Cor-
mac Gallagher's unauthorized translations (rev. Mary Cherou-
Lagreze) of unedited French transcripts, by section and page
number.

and food supply, but also by the social forms that derive from and embed these supposedly extra-social factors— for example, the expectations my parents have of me ("angel," "baby," "daughter"), expectations that impress themselves on me (the *agalma* of Lacan's *Seminar X: Anxiety* [1962/63, XIV.124]). What happens, then, to the rest of me? I can't say, though I know it used to be here, and probably went somewhere. But wherever the rest of "me" has gone, "I" exist as a signifier in the discourse of the Other ("baby," "daughter"). I already have a very strong sense of this when, upon being born, the importance of interpreting (and being interpreted) skyrockets. *To breathe (and to sob, scream, shriek) is to be on display.* "[T]he expiration in sighing (in Spanish *desahogo*, . . . de-choking) is a recovery from . . . discouragement," says Chiozza (1988, 31). Infants play with respiration, "breathing quickly then slowly, shallowly then deeply—their attention obviously concentrated on the game" (Forsyth 1921, 124).

In 1893 Freud and Breuer laid out a still-powerful rationale for thinking psychosomatically:

> The fading of a memory or of its affect depends . . . on whether an energetic reaction . . . supervened . . . . By *reaction* we here mean the whole range of voluntary and involuntary reflexes by which . . . the affects are habitually worked off—from weeping up to an actual act of revenge. (Breuer and Freud [1893] 1955, 7)

Abreactions like sighing, crying and shouting occur frequently in analysis, and are often transformative. Abreaction is *expressive* activity, in both senses: it *pushes out* bad affects, and *displays* them. I "spit it out," "cry my head off," "get it off my chest." (In English, the word "express" means both "*to* express," "to press out [an essence]," and also "to signify"). The expression and "regulation" of affect is directly linked to physiological changes in the body (respiration, heart rate, blood pressure), changes which in turn give rise to signals that are fed back into the brain and influence ongoing processing (Ledoux 2002, 288). The brainstem mechanisms that mediate "suffocation alarm," and are activated during panic, are very ancient (Panksepp 2005, 147). The amygdala has "output connections" to the brain systems that initiate defensive responses (like "freezing"). A network of processes that links ancient brainstem to limbic to cortical activity has taken a long time to evolve.[5] While, phenomenologically, the affect of anxiety seems to us both unmistakeable and unvaried, it is really much more of an assemblage and much more of an achievement, so to speak, than is generally recognized. Because it "requires, at a minimum, networks involved in arousal (monoamine systems), emotional (amygdale . . . extended amygdale), and cognitive (prefrontal cortex, hippocampus) functions," according to Ledoux, it "is best thought of as a property of the overall circuitry rather than of specific brain regions"—i.e., it is best thought of holistically (Ledoux 2002, 290).

"Holistic" means (in this context) *generated by a complex system*. If "neurons that fire together, wire together" (Hebb's Law), what is decisive in affect-formation and expression is the factor of *time*. Bodily registration of affective experience is neither "deeper" nor "truer" than its registration in the order of the signifier. Affects arise as a consequence of *connections* between conscious and unconscious (or "implicit") processing, connections that take shape, in the forms of linguistic registration, facial display, vocal patterns (including contour, pitch and volume), gestural language (slumping vs. pacing), and levels and kinds of arousal, defined by Beebe and Lachmann as "pattern[s] of physiological indices such as EEG, heart rate, and respiration" (Beebe and Lachmann 1994, 129). For Freud, affects *are* psychosomatic phenomena, not disembodied emotions: combinations "of certain feelings in the pleasure-

---

[5] See Ledoux on the connectivity between the brain's cortical, motivational, and emotional systems (2002, 323).

unpleasure series with the corresponding innervations of discharge *and a perception of them*, but probably also the *precipitate* of a particular important event," namely birth—"at the time of which [we felt] the effects upon the heart's action and upon respiration characteristic of anxiety" (Freud [1933] 1961, 80; my emphasis).

Affects are expressive.[6] Expression *is* action that shapes, and is shaped by, states of arousal: "[A] particular facial or vocal pattern is always associated with a particular arousal state" (Beebe and Lachmann 1994, 129)—for example, the "increased sensory attention and motor tension" characteristic of "preparedness" (Freud [1933] 1961, 80–81). Infants listen, and scan faces, to identify/affect parents' states of arousal. In turn, "[h]eightened affect" "lead[s] to the formation of representations" (Beebe & Lachmann 1994, 129; cf. also Anzieu 1979, 75). The mediation of "somatopsychic experiences" of trauma (for example, the compromise of the noradrenergic system, which regulates respiration) is accomplished in part through the "reintroduction of ideational representation" (Marans 1996, 536–537). *Respiration both is, and precipitates, expressive and interpretive activity, nonverbal as well as verbal.*

Living is artful. J. Z. Young points out that art "has the most central of biological functions, 'of insisting that life be worthwhile, which, after all, is the final guarantee of its continuance" (Young 1971/74, 360; see also Dissanayake [1998] 2002, 70). And there are few species for which "worthwhile" has no social dimension whatsoever. For us, sociality is paramount. Expression acknowledges the "relational field" of "the Øther"—Lacan calls it a "ceding" (of imaginary sovereignty). "I am always a cedable object, . . . an object of exchange" (Lacan 1962/63, XXV.232). Ceding is adaptation: I am aware of the world around (and in) me, and if I want to live (well), I must realize that my

---

[6] Damasio's understanding of the emotions as incompletely voluntary but profoundly socially expressive is relevant here (2003, 29 ff.).

power over my environment has its limits. "If I want to live" is the key: I cede because I want to make a deal; I need something I don't have, someone else has got it, I need to get it out of them. Again, expression acknowledges the "relational field" of "the Øther": when I act out, I act *out*. I *open, unfurl* my best feathers, because I want you to notice me. This is the import of Foghorn Leghorn: "For—I say, fortunately, I always carry a spare set of feathers."

Respiration marks our constitutive permeability, our embeddedness in the Øther. So changes in respiration mark our attempts to struggle against, or settle into, that permeability. Respiratory disturbances express changes in the rhythms of analysis (Guignard 1995, 1083). One of my own analysands arrives in a state of agitation, choking and/or hyperventilating, broadcasting speechlessness and helplessness. Sighs follow her expressions of pain, as if the reward for verbal effort were deep breathing. The pleasure is partly that of letting oneself be changed; in analysis, the sigh is an act of ceding, which is also a bid for life—ceding not to the analyst, but to the Øther.

Respiration marks and is an experience of intersubjectivity. One of Gardner's analysands made efforts at "dyadic respiratory union" that were "like a dream," as they displayed the analyst's own, at that time, unknown "pulmonary disorder" (Gardner 1994, 930, 933). Anthi explains the blocked respiration of one of his patients as a suppression of the urge to scream and cry (Anthi 1995, 36–37). As with all symptoms, styles of breathing can express many different affective experiences; they are created by (our) history. Inhibition (or hiding) can serve the refusal to cede, just as exhibition (or showing) can serve to distract attention from the hidden treasure the subject dreams of keeping forever. An analysand of Mitrani's experienced exhalation as "losing herself" "to a gaseous state of invisibility"; "broncho-constriction" was an "effort aimed at holding a self, equated with life's breath, safely inside her lungs" (Mitrani 1993, 331). Note that display and reserve are repeat *performances*, not just repeated experience. They announce, to the O/Øther, aliveness, through the cry for attention, the cry for help, which must also at times be smothered in the mode of camouflage.[7]

The cessation of screaming and crying is the cornerstone of our sentimental educations. My parents may not like it when I scream and cry; maybe if I choke back "unbearable psychic pain, sorrow and anger," I'm *more* likely to be comforted, not less. Or, I might "hold my breath" in anticipation of the return of the abandoning object. There are strong clinical connections between unconscious breath-holding and "obstinacy"—i.e., the refusal to cede one's position, to leave behind any "remainder": "when annoyed, infants will obstinately hold their breath, even to the point of becoming convulsed and comatose" (Forsyth 1921, 124). Withholding is always withholding *from* the Other. The best revenge may be a dish served cold, but it is never eaten alone:

> An insult which is returned, if only in words, is remembered differently from one endured in silence. Common speech also recognizes this difference in the psychical and bodily consequences, and . . . designates silently endured suffering as a . . . wound, injury, mortification. (Freud [1893] 1962, 36)

Classical and medieval traditions of poetic complaint do not allow the spurned to suffer in silence for very long. At the same time, complaint is always haunted by its putative excessiveness and futility, and thus by the unbearability of listening to it. Dido, the queen who refused to lose, knows her "compleyninge" letter—her last words to Aeneas, in Chaucer's *Legend of Good Women*—will not change the will of the gods. But that does not stop her.

---

[7] See Szpilman (1945/2000, 103–104); the anecdote, about a mother forced to smother her crying baby while hiding from the police, is related in Roman Polanski's film *The Pianist*.

Since she also has nothing left to lose, she is free to "lose a word on" Aeneas, whose inconsistency renders him less than the smoke that will shortly bear her remains *into the atmosphere*:

> "But sin my name is lost through yow," quod she,
> "I may wel lese a word on yow, or letter,
> Al-be-it that I shal be never the better;
> For thilke wind that blew your ship a-wey,
> The same wind hath blowe your fey a-wey."
> (ll. 438–442)

> ["But since my name is lost through you," said she,
> "I may [as] well lose a word on you, or letter,
> Although for that I shall be never the better,
> For that wind that blew your ship away,
> That same wind has blown your faith away."][8]

The wind can blow us anywhere: on our imperialist way, into the annals of shame, to the far corners of the world, home.

Air has an "*a*" quality; it is full of our leavings (carbon dioxide); full of our transmissions (pheromones); full of organisms seeking to breach our defenses. Since we all breathe the same air, it (materially) has, and expresses, social significance. Respiration stocks the "olfactory unconscious" and transmits hormones and pheromones as well as pathogens (see Brennan 2004). *Because* intangible and protean, air's power of alteration is immense. For Aristotle it is the epitome of unseen force; in Chaucer's *House of Fame* it is the medium of the Øther, the "barred" symbolic order—of scandal, rumor, notoriety, (un)deserved reputation, the phantasms that haunt Anzieu's "sound-image of the self" (Anzieu 1979, 26).

In Lacan's meditation on the *shofar*, the voice be-

---

[8] All citations of Chaucer's poetry are from Benson's (1987) edition; all translations are mine.

comes *a* when air is concentrated (cf. the sail), and its propulsion rhythmically timed. The stylization and magnification of sound creates the *a* as Echo, what is rejected but can't be effaced (as in Dido's complaint), and continues to seek some way of announcing, "here I am, look at me, *pay attention to me,*" the mode of address of so many medieval lyrics: "have reuthe on me, ful of murnyng."[9]

> Der Schrei, dendas kind bei der Geburt ausstößt, ist das Signal seines Eintritts in die Welt der Sprache, ich würde sogar sagen, es ist ein Eintritt im Atemstillstand.

> [The scream that the child utters at birth is the signal of his entry into the world of language. It is an entry into respiratory arrest.] (Samson 2012, 30; my translation)

Respiratory action is a bridge between affect and language. Schreber writes that he is "forced to emit bellowing noises" when the "muscles serving the process of respiration are set in motion by the lower God" (noted by Ferenczi 1910, 225n10). Bellowing (Lat. *follis*, 'bellows') and horn-blowing both need air. During phonation, sensitivity to carbon dioxide decreases notably, so intertwined are respiration, outcry *and* language. Chiozza suggests that "through audible language we attempt to re-establish the original union that was lost" (Chiozza 1998, 32n5, referencing Murray 1983). Since there is no original union to lose, let's say instead it is the way we display ourselves and participate in the field of the Other.

The intersubjectivity of breathing is foregrounded in emergency work, when the paramedic "breathes for" the distressed, a merging of functions inbetween life and death, for

---

[9] "Have pity on me, full of mourning"; from "Mary at the Foot of the Cross," ed. Karen Saupe, TEAMS Middle English Texts Series, gen. ed. Russell Peck, http://www.lib.rochester.edu/camelot/teams/mary.htm.

which we are to be grateful: the gift of life/death (resuscitation so often brings back to life an organism it also ages). Since air is always exchanged, so it can be a gift: infants "conceive of breath, the stimulus object, as a concrete thing, and this well into childhood, as shown by a boy of six who offered a handful of breath to another child panting after a race" (Forsyth 1921, 124). Respiration is bound to oral experience, and begins to help with excretion in later infancy. Forsyth suggests that the respiratory zone (which . . . plays an excretory as well as a nutritive role) may influence character-formation in a way comparable to that of the anal zone" (Forsyth 1921, 126). Again, air has intersubjective significance; Forsyth identifies breath as one of "the original objects . . . of an infant's love," one of the mother's "outstanding rivals" (Forsyth 1921, 134).

Obstfeld contends that the pulmonary function implies "sharing something in common," and "is connected to the capacity for empathy and the desire for deep understanding" (referenced by Chiozza 1998, 32–33). But respiratory experience will inevitably entail aggression as well as love. The air may be pure, but one does not for all that breathe so easily in Fiesole, when down below people are dying in the plague-ridden atmosphere of Firenze.[10] Our folklore tells us breathing has to be "started" by the Other: the gift of life/death. So we also recognize the dimension of horror here. It's the Other who gives me oxygen, or makes me struggle for it, the father as much as the mother. The father of one of my patients "sucked up all the oxygen in the house"; the children all kept their mouths open and were shamed for it (she is bulimic). Just so Sylvia Plath barely dared to breathe or 'achoo' when she was living like a poor white foot in Daddy's shoe.[11] Infants readily re-experience the dying that is also the experience of birth, via suffocating experiences in early

---

[10] The reference is to Boccaccio's *Decameron*.
[11] Sylvia Plath, "Daddy," in *Ariel: The Restored Edition* (New York: HarperCollins, 2004), 74–76.

childhood (attacks by smothering breasts, bedding and bath-water, and respiratory infections).

Contending against Fenichel's sourcing of asthma in "a sexualization of respiration owing to a regression of Oedipal drives," Adroer suggests that "asthma depends on fixations at the level of the breast," the aim of which is to avoid collapse of self (Adroer 1996, 787; citing Fenichel 1931). Fears of "suffocating containment" are expressed by the body via oscillations between contact and withdrawal (Cooper 2004, 158, 162). Containment can protect the subject from the suffocating effects of others' "demands, deficiencies, or deadness" (Cooper 2004, 162), but can also be suffocating in its own right. The ambiguities of containment appear in the transference and countertransference: Ogden reports an analysis in which "feelings of being foreclosed from all that is human [were] experienced in the form of images and sensations of suffocation"; at the same time, to inhale what was formerly feared was also suffocating (Ogden 2004, 180). Wolson suggests that, "[w]hen the infant merges with the primary maternal object, the fear of psychic death is experienced as the fear of entrapment, suffocation and ego dissolution" (Wolson 2005, 684).

What enables communication also enables vulnerability to haunting and possession. A medium is a medium— the Other is always at the other end. The point is not to demystify exchange—we are very familiar with its ironies—but rather to underscore sufficiently that exchange is the *sine qua non* of living (and its vicissitudes). Not simply the formation of a sac, but also osmosis, "ecosystemic connection," the permeability of that sac (as is replicated over and over in the structure of the lung), is essential to vitality (Chiozza 1998, 34).

Birth is often understood to entail a traumatic loss of union with the uterine environment. But if the "core" self begins to develop in the womb, and maintains its coherence during the birth process, perhaps, as Mancia suggests, it's not so bad as all that: "since even the most primitive form of memory can be retained after birth thanks to its affective component," "we are justified in thinking that the processes which organize this function *before* birth . . . lend a sense of continuity to the affective nucleus of the [postnatal] self"—this despite the "undeniably traumatic" aspects of birth, such as "the move from the watery environment of the womb to the 'dry land' of the outside world, from one type of respiration to another" (Mancia 1989, 1065). Despite all this, "birth does not interrupt the continuum of mental development"; it is "a process of continuous transformation." But should we not also note that an experience of rupture depends on a prior experience of *linking*, if not continuity?

Borning is aporetic, a certain epitome of the experience of coming-into-being without knowing what or where we are or were. The subsistence of an affective nucleus throughout the birth process accords with ultrasound studies of prenatal behavior; but this affective nucleus can undergo fragmentation and reconstitution nonetheless. Either way, when an affective nucleus finds herself subject to gravity and sick with too much carbon dioxide, she has to start living in an environment capable of overwhelming and traumatizing her. She has to cede, attend, link herself to, that environment. Birth remains a stunning emergence/y. At minimum, the demand on the infant's intellect is massive; to start breathing is to start interpreting, for life, and for the O/Øther. "In the few minutes required by the placenta to separate from the uterus, the newborn must activate the central and autonomic nervous systems, replace the liquid filling the lungs with air, and establish and reorganize the direction of the blood flow through the heart and main blood vessels"; this is indeed a rapid series of "adaptations" (Chiozza 1998, 29–30). It is exactly the series to which Freud refers when he defines the "state of anxiety" as a reprise of "the combination of unpleasurable feelings, impulses of discharge and bodily sensations" experienced by the borning infant and caused by "the interruption of the renovation of the blood (internal respiration)" (Freud 1917, 395). *Angst, angustiae, enge*: restriction, narrowness, narrow straits.

When placental circulation is interrupted, "a condition of partial suffocation is produced, and this increases in intensity until the child draws its first breath, often not for several minutes" (Forsyth 1921, 124). Anxiety attacks, Freud notes, are interpreted in accordance with ideas "nearest to hand," such as the "extinction of life" or a disturbance of bodily functions "such as respiration" (Freud [1895] 1962, 92–93). Panic attack mimes the dying, the succumbing to catastrophe, that the subject believes is already happening to her. Panicked bodies performatively and perhaps apotropaically "act out" annihilation; they "believe that what they fear . . . *is already taking place*" (Masi 2004, 311, 313). Oscillations between intimacy and separation are "existentially motivated," writes Wolson (2005, 684). The (affective traces of the) birth process force upon us adaptations—cedings—that resemble life's evolutionary transition from one means of oxygenation to another, and anticipate the organism's acquisition *and* loss of autonomy in the field of the Øther. Not self-continuity, but rather the giving up of one way of life for another, is the import of birth for Lacan (1962/63, XXV, passim).

Freud tells us that anxiety is a signal of danger—the danger, in Lacanian terms, that enforces the "ceding" of the *a*, that of the suspension of the "renewal of blood," namely, *ceasing to be as one was* (Freud, [1933] 1961, 84). The *a* can be thought of as the remainder of the process of striving for life. Affective display accompanies these changes, and is always showy compared to that little thing (the afterbirth, the legendary "meconium") we leave behind. We never really forget it; nor does it ever seem to forgive us. So, at the moment of "my" origin, I become a signifier in the symbolic order, *and* something abandoned and unmentionable—something with gills, Thingy, an extinct mode of viability, but re-membered by my body, non-conscious.

The Øther, says Lacan, is always there in its "full reality," whether we are conscious of this or not. When the Øther's reality acquires subjective presence, it makes itself felt, as insistent but immense and obscure patterning. Nonetheless, at least we have something to talk to, even if its replies, like those of any oracle, are highly ambiguous. The payoff for being impressed is the ability to express, and hence to impress others. I find myself in a very different world, needing new kinds of support, from entities I am ready to know but am not sure how to approach. But I have new, enhanced ways of "expressing" my emotions, of abreacting. Laughter takes me a while to learn, I have to do a lot of smiling first. Comedy is linked to ceding, as Ernst Kris points out: the face contorted by the grin and/or by laughter is just one step away from the "grimace" (Kris 1940, 323). I might snarl, but if I "recognize" you, I might start smiling instead. If I recognize you, I might even enjoy you, perhaps laugh at your jokes. I acquire a sense of humor. I yield to having ("lost") some part of myself at sea, or in the primeval swamp, or in a Devonian pool (Fortey 1998, 137–166). Then, the "I" knows it is where "it" once was: not immortal, omnipotent, or eternal, except for, possibly, the effects of its signifiers on the Ø. If the "I" cedes, however, "I" can desublimate being and instead *become,* before, during and after my whole life long. Of course *we* don't "*know*" what's back there. So what? How should that limit constrain us?

The value of what I give up can't be determined exactly, except for the fact that, whatever it is, I decide it isn't worth (social) annihilation. And there's always something new to adapt to. Anxiety signals these advents of the "I," signals every *re/constitution* of the "subject," every adaptation to (new) life. We become breathless with anticipation as well as dread. We inflate and deflate ourselves when we reach extremes of feeling—we horripilate, or make ourselves small. So when we change, we change our breathing, and change we must. Anxiety can readily kick off this appeal: "I'll do *anything* to make myself recognizeable to you. But what do you want to see in me?" I abandon (part of) my being so that I can be loveable to the people I depend on. If I want to survive as a subject, an "I," I have to make myself loveable in the eyes of my caregivers; I can't simply eat them. I have a lot of incentive to put energy into my aestheticization; only if I'm sufficiently entertaining (and/or terrifying) will my needs be addressed. Therefore, "I" take shape according to my self-states' various interpretations of the desire of the Øther. Unfortunately, my self-states do not and never will know for certain what "I" am (or *a* is) before the desire of the Øther (it doesn't know either, because it isn't really an entity, whether we know it or not). Anxiety marks the moment when the Øther's desire for us seems to fail. So "I" experiment some more. It appears that "my" desire can't be satisfied because I can't afford to stop enchanting my nurses. At the same time, I know the nurses don't know everything. They can't see the future either. So there's always a chance I can get into the game.

How the subject accesses the reality of the Øther is subject to change. Lacan imagines these anxiety-inducing processes as a series of stages, where each stage leaves something ineffaceable behind—ineffaceable, because it has changed (things) forever. At the first stage, says Lacan, the reality of the Other is "presentified" through need (Lacan 1962/63, XXV.229). Need makes us aware that we are not self-contained; the feeling of need is an intrusion of lack (cf. Chiozza 1998, 32). But there's more to come. At the "second level" (the anal), something detaches itself from "my" being, in order to answer the Other's demand that we release our feces when It wants us to—a demand made in and by language, "which [we] hear from the Other" (Lacan 1962/63, XXV.229). Signifiers have power over our bodies; that's how they turn us into splendid wholes and murky, rhizomatic embarrassments. But we can recover somewhat from mortifications (if not from vulnerability thereto), by "talking back," being a "smartass." (The simultaneous registration of vulnerability to mortification and the power of backtalk is the import of the jester.) Psychobiological history is one of constantly trying to find new ways to live, in response to new seductions or irritations. It's the story of the creature's entry into the field of the Øther: of an "original anxiety" traumatically related to "the emergence of the organism . . . into a certain world where it is going to live" (Lacan 1962/63, XXV.229). You could say that the environment is the first remainder. That's how we treat it, anyway.

It is "something unbelievable," it's really amazing, how this works, Lacan feels (1962/63, XXV.229). Don't take it for granted. Some might compare fetal suspension in amniotic fluid to the situation of the brachiopod, ensconced in and caressed by plankton-bearing ocean-water (Lacan 1962/63, XXV.229). But there's a difference: brachiopoda are osmotic—directly hooked-up to sea-water. They get food and oxygen directly from the water surrounding and flowing into them. Lacan, however, thinks the human fetus does not exchange anything with the fluid surrounding it. It gets everything it needs from the placenta through the umbilical cord. The fetus is self-contained with respect to its *surround*. Lacan emphasizes this formulation because it dramatizes an extra strangeness for the human being—namely, that it must "take in" something as foreign as air. The "birth trauma" ("there is no other one") means that an other element intrudes, preceded by a "stifling" (Lacan 1962/63, XXV.230).

The organism with, on its borders, "a certain number of chosen points of exchange," is not like the fetus. "The most basic schema of vital exchange is . . . created by the function of this wall, of this border, of this osmosis between an outside milieu and an inside milieu, between which there can be a common factor" (Lacan 1962/62, XXV.229). By contrast the fetus is cradled in, but separate from, its "outside" milieu. It is a question of a style of intake, whereby the human fetus is perhaps more surprised by birth, by the difference between itself and its environment, than brachiopoda. We are to wonder at the "strangeness" of "our" long-ago passage "into the air," and its corollary, the "radical intrusion [at birth] of something so other to the [fetal] human being" as air, where suddenly we are starved for something, but we do not know what. This experience of need is thus doubly invasive: the irruption of the feeling of need, *and* the intake of—the satisfaction of the need by—something alien to me. Breathing out is similarly involuntary but manipulable; we can take in plenty of oxygen, but if we can't expel carbon dioxide, we die just as surely. Breathing is an experience of (embodied) extimacy: the "me"-ness of a strange element, the strangeness of what is in me.

Lacan stresses that the fetal pulmonary system's ability to process air is irrelevant to the fetus's survival. What need accounts for the emergence of the lung? What prepares us for the "strangeness of the leap by which living beings have emerged from their primitive milieu, have passed into the air" with the help of an organ of "arbitrary character" (Lacan 1962/63, XXV.229)? Life begins (again) by differentiating itself from its surroundings, a process that paradoxically enables exchange with those surroundings. Living is in fact an unending process of differentiation. The transition from water to land recapitulates this phenomenology. Life grows on the edges, in the pools nesting along the fault lines of the Devonian Period. It depends on the passage of flows between water, earth, air and fire.

But to what end? Lacan insists on the arbitrary character of evolution, as he does on the *ex nihilo* of verbal language. While playing at the edges of pooling streams, couldn't our marine ancestors just as easily have experimented with flatness, or eyes on stalks, or snorkels? The intrusion within the organism of the respiratory neo-formation of lungs is just as strange as its later technological avatars: the iron lung, or the spacesuit, also a "reserve of air" (Lacan 1962/63, XXV.229). Anxiety signals the human being's emergence from what thereafter is (re)constituted as a remainder. But this emergence depends also on "the aspiration into oneself" of a "different milieu." "I" cannot emerge, come out, without taking in. So, in the world she must enter, the "little neo-natal subject" is

> what [s]he has first of all to give; and it is to this object that there is appended, as to a causal object, what is going to identify [her] primordially to the desire to retain. The first developmental form of desire is thus and as such akin to the order of inhibition. (Lacan 1962/63, XXV.230)

What is sacrificed turns into the "cause" of my desire, which unleashes chains of substitutions and signifiers by means of which I (re)discover the *a* in my surroundings. Cordelia, however, won't heave her heart into her mouth, or give in to anything that isn't a square deal—and we know how many of those there are around.[12] We also know Hamlet can't do or say anything except folly, at least until the jester's skull shows up as remainder and reminder of the vanity of human wishes (*Hamlet* V.i; the *follis* is a purse, a bag, an inflated ball, "windball," but also a small coin; on the theme of vanity, see Lacan 1962/63, XXV.232). We learn at the same time that the remains of Caesar are airborne. Sooner or later, (desire for) the *a* will "fall off" (roll off? blow away?) any stage it is foolish ("imprudent," "lacking in foresight") enough to mount (Lacan 1962/63, XXV.232).[13] Ophelia learns this the hard way, according to Gertrude's report: while not-herself, Ophelia plays on the edge of a stream, she's out on a limb; when she falls in, her clothes lose their buoyancy and pull her down (*Hamlet* IV.vii). Again, life emerges and *re-*merges at the edges of water, land, air. The subject's continuing dependence on the sacrificed remainder is also unbearable for Lear, who, buffeted by the winds like any

---

[12] In William Shakespeare's *King Lear*; see especially Act I, Scene i.

[13] See also Lacan's discussion of the world, the stage, and *Hamlet* (1962/63, III.24–28).

poor houseless creature, cries to them to blow and crack
their cheeks.

In Shakespeare's *Twelfth Night* (III.i), Feste says he is
Olivia's "corrupter of words" (*corrumpo*, "to break to
pieces," hence "to bring to naught"). Inspector Clouseau
has no native language, he is clueless, his inflated hump
flies the friendly skies of Paris.[14] Education or exposure of
vanity (anamorphosis) is also a tragic theme—"I eat the
air, promise-crammed" (*Hamlet* III.ii). But tragedy resub-
limates by rendering desublimation horrifying, as though
the real could be bothered with our little disappoint-
ments. Coming after Lacan's seminar on *Hamlet*, Seminar
X is in part a poetics of comedy, to which anxiety is inti-
mately related.[15] The *a* must fall off the stage "through the
test of what it will have left there in a relationship of tragedy, or more often of comedy" (Lacan 1962/63, XXV.
232). Further, it's not the (comic) role that counts, "but
what remains beyond this role"—a remainder that is
"precarious" but unavoidable for all that. The comic actor
acts this out: the missing piece is always in another universe, outlined by the play's designs, but unknowable to
consciousness ("I" don't visit behind *that* scene). The
comic actor acts out the connection between this split and
the experience of ceding to exchange, to the role of signifier in the desire of the Other, to our piecemeal nature.
The comedy itself is but the "vase" of Seminar VII, whose
shape is designed to call our attention to the emptiness
inside (Lacan 1992, 120).

Comic plots ask us to find pleasure in our often-
baroque ornamentations of the air we breathe—pleasure
that includes some understanding of the meaning of ornamentation. So there must be inflations—the rhetorical

---

[14] In *The Pink Panther Strikes Again.*
[15] Miller (1990) notes that Lacan thought comedy even more
important than tragedy, especially with respect to analytic process. See also Galligan's (1984) emphasis on comedy as a technique of living. Thanks to Peter Van Summeren for drawing my
attention to these works.

term is *amplification*—to deflate. The comic plot, the "rhythm" of comedy, alternately inflates and deflates. Boasting competitions have a similar rhythm. Satiric genres—the troubadour *sirventes*, the Scots "flyting"—foreground "backtalk." The "sirventes" are so-called because the poet's persona is a servant—and service to the Øther is something we all owe, for which we (foolishly) expect compensation. The question of class is embedded in subject-formation (e.g., the "family romance," hence the tragedy of Oedipus [Freud, 1910]) and in comedy—hence antique comedy's famous "lower" characters; the humble origins of "Plautus" (a self-deprecating nickname) and Terence (a freed slave); and the *querelle* that blew up in the name of these names in Renaissance debates about comedy (Hardin). The buffoon is all puffed up; Ecclesiastes says "All is vanity"—in Hebrew, "vanity" is "*ruach*," "which means wind, or again breath, a mist, if you wish, something which is effaced" (Lacan 1962/63, XXV.232). "Imagination blows" the windbag Malvolio after he reads the love letter he believes to be from his employer Olivia (*Twelfth Night* II.v). Because he denies his servile status, he is a fool, and made a fool of; the windbag is "shot down," deflated. But wordplay is also just this sort of nothing; hence Feste lets the signifier keep going and going, which reminds us that we all eat the air, or that nothing is ever completely down-to-earth, or that even the clever can fly too high.

Hamlet's atmosphere of rueful wisdom comes down to this: the ceding, the yielding to change, the "readiness" (V.ii). Lacan remarks that the Hegelian fight to the death for pure prestige "has indeed the accent of meaning the fight for *nothing*" (Lacan 1962/63, XXV.232; my emphasis). Satirized in Shakespeare's *Troilus and Cressida*, the fight over nothing is the centerpiece of *Twelfth Night* as it is that of *Hamlet*. Act III is consumed by Fabian and Sir Toby's efforts to entertain themselves by starting a fight, a duel of honor, over nothing, over the *a*, between Viola and Sir Andrew the "manikin" (as Fabian calls him in

III.ii). "Anxiety, at the level of castration, represents the Øther, since encountering a weakening of the apparatus gives us the object . . . in the form of a lack (*carence*)" (Lacan 1962/63, XXV.233). And "[w]ho is the one who gives us the first example of a castration, attracted, assumed, if not desired as such, if not Oedipus?" (Lacan 1962/63, XXV.233)—Oedipus the fool, like all the melancholy men who follow him in subliming their basic fault(s) (for example, Duke Orsino, Hamlet). What misses or is missing is enlightenment: Oedipus wants to see the satisfaction of his desire because he wants to see what's beyond it; his real desire is for knowledge, says Lacan. But Oedipus doesn't know about the unconscious/Ø.

Evolutionary theory is full of aspirational (and pathetic) narratives about radical eco-biological change; the development of the lung, the transition from water to land, is only one of them. Another goes as follows:

> The leap from anaerobic (non-oxygenating) to aerobic metabolism . . . reflected one of those synergistic processes wherein life forms transformed the environment to which they were adapting. By giving out oxygen as a byproduct, photosynthesis 'created an atmosphere which made the development of respiration possible'. . . . Later life-forms realized a 'windfall profit,' so to speak, and developed *respiration and the refined visual capacities we associate with anticipatory movements*. (Mahoney 1991, 130–131; my emphasis)

Breathing, vision, foresight, synergy: it's all there. Oedipus sees his own eyes lying bleeding on the ground. But what does he see with? The import of this mystery is the impossibility of seeing ourselves as the Øther sees us, which includes "the way we look to us all" (Simon 1986). The wisdom that asks us to bear the knowledge of our limitations can't help at this vanishing point, where nothing and no one can see us in all our foolish guises. But we needn't be so literal about it, says Lacan; the "bloody ritu-al" is "not necessary—and this is why the human drama is not tragedy, but comedy: [we] have eyes in order not to see—it is not necessary for [us] to tear them out" (Lacan 1962/63, XXV.233). Psychoanalysis prefers me to "posit [my]self as a finite object to which are appended finite desires, which only take on the appearance of becoming infinite in so far as by escaping from one another . . . they carry the subject away further from any authentic realiza-tion" (Lacan 1962/62, XXV.237). What do I get out of putting the brakes on substitution? I get an interpreta-tion—not "a confrontation with anxiety," but "an over-coming of anxiety when the Øther has named [her]self" (Lacan 1962/63, XXV.237). If talking makes me feel bet-ter, it is because doing so enhances my capacity for dis-play, for expression, not simply because the Other who I address may be capable thereby of experiencing what I experience, but because the Ø/other to whom I address myself is situated in its own inability to avoid impression, change, and misprision.

What we find in Lacan's *Seminar, Book X: Anxiety* is a reduction of the antinomy between Mahler's (1974) em-phasis on autonomy and Bowlby's (1969) on attachment, where such reduction takes the form neither of "optimal frustration" nor a sentimentalized intersubjectivity. It is more a question of our mutual dependence on the ether, our mutual reference to an apparent invisibility—a Third, an Øther—that mediates our living and waves on the sig-nifiers that will take up that task on another level of func-tioning.

* * *

It seemed to me a cloud encompassed us,
Luminous, dense, consolidate and bright
As adamant on which the sun is striking.
Into itself did the eternal pearl
Receive us, even as water doth receive
A ray of light, remaining still unbroken. (Dante, *Paradiso*)

And what is the situation of our own discourse? Are we witnessing in our current moment a semiotic transformation of the life sciences, or a biologizing transformation of semiotics? The critique of "representation," never more "scientific" within the disciplines of the humanities, has renewed its adolescence (for example, see Massumi 2002, passim); but representations of relationships are at the forefront of the contemporary life sciences. Current ethological research presents much animal display as open system, not fixed repertoire; as learned signaling as well as inherited, innovative as well as traditional (see, for example, Boyd 2009, 159). If Lacan's distinction between the animal and human orders seems to explain less and less, his respect for unpredictability and improvisation in symbolic process (Ø) is nonetheless a point at which exchange between his work and the new life sciences becomes possible.

References

Adroer, S. (1996). "Fixation of Asthma and Sexual Impotence at Different Pregenital Stages." *International Journal of Psychoanalysis* 77: 787–802.

Anthi, P.R. (1995). "Resistance Analysis and Psychic Reality." *Psychoanalytic Study of the Child* 50: 32–47.

Anzieu, D. (1979). "The Sound Image of the Self." *International Review of Psychoanalysis* 6: 23–36.

Beebe, B. and Lachmann, F.M. (1994). "Representation and Internalization in Infancy: Three Principles of Salience." *Psychoanalytic Psychology* 11.2: 127–165.

Benson, L.D., gen. ed. (2008). *The Riverside Chaucer*, 3rd edn. Boston: Houghton-Mifflin.

Bowlby, J. (1969). *Attachment and Loss, Vol. 1: Attachment*. New York: Basic Books.

Boyd, B. (2009). *On the Origin of Stories: Evolution, Cognition and Fiction*. Cambridge, MA: Harvard University Press.

Brennan, T. (2004). *The Transmission of Affect*. Ithaca: Cornell University Press.

Breuer, J. and S. Freud. ([1893] 1955). "On the Psychical Mechanism of Hysterical Phenomena: Preliminary Communication." In *The Standard Edition of the Complete Psychological Works of Sigmund Freud*, Vol. 2, ed. and trans. James Strachey, 1–17. London: Hogarth Press. [Hereafter referred to as SE = Standard Edition.]

Chiozza, L. (1998). *Hidden Affects in Somatic Disorders: Psychoanalytic Perspectives on Asthma, Psoriasis, Diabetes, Cerebrovascular Disease, and Other Disorders.* Madison: Psychosocial Press.

Cooper, P.C. (2004). "The Abyss Becoming Well: Psychoanalysis and Reversals in Perspective." *Psychoanalytic Review* 91.2: 157–177.

Damasio, A. (2003). *Looking for Spinoza: Joy, Sorrow, and the Feeling Brain.* New York: Harcourt.

Dissanayake, Ellen. ([1988] 2002). *What Is Art For?* Seattle: University of Washington Press.

Eisler, M. J. (1922). "Pleasure in Sleep and Disturbed Capacity for Sleep—A Contribution to the Study of the Oral Stage of the Development of the Libido." *International Journal of Psychoanalysis* 3: 30–42.

Fenichel, O. (1931). Hysterien und Zwangsneurosen. Vienna: Internationaler Psychoanalytischer Verlag.

Ferenczi, S. (1993). Letter from Sandor Ferenczi to Sigmund Freud, October 10, 1910. In *The Correspondence of Sigmund Freud and Sandor Ferenczi, Vol. 1: 1908-1914,* eds. E. Brabant, E. Falzeder, and P. Giampieri-Deutsch, trans. Peter Hoffer, 224–226. Cambridge, MA: Harvard University Press.

Fonagy, P. and M. Target. (2007). "The Rooting of the Mind in the Body: New Links Between Attachment Theory and Psychoanalytic Thought." *Journal of the American Psychoanalytic Association* 55: 411–456.

Forsyth, D. (1921). "The Rudiments of Character: A Study of Infant Behavior." *Psychoanalytic Review* 8: 117–143.

Fortey, R.A. (1998). *Life: A Natural History of the First Four Billion Years of Life on Earth.* New York: Knopf.

Freud, S. ([1893] 1962). "On the Psychical Mechanism of Hysterical Phenomena: A Lecture." SE, Vol. 3, 25–39.

Freud, S. ([1895] 1962). "On the Grounds for Detaching a Particular Syndrome from Neurasthenia Under the Description 'Anxiety Neurosis.'" SE, Vol. 3, 85–115.

Freud, S. ([1910] 1958). "A Special Type of Choice of Object Made by Men: Contributions to the Psychology of Love I." SE, Vol. 11, 163–176.

Freud, S. ([1917] 1963). "Lecture XXV: Anxiety." *Introductory Lectures on Psychoanalysis (Part III)*. SE, Vol. 16, 241–463.

Freud, S. ([1933] 1961). "Lecture XXXII: Anxiety and Instinctual Life." *New Introductory Lectures on Psychoanalysis*. SE, Vol. 22, 1–142.

Galligan, E.L. (1984). *The Comic Vision in Literature*. Athens: University of Georgia Press.

Gardner, M.R. (1994). "Is That a Fact? Empiricism Revisited, or a Psychoanalyst at Sea." *International Journal of Psychoanalysis* 75: 927–937.

Guignard, F. (1995). "The Infantile in the Analytic Relationship." *International Journal of Psychoanalysis* 76: 1083–1093.

Hardin, R.F. (2007)."Encountering Plautus in the Renaissance: A Humanist Debate on Comedy." *Renaissance Quarterly* 60: 789–818.

Havlicek, J. and S.C. Roberts. (2009). "MHC-correlated Mate Choice in Humans: A Review." *Psychoneuroendocrinology* 34: 497–512.

Isaacs, S. (1952). "The Nature and Function of Phantasy." In M. Klein, P. Heimann, S. Issacs, and J. Riviere, *Developments in Psychoanalysis*, 67–121. London: Hogarth Press.

Jenssen, T.A. (1977). "The Evolution of Anoline Lizard Display Behavior." *American Zoologist* 17: 203–215.

Kris, E. (1940). "Laughter as an Expressive Process: Contributions to the Psychoanalysis of Expressive Behavior." *International Journal of Psychoanalysis* 21: 314–341.

Lacan, J. (1962/63). *The Seminar of Jacques Lacan, Book X: Anxiety*, trans. C. Gallagher, rev. M. Cherou-Lagreze, http://www.lacaninireland.com/web/?page_id=123.

Lacan, J. (1992). *The Seminar of Jacques Lacan, Book VII: The Ethics of Psychoanalysis (1959-60)*, trans. Dennis Porter. New York: W.W. Norton.

Lacan, J., J.-A. Miller, and J. Hulbert. (1977). "Desire and the Interpretation of Desire in *Hamlet*." *Yale French Studies* 55.6: 11–52.

Lakoff, G. and M. Johnson. (1980). *Metaphors We Live By*. Chicago: University of Chicago Press.

Ledoux, J. (2002). *Synaptic Self: How Our Brains Become Who We Are*. New York: Penguin.

Mahler, M.S. (1974). "Symbiosis and Individuation: The Psychological Birth of the Human Infant." *Psychoanalytic Study of the Child* 29: 89–106.

Mahoney, M.J. (1991). *Human Change Processes: The Scientific Foundations of Psychotherapy.* New York: Basic Books.

Mancia, M. (1989). "On the Birth of the Self." *Rivista Psicoanalytica* 35: 1052–72.

Marans, S. (1996). "Psychoanalysis on the Beat: Children, Police and Urban Trauma." *Psychoanalytic Study of the Child* 51: 522–541.

Masi, F.D. (2004). "The Psychodynamic of Panic Attacks: A Useful Integration of Psychoanalysis and Neuroscience." *Journal of the International Psychoanalytic Association* 85: 311–336.

Massumi, B. (2002). *Parables of the Virtual: Movement, Affect, Sensation.* Durham: Duke University Press.

Miller, J.-A. (1990). "L'ecole et son psychanalyste," "Dispositif du Passe," and "Du tragique a la comedie," *École de la Cause freudienne,* http://www.causefreudienne.net/index.php/ecole/textes-fondateurs/l-ecole-et-son-psychanalyste.

Mitrani, J.L. (1993). "'Unmentalized' Experience in the Etiology and Treatment of Psychosomatic Asthma." *Contemporary Psychoanalysis* 29: 314–342.

Murray, J.F. (1985). "Crecimiento y desarrollo del aparato respiratorio." In L.H. Smith and S.O. Tier, eds, *Pathophysiology: The Biological Principles of Disease.* 2nd edn. International Textbook of Medicine, Vol. 1. Philadelphia: W.B. Saunders.

Obstfeld, E. (1975). "Psicoanalisis del trastorno diabetico." *Eidon* 5: 33–59.

Ogden, T.H. (2004). "The Analytic Third: Implications for Psychoanalytic Theory and Technique." *Psychoanalytic Quarterly* 73: 167–195.

Panksepp, J. (2005). "Commentary on 'Integrating the Psychoanalytic and Neurobiological Views of Panic Disorder'." *Neuropsychoanalysis* 7: 145–150.

Premack, D. (1985). "'Gavagai!' or the Future History of the Animal Language Controversy." *Cognition* 19: 207–296.

Samson, F. (2012). "Das Objekt der Angst." In *Angst: Lektüren zu Jacques Lacans Seminar X*, ed. Michaela Wüensch, 13–23. Wien-Berlin: Verlag Turia + Kant.

Simon, P. ([1986] 2012). "The Boy in the Bubble." In Paul Simon, *Graceland* (CD). Legacy Recordings.

Steen, F. (In Preparation). *Incorporating Consciousness.*

Szpilman, W. ([1945] 2000). *Death of a City*; republished in English as *The Pianist: The Extraordinary True Story of One Man's Survival in Warsaw, 1939-1945*, trans. A. Bell. New York: Picador.

Wolson, P. (2005). "The Existential Dimension of Psychoanalysis (EDP): Psychic Survival and the Fear of Psychic Death (Nonbeing)." *Psychoanalytic Review* 92: 675–699.

Wyss, W. ([1947] 1974). *Cuerpo y Espiritu.* Barcelona: Manuel Marin.

Young, J.Z. (1971/74). *An Introduction to the Study of Man.* Oxford: Oxford University Press.

The Object Breath

Ruth Evans

Breathing my mother in
Breathing my beloved in
Breathing
Breathing her nicotine
Breathing
Breathing the fall-out in
Out, in, out, in, out, in, out, in
Out, in, out, in, out, in, out
(Out, out, out, out)

                Kate Bush, "Breathing" (1980)

BREATHING WITH "BREATHING"

Respiration is habitual, so we do not normally notice it. Voice—what Steven Connor calls "shaped breath"—claims our attention, but breathing, because it is second nature, slips under the radar (Connor 2008a). Breath is nature to voice's culture. Yet respiration is "meaning-making," as Aranye Fradenburg rightly insists in her marvelous, erudite essay: our first gulp of air is an involuntary response to a traumatic change in our environment, but that change catapults us from safety to profound anxiety, provoking and developing our skills of interpretation and expression, as we take in that novelty and push it out again in our cries, our laughter, our words. Breathing is the making of us, just as we come to know and make the world through breathing.

I want in this essay to take up Fradenburg's two provocative claims that "the Lacanian *objet a* is a striking conceptualization of the embodied mind's experience of change" and that this conceptualization "trenches on the psychosomatic nature of rhetorical activity." My purpose in this response is to breathe with "Breathing" by elaborating on the wide-ranging implications of these claims: for psychoanalysis on the one hand and for reading literature and art on the other. I end by considering Fradenburg's crucial question about the interrelationship of the life sciences, psychoanalysis, and the humanities as a question about the "representations of relationships," and thus about the nature of creatureliness.

As Fradenburg reminds us, although breathing is an autonomous physiological process, it can also be enlisted by the mind, consciously or unconsciously, to serve its ends. I *have* to breathe, but breathing is also "me," insofar as the *objet a* that constitutes "me"—driving me to act, organizing my desire—is shaped by the anxieties that attend change, of which the neonate's encounter with the real of the *pneuma* is paradigmatic. Fradenburg's highly original contribution to the neurobiological and psychoanalytic literature on anxiety lies in her argument that the origins of the *objet a* lie as much in breathing—let's call it the respiratory stage—as in the oral, anal, and genital developmental stages. As Fradenburg argues, "[a]nxiety signals the human being's emergence from what thereafter is (re)constituted as a remainder": the lost object. In

Lacanian theory the object is "both the hole and that which stops it up" (Adams 1996, 104)—it hollows out a space inside me (creating lack) and it covers it up (screening that lack). We might see the action of the lungs, pushing air in and out, as a dynamic version of this paradoxical topology. Although breathing is not an object, clinical symptoms that involve respiratory mechanisms (choking, sighing, panic attacks, breath-holding) demonstrate that breathing embodies unconscious desire, and is thus connected to the object.

Maureen McLane beautifully connects breathing and desire when she observes: "It's only humans as far as we know who can use words to get bodies together. The word as the body evanesced in a breath, a breath bearing intelligible sound" (McLane 2012a, 8). Words—signifiers—literally get bodies together, via calls, emails, texts, love-letters, but also metaphorically, through literary forms, which people worlds with strangely alive, absent presences. Signifiers are fleeting, like breath, vanishing from one to the other in the signifying chain, bearing witness to the absent body—"intelligible sound"—but never making that body fully present ("the body evanesced in a breath"), just as desire moves ceaselessly from signifier to signifier, never finding its final satisfaction. McLane's words imagine breathing as both expressive *of* desire and as behaving *like* desire.

Now psychoanalysis associates desire with the Freudian partial objects around which the drive turns. I want to argue that Fradenburg's essay opens up the possibility of theorizing breath—as distinct from breathing—as another partial object, as "a catalyst that sets off love" (Salecl and Žižek 1996, 3). Why argue this?

In western culture, breath has many dimensions. On the one hand, it is inferior to *logos*, insubstantial, not even (like voice) a vibration in the air. God made his creatures with his Word, but he *breathed* life into Adam. St Augustine worries about the (lack of) substance of God's breath: "But we must not think that the creatures He made by a word are better than what He made by a breath, in view of the fact that *a word is better than a breath in us*" (Augustine 1982, 5; my emphasis). Word—voice—trumps breath in the hierarchy of air-related phenomena. And yet, Augustine concedes, "to produce a breath is to produce the soul" (1982, 5). Breath is life and death. For Søren Kierkegaard, breathing opens onto the dimension of possibility: to pray is to breathe, "and possibility is for the self what oxygen is for breathing" (1989, 33). Kierkegaard's is a religious understanding of the adage attributed to Cicero: *Dum spiro spero* ["while I breathe, I hope"]. But Fradenburg's question—"What gives 'me' life/ death?"— is not about breath as substance or possibility, nor is it really about what Connor calls "the intense work of fantasy that attaches to the human breath, which is both demonic and divine, both flatulence and afflatus" (Connor 2008b). Rather, it concerns breath as the Lacanian object: that which constitutes the self, that which is invested with love.

BREATH AS *OBJET A*

Is breath a love object? Sigmund Freud (1962) identified a number of so-called "partial objects," elements that the child imagines as separate from the body: the most important of these are the breast, faeces, and phallus. To these Lacan (1979) added a further two: gaze and voice. These last two are, in Renata Salecl's and Slavoj Žižek's words, "love objects par excellence," because they are "a medium, a catalyst that sets off love" (1996, 3). These partial objects are "partial" not because they are part of a total object—the body—but because they represent only partially the function that produces them: the breast is a love object because it represents more than food. They are "something that is separated from [the subject], but belongs to him and which he needs to complete himself" (Lacan 1997, 195), avatars of the lost object (Lacan's *objet a*): a hole in the symbolic, but also the cover-up of that hole. The partial objects are all associated with the body's erotogenicized, rim-like structures: orifices and apertures that act as "the source and departure of a certain drive"—the mouth, the anus, the umbilicus (Lacan 1997, 169, 172). The drive (oral, anal, scopic) emerges from a rim as it aims at the object of desire [Fig. 1] and then returns, but it never "hits" the object (*a*): it always circumvents it. The shape that the drive describes as it moves around the object—as the object rises "in a bump"—is "like the wooden darning egg in the material which, in analysis, you are darning: the *objet a*" (Lacan 1979, 257). Lacan links these rim-like orifices, which open and close, to the opening and closing gap of the unconscious (1979, 200).

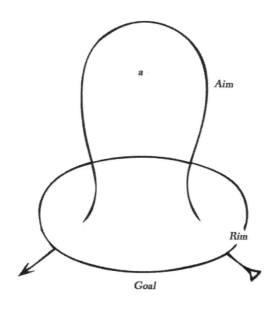

Figure 1. The partial drive and its circuit

But breath, unlike the other partial objects, is not connected with developmental tasks and breathing has nothing to do with the drives: it is a (semi)-autonomous physiological process. Breathing satisfies a need, not a demand. Yet, as Fradenburg amply demonstrates, breath represents more than our need for air. The clinical literature and cultural history suggest that breath *is* an object that can be detached from the body and invested with love.

The Greeks considered air to be the substance of the self. Herakleitos says that "[t]he stuff of the psyche is a smoke-like substance of finest particles that gives rise to all other things; its particles are of less mass than any other substance and it is constantly in motion" (Herakleitos 1976, 18). As Devin Johnston notes, "For the Greeks, bodily odor and breath carry the effluvia of essence, undiminished while the organism lives, the sole continuity of the psyche when it dies" (2009, 6). After death we will go on as breath; while we live we are constituted by the dynamic of respiratory exchange: "Breathing my mother in / Breathing my beloved in / Out, in, out, in, out, in, out," as Kate Bush has it. Contrary to Augustine's view of breath as insubstantial, medieval vernacular traditions held that breath is composed of one of the four elements that are basic to all living things: earth, fire, air, and water. As *The Early South-English Legendary* (c. 1300) puts it: "Man hath of eorþe al is bodi: and of watere he hauez wete, / Of þe Eyr he hath breth and wind: of fuyr he hath hete" ["Man's body is entirely of earth; he has moisture from water; from the air he has breath and respiration; from fire he has heat"] (Horstmann 1887, 318). Breath is me: it is elemental. A gaseous wave of bodily flotsam and jetsam, breath is a delirious, sometimes poisonous, mix of self and other, slag and allure: cigarette smoke, ketones, dust, microbes, pheromones, sweetness, "plumes of particulate matter" (Johnston 2009, 5).

In our sensual engagement with respiratory mechanisms, breath is both eroticized and charged with desire.

We taste the other's breath in kissing. CPR is the "kiss of life." We respond with emotion when we hear the sudden intake of breath, the sigh, the sound of panting, heavy breathing, rasping breath, the death rattle, a laboring woman's butterfly breathing. We feel warm breath fluttering and the swoosh of snorting on our skin. We see with relief the chest rising and falling, the feather held to the lips trembling. We smell, with disgust or delight, bad breath, garlic breath, sweet breath, the Cook's breath that "ful soure stynketh" (Chaucer, *The Manciple's Prologue*, IX.32).[1] And what do we make of the fact that respiratory rate is one of the vital signs of life, and yet in triage is almost never measured accurately (Lovett et al. 2005)? That we need better instruments? That we need better methods of auscultation and observation? Or that poor inter-observer agreement argues for an element of desire in the interaction: a residue that distorts the measurement? As Fradenburg argues, air "has an '*a*' quality": it is like the remainder around which the drive moves.

FLA(I)RING NOSTRILS

We use two orifices to breathe—the mouth and the nose. But nostrils seldom enter cultural history. Maybe this is because we associate the nose primarily with smell and with disgust (snot, sniffles), or because we are obsessed with the oral. Or because we find the mouth infinitely expressive, whereas the poor nose isn't. A nose doesn't give much away (unless it has an imagined shine on it). "To hold one's nose" means to block a smell, not to arrest breathing; "to look down the nose at someone" refers to an action of the eyes, not the breath. Yet the nasal cavities play a starring role in western culture: in Genesis 2.7 God's ex-spiration brings Adam to life solely through his

---

[1] All citations of Chaucer's poetry are from Benson's (1987) edition, *The Riverside Chaucer*, by fragment, book, and/or line numbers; all translations are mine.

nostrils: "And Jehovah God formed man of the dust of the ground, and breathed into his nostrils the breath of life; and man became a living soul" (Douay-Rheims Bible). Although the mechanics of divine CPR remain somewhat obscure—does God breathe life into Adam through His nostrils or His mouth?—the human nares are privileged here as a dual point of entry for the *pneuma*.

In the psychoanalytic tradition, the nasal fossae are associated overwhelmingly with the olfactory (Sharon-Zisser 2004). Freud famously sees "nostrils with scabs" in Irma's throat, but these are reminders of his own cocaine use (Freud 1999, 88–90) and are unconnected to breathing and its affects. I'm struck by the fact that the nostrils are rim-like structures, and yet Lacan does not include them in his list of eroticized bodily orifices that function as specific sources for the drive, namely, "the two rims concerned in the digestive tract . . . the rheumy rim of our eyelids, our ears, our navels" (1979, 172). But breathing is not associated with a drive (or is it?), and the nostrils do not open and close like the other orifices (or do they?), which, as Lacan observes, "are linked to the opening/closing of the gap of the unconscious" (1979, 200).

Why do our fantasies of breathing make so little reference to the nostrils? The nose is a complex organ that plays an important role in breathing. A normal adult nose processes on average 10,000 liters of air in 24 hours. The nose contains structures called turbinates that streamline the air that passes around them, humidifying, heat-exchanging, filtering, sensing, and controlling the airflow. The turbinates are crucial for maintaining nasal and sinus health and physiology (Wolf et al. 2004). They contain erectile tissue that swells and engorges in response to congestion or as an immunological defense. Anxiety interferes with nasal respiratory functions: vasomotor rhinitis can be caused by emotional stress. As we say, people get up our noses. Psychoanalysis needs to begin to theorize the nostrils *qua* air-passages, as opposed to olfactory or-

gans, or at the very least to account for why these apertures are largely absent in fantasies of the psychical body.

Lacan's list of the bodily orifices associated with desire
doesn't rule out the possibility of adding the nostrils to
that list—as the source and departure of a certain drive—
and of positing breath as the object of a drive. The nostrils are, after all, differentiated by their rim-like structure
and they are, in relation to certain dimensions of respiration, erogenous zones. Sneezing is reported as a fetish.[2]

Is the infant's game of respiration—"breathing quickly then slowly, shallowly then deeply" (Fradenburg, citing
Forsyth)—a version of the *fort-da*, the game with the cot-
ton reel that Freud's grandson invented to represent the
appearance and disappearance of the mother? For Lacan,
"This reel is not the mother reduced to a little ball . . . it is
a small part of the subject that detaches itself from him
while still remaining his. . . . [M]an thinks with his object
. . . . To this object we will later give the name it bears in
the Lacanian algebra—the *petit a*" (Lacan 1979, 62). In
this sense, the infant plays with its breath as if it were an
object: a part of ourselves that detaches itself from us while still
remaining ours. "Love makes its object from what is missing in the real" (Florence 2011). David Forsyth identifies
breath as one of "the original objects . . . of an infant's
love," one of the mother's "outstanding rivals" (Forsyth
1921, 134, cited by Fradenburg).

"Nostril" is from Old English "nos-þyrel." The etymology of *þyrel/thirl* is "[a] hole, bore, perforation; an
aperture" (*Oxford English Dictionary*). A nostril is a hole
bored into each side of the fleshy protuberance that is the
nose. Chaucer twice describes the grief that Queen Anelida experiences when her false knight Arcite betrays her
love as analogous to being "thirled" ["pierced"] by memory. Here's Anelida, lamenting: "So thirleth with the poynt of

---

[2] See Sneeze Fetish Forum: http://www.sneezefetishforum.org/
forums/.

remembraunce / The sword of sorowe . . . / Myn herte"
["The sword of sorrow has so pierced my heart with the
point of remembrance"] (*Anelida and Arcite*, 211–213).
And here's the narrator, in sympathy with her: "So singe I
here . . . / Howe that Arcite Anelida so sore / Hath thirled
with the poynt of remembraunce" ["how Arcite has pierced
Anelida so sorely with the point of remembrance"] (*Anelida and Arcite*, 348–350). The image of memory, the
sword's tip, piercing Anelida's heart is an exquisite metaphor for the desire that does not—that cannot ever—
attain its object: the physical sensation of loss is felt as a
perforation in the body's defenses. *Thirl* is also *thrill*
(*OED*). Anelida is thrilled: emotionally pierced. I imagine
a poetics of the nostrils in which the cavities of the nose
are also "thirled" with remembrance, pierced by desire.

Insofar as breath is invested with remembrance, so it
functions as an object of desire. Breath as an object surfaces with peculiar force in accounts of anorexic desire.

STARVED OF BREATH

In his study of anxiety, *On the Nightmare* (1931), Ernest
Jones notes that one of its cardinal physical symptoms is a
"sense of oppression or weight at the chest which alarm-
ingly interferes with respiration" (Jones 1931, 12). Anxiety feels like the physical torture of *peine forte et dure*
(being pressed to death by having heavy stones heaped on
one's chest): the breath is squeezed out of the body. The
rhetoric of suffocation is often invoked in descriptions of
anorexia nervosa. The narrator of Marya Hornbacher's
Wasted: A Memoir of Anorexia and Bulimia speaks of her
elaborate food-system—dividing food into 80-calorie
units—as a form of respiratory stifling: "systems, like corsets, keep shrinking, tightening around the body, pressing
the breath out of you" (1998, 246). These food-systems
provide control over chaos, but the narrator's anxiety—
expressed in terms of a symbol of constricting, female
clothing (but that symbol should not be read over-simply

in sociological terms)—shows that what's also at stake in the establishment of the food-system is the loss of an object. Containment, in corsets or diet plans, protects the subject from the suffocating effects of others, but is suffocating in its own right (as Fradenburg notes).

The recovering anorexic/bulimic narrator of Janice Galloway's *The Trick Is to Keep Breathing* declares on the last pages of the novel: "I'm gawky, not a natural swimmer. . . . I read somewhere the trick is to keep breathing, make out it's not unnatural at all. They say it comes with practice" (Galloway 2003, 235). Unable to completely control her respiration, to breathe with her desire, the narrator feels like a fish out of water, in an alien environment. She can't breathe properly, and things are not going swimmingly. But is the alien environment the one she has been in or the one she is about to dive into? When the infant starts breathing, "[f]or the very first time, he is traversed by something outside of himself. . . . [and] that particular experience constitutes the first encounter with the real of the ex-uteros, the real of the *pneuma*" (Florence 2011). Withholding her breathing has been a strategy of control, a way of refusing the real of the *pneuma*. It's another form of ambiguous containment: not breathing allows the narrator to escape the real but she risks drowning in the effort.

Crying is also a function of respiratory physiology. One of Hilde Bruch's anorexic patients "determinedly refrained from crying for [her parents] when she awoke from naps in her crib" (cited in Brown 1991, 195). The anorectic does not want to be noticed: she does not want to *open*—as Fradenburg writes, to *unfurl* her best feathers. She voluntarily curbs her respiratory processes, not because she wants to die but because she wants to play with the phantasy of her own death, her own disappearance. This is not self-effacing; it's an aggressive refusal to accede to the Other. As Lacan observes of anorexia nervosa, "the phantasy of one's death is usually manipulated by the child in his love relations with his parents" (1979, 215). As Fradenburg writes, since "[i]t's the Other who gives me oxygen, or makes me struggle for it, the father as much as the mother," to express myself by crying would be to acknowledge the relational field that I do not want to be caught in. Lacan's remark that we must seek correlations for the infant's refusal of the breast, for "the first forms of anorexia," at the level of the big Other (Lacan 1962/63, 303–304) finds its echo in Galloway's narrator's references to this structuring Other: "I read somewhere . . . . They say . . . " (2003, 235). Our desire to keep breathing—or not to breathe—is the desire of the Other.

The anorectic does not eat nothing, as those medieval fasting saints understood only too well. Inanition can be a feast. Air is full of the remainders of our desire. Sylvia Plath's resurgent "Lady Lazarus" triumphantly reveals her vengeful meal plan: "Herr God, Herr Lucifer / Beware Beware. / Out of the ash I rise with my red hair / And I eat men like air" (2005, 17). Fire consumes (h)air, leaving ash, but what is consumed (air) becomes in turn the object of consumption, in a marvelously comedic reversal of the gendered status quo. Gods and devils are airy nothings; anthropophagy is effortless. Air is the chameleon's dish, "promise-crammed" (*Hamlet*, 3.2): the carrier of Hamlet's desire to avenge his father's death, of Lady Lazarus's desire to feast on the delicious nothing of her revenge on the primordial forbidding father, on the *nom-du-père*.

PNEUMATIC FORMS

Respiration, Fradenburg tells us, "links the history of what and how the body takes in, and why, to narrative structure, comical or tragical." The metaphors and locutions associated with breathing point to a respiratory basis for genres: a literary psychosomatics, if you will, that connects the embodied mind's experience of change to rhetorical forms. Samuel Beckett offers a brilliant epitome of this process in his 35-second play *Breath*:

Curtain.

1. Faint light on stage littered with miscellaneous rubbish. Hold for about five seconds.

2. Faint brief cry and immediately inspiration and slow increase of light together reaching maximum together in about ten seconds. Silence and hold about five seconds.

3. Expiration and slow decrease of light together reaching minimum together (light as in 1) in about ten seconds and immediately cry as before. Silence and hold for about five seconds.

   Rubbish. No verticals, all scattered and lying.

   Cry. Instant of recorded vagitus [the cry of a newborn infant]. Important that two cries be identical, switching on and off strictly synchronized light and breath.

   Breath. Amplified recording.

   Maximum light. Not bright. If 0 = dark and 10 = bright, light should move from about 3 to 6 and back.
   (Beckett 1970?)

First there is a "faint light," amidst the trash, held (like the breath) for about 5 seconds, in uncertainty or perhaps anticipation, and then the "faint brief" cry of a newborn baby, followed by "inspiration" (inhaling/stimulation/divine influence/(Romantic) poetic motivation) as the light gets stronger (*fiat lux*! a comic reference to creation). The intake of breath and the light swell together in diapason, and are then both suspended (the breath holds its breath, the light holds its breath) before the breath is slowly expelled and the light slowly fades; the first birth-cry is repeated, and then there is silence, again suspended: uncertain, nervous. There is no consolation and no transcendence.

The first cry mimes the moment when the child takes its first breath, and is invaded by something alien; when "the foetus, upon birth, goes from one topology to another" (Florence 2011). As Freud argues, this violent topological shift means that "the act of birth, as the individual's first experience of anxiety, has given the affect of anxiety certain characteristic forms of expression" (Freud 1990, 12–13)—that is, respiratory expressions. In Beckett's play, birth, life, and death are condensed into a few brief, pulsating moments on a bleak, chaotic stage. The viewer does not know if the events that unfold are tragic or absurd, providential or doomed, does not know if she should celebrate the life that appears so briefly or mourn its swift passing. The fleeting life is heralded by a cry, but it fades fifteen seconds later with the same cry, as if the infant expires almost as soon as it has been born (tragedy), or as if life merely lasted for as long as it takes for one breath to be inhaled and exhaled (which is comic in its reductiveness). Expression and interpretation are pared down, but are nevertheless present: the degree zero of the recognition that "[r]espiration both is, and precipitates, expressive and interpretive activity, nonverbal as well as verbal" (Fradenburg's words). There is chaos, somewhat illuminated; there is the pattern of a repeated cry. The second cry is the same as the first, but it does not mean the same because we encounter it as part of a narrative that unfolds in time. We register a barely perceptible but meaningful change between them: a slide, perhaps, from hope to tragedy to comedy. It never gets really dark. Somehow we'll keep going.

The physical dynamics of breathing take many (literary) forms. Laughter, in physical terms, is repeated sharp breaths. It is a "dynamic response of the respiratory system" (Filippelli et al. 2001, 1446), shaped by the expiratory muscles and the diaphragm. The myriad permutations of the laugh are a dazzling catalog of literary subgenres: the chuckle, the titter, the giggle, the chortle, the cackle, the belly laugh, the sputtering burst, breathless laughter, the snicker, the snigger, the guffaw, the snort, the hoot, nervous laughter, embarrassed laughter. One can roll with laughter, whoop with laughter, or cry with laughter. Chaucer's *Sir Thopas* is a chortle or a knowing snigger; the *Miller's Tale*, at the moment of Alison's "Teehee," is a joyful hoot.

So also the cough, which is, as Connor remarks, "closely twinned with and often implicated in the laugh, and indeed, we might say that laughter is the orchestration of the reflex action involved in the cough" (Connor 2008a). The embodied dimension of the signifier is evident in Connor's "crew" of "creole quasi-locutions: the lisp, the gasp, the sigh, the rasp, the whistle, the hiss, the brrr, the purr, the snore, the sniffle, the crepitus, the croak" (Connor 2008a). There is also the whoop of pertussis and the self-conscious "ahem." Like laughter's array of forms, this tussive litany is a lexicon of literary subgenres. Other breath-related phenomena are hiccups, yawns, sneezes, gulps, wheezes, puffs, and pants. The various prologues of the *Canterbury Tales* are models of some of these respiratory mechanisms: the Wife of Bath's is a gloriously protracted, mock-apologetic throat-clearing, the Prioress's a pious sniffle, the Manciple's words to the Cook an irascible hiss.

The literary as a moment of evanescent breath is given form in Frank O'Hara's magnificent poem "The Day Lady Died," in which the poet, shocked to learn accidentally of Billie Holiday's death by seeing a *New York Post* "with her face on it," finds himself suddenly sweating a lot and thinks of "leaning on the john door in the 5 SPOT / while she whispered a song along the keyboard / to Mal Waldron and everyone and I stopped breathing" (1995, 325)—there is no final punctuation. Like "Mal Waldron and everyone and I," the poem stops breathing, as if the air had been squeezed out of it by the realization that Holiday is dead. This is breathing begetting tragedy. But the poem is also at that moment vividly, intensely alive: it is breathing. This is breathing begetting comedy.

The syntactic ambiguity—Holiday "whispered" her song to "Mal Waldron and everyone" *and* "Mal Waldron and everyone and I stopped breathing"—creates a moment of *après-coup* that transforms the rapt listeners of Holiday's song into grieving subjects, and simulates a double exhalation, so that Holiday's entrancing, lyrical whisper, her breathing out, is then belatedly understood as a dying sigh. O'Hara does not make his poem a monument to Holiday (although it *is* this): he offers nothing as grand or self-aggrandizing as Shakespeare's assertion to his beloved in Sonnet 18: "So long as men can breathe, or eyes can see, / So long lives this, and this gives life to thee." O'Hara's poem does not live in order that the dead live on. Instead there is a quiet exhalation and inhalation: the poem stops—what McLane calls "lyric arrest" (2012b, 22)—and then starts again: a new cycle, life, art.

Margery Kempe's performance of Christ's death at Calvary is a startling example of one extraordinary medieval woman's ability to make breathing serve her ends. To understand that performance we must go back to Kempe's first-recorded traumatic episode: not her own birth but the events that accompany the birth of her first child. Believing that she might die after a difficult pregnancy and delivery, Kempe sends for her confessor so that she may express an old, unconfessed sin. But while she is revealing it, her confessor cuts her off: he "gan scharply to vndyrnemyn hir er þan sche had fully seyd hir entent" ["sharply reproved her before she had fully said her meaning"][3] (Meech and Allen 1940, 7). Stifled by him, she "wold not more seyn" ["wished to say nothing more"], and the sin goes unshriven.

The effect of this is that she "went owt of hir mende" ["out of her mind"] (7); for more than half a year she is vexed with spirits, and sees "deuelys opyn her mowthys al inflaumyd wyth brennyng lowys of fyr as þei schuld a swalwyd hyr in" ["devils opening their mouths, all inflamed with burning flames of fire, as if they must swallow her in"] (7). Her fear of being ingested by the Other is primarily an oral fear of being eaten alive but also a fear of being inhaled, a fear that is typical of ego dissolution. It's what Kate Bush protects herself against when she changes the steady rhythms of "*Out, in, out, in, out, in, out*" (where the focus is already on the exhaling) to an anxious panting as she rids herself of the breath that is poisoning her: "*(Out, out, out, out)*" (1980). What shall we call this? Not abjection: ab-halation?

Calvary is where Kempe symbolically gives birth to Christ and simultaneously experiences his death, where she first begins her extravagant "krying & roryng" (68). Her bellowing needs air; it's her attempt to reverse being stifled by her confessor. But this time her breathing is within her control; she knows, for example, that this crying irritates people: "sche wolde kepyn it in as mech as she myth þat þe pepyl xulde not an herd it for noyng of hem" ["she wished to keep it in as much as she was able so that the people might not hear it because it annoyed them]" (69). This withholding sometimes causes her to "wax as bloo as any leed" ["become as blue as lead"] (69), as if she were being suffocated: a withholding that replicates the original withholding of her sin from her confessor, but which, given her recognition of her fellow-Christians' hostility to the practice, is (for her) satisfyingly ag-

---

[3] All citations of *The Book of Margery Kempe* from Meech and Allen's 1940 edition, by page number; translations are mine.

gressive. If she is acting out, then we can also understand this as a response to trauma. If "[a]nxiety marks the moment when the Other's desire for us seems to fail," as Fradenburg argues, then it is gratifying to Kempe that Christ can reassure her that he has not forsaken her, that he knows what *a* "she" is. Kempe's behavior is a magnificent improvisation, a gloriously comic response to anxiety, a way of turning unpleasure into pleasure, and into form: her *Book*.

BREATHING MY BELOVED IN: SMITH/STEWART AND THE OBJECT BREATH

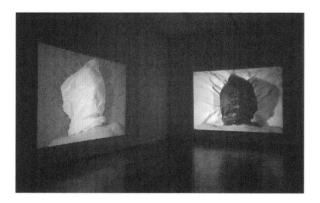

Figure 2. Smith/Stewart, *Breathing Space* (1997); with permission from the artists.

The link between (artistic) expression and respiration is strikingly dramatized in the work of the Glasgow-based artists Stephanie Smith and Edward Stewart. Smith/Stewart's artworks are preoccupied with the struggle to breathe. *Breathing Space* (1997),[4] a looped, two-channel color video projection installation [Fig. 2], shows Ms. Smith's head and shoulders on one screen; she is lying on a red sheet

---

[4] Smith/Stewart, *Breathing Space* (1997): http://www.smithstewart.co.uk/selected-works/breathing-space/.

and has a white plastic bag tightly fitted over her head. The other screen shows Mr. Stewart's head and shoulders; he is lying on a white sheet, with a black plastic bag over his head. As each artist slowly inhales and exhales, the plastic bags are sucked in and out, sticking to their faces. Microphones inside the bags amplify their breathing, which becomes increasingly panicky.

The viewer is both fascinated and distressed. Are they breathing together or dying together? The artists are united by their shared experience of anxiety, but kept apart on their separate screens. In its rigidity, repetition, and compulsion, its referencing of torture and masochism, the performance sexualizes respiration, but the viewer does not know if this is a game or a punishment, nor who is in control. The artwork is not only a trap for the gaze but also a trap for the breath: the artwork sucks the oxygen from the viewers by producing within them the anxiety experienced by the artists.

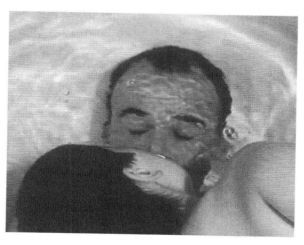

Figure 3. Smith/Stewart, *Sustain* (1995); with permission of the artists.

Sustain (1995), another two-channel color video projection installation, is concerned with the intersubjectivity of breathing and with what Fradenburg calls "the dimension of horror" in our reliance on the Other to give or withhold our oxygen. In the lower screen Mr. Stewart, fully clothed, is submerged under water in a bathtub, holding his breath and staring up at Ms. Smith, who is leaning over him [Fig. 3].[5] His only means of survival is Ms. Smith, who repeatedly bends over him to breathe into his mouth, resurfacing to take another breath while he remains underwater. Mr. Stewart makes no attempt to get out of the tub. Nothing appears to compel him to stay there (elements of torture and coercion are absent), but Ms. Smith makes no attempt to pull him out.

This underwater mouth-to-mouth resuscitation eroticizes breathing, and makes breath a love object that keeps the other alive. Even though Mr. Stewart displays no anxiety about whether she will return (she never disappears), it's a matter of life and death for him that the mother give him the gift of breath. To stay alive through the gift of the other's breath is terrifying, evoking suffocation, death, drowning, sex, the death drive. Breathing exists on a borderline: one is always poised to be alive or dead. Exploiting the medium of video, the looped tape, with its soundtrack of heavy-breathing, emphasizes that breathing goes on and on—in/out, in/out: it is the original binary code, 0 + 1, ones and zeros, off/on, but it's binary code made dangerous by positing it as fragile, perilous, finite.

Sustain calls to mind a performance artwork by Marina Abramović and Ulay, *Breathing In/Breathing Out* (performed twice, in Belgrade in 1977, and in Amsterdam in 1978), in which the two artists blocked their nostrils with cigarette filters, taped microphones to their throats, and pressed their mouths together [Fig. 4]. Each was able to inhale only the exhaled breath of the other. As carbon di-

---

[5] Smith/Stewart, *Sustain* (1995), http://www.smithstewart.co.uk/selected-works/sustain/.

oxide filled their lungs, they began to sweat and be visibly distressed, agitating their bodies in their attempt to cope with their slow suffocation. Viewers were able to sense their agony through the projected and amplified sound of breathing. It took nineteen minutes in the first performance and fifteen in the second for them to use up all the oxygen in that one breath and reach the point of passing out.

Figure 4. Marina Abramović and Ulay, *Breathing In/ Breathing Out* (1977-78)

Abramović and Ulay's work uses respiration to express the heterosexual couple as a monstrous unity, and collaborative work as potentially deadly: a parody of mutual sustenance. In Smith/Stewart's work breathing is not reciprocal; one gives and the other takes. Mr. Stewart is a newborn, utterly dependent on Ms. Smith for sustenance. What if she didn't return? The apparent generosity and selflessness of her action is belied by the ambiguities of "breathing for the other," by the aggression as well as love that lurks beneath it. Your breathing calls to me, but I might refuse to call you *back*, or I might call you *out*. Breathing tests our courtesy, our hospitality (or hostipitality, as Jacques

Derrida would have it). I live by your breath, but equally I may feel—as a neonate does—invaded. And so you by me. Which is to say that living is anxious.

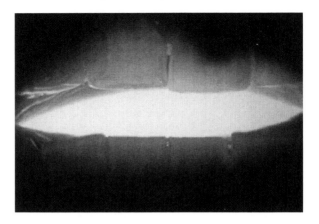

Figure 5. Smith/Stewart, *Inside Out* (1997); with permission of the artists.

In another installation, *Inside Out* (1997), a camera is placed inside a mouth so that the viewer looks out from within the mouth cavity [Fig. 5].[6] As the mouth rhythmically opens and closes, light appears and disappears, by turns lighting up and plunging into darkness the cavity of the mouth, in a visual presentation of inhalation and exhalation. The teeth that open and close function like a camera shutter or obturator. Just as the obturator in desire blocks and lets in the gaze, the voice (Lacan 1979, 147, 159), in accordance with the pulsation of the unconscious as it opens and closes, so here the teeth alternately block and let in the breath-as-light. Breath is here imagined as object-like: both the hole, when open, and the *bouchon*, the stopper for the hole, when closed (Adams

---

[6] Smith/Stewart, *Inside Out* (1997): http://www.smithstewart.co.uk/selected-works/inside-out/.

1996, 104). And isn't it the case that in Lacan's trajectory of the partial drive [Fig. 1], the path described by the drive as it circles around the object looks like a windbag?

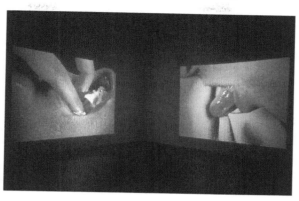

Figure 6. Smith/Stewart, *Gag* (1996); with permission of the artists.

In *Gag* (1996), another looped, two-channel color video projection installation, with amplified sound, each screen shows a close-up face with a piece of cloth over its mouth [Fig. 6].[7] The fingers and tongue of each subject methodically poke and force the cloth into the other subject's mouth: a slow gagging, intimate, perverse. Tongues and fingers lick, probe, and push; the viewer focuses on the mouth as a rim, and on the process of gagging the breath, closing the hole of desire with the cloth but also making the hole appear. The subject reveals and conceals herself. Gagging not only prevents us from breathing, but also stops our talking, stops us emitting signifiers, excludes us from the symbolic, the Other. And yet the act of poking or pushing the fabric down into the mouth with the tongue or fingers functions like the *point de capiton* (upholstery

---

[7] Smith/Stewart, *Gag* (1996): http://www.smithstewart.co.uk/ selected-works/gag/.

button; anchoring point) that nails down meaning. Each artist seeks to arrest the movement of signifiers/breath in order to create meaning, linking breathing to the signifier and to rhetoric.

Smith/Stewart's work takes breathing out of the habitual and the biological, to the point where it becomes part of the drive, which, as Freud insisted, could only be known through its representations (Adams 1996, 124). In their artworks, breathing is both intimate and "foreign," replicating the trauma of birth, offering in Fradenburg's words, "an experience of (embodied) extimacy: the 'me'-ness of a strange element, the strangeness of what is in me."

BREATHING WITH IT: UNPREDICTABILITY AND IMPROVISA-TION

Fradenburg's rigorous, subtle, moving work has prompted me to engage closely with the astonishing "unpredictability and improvisation in symbolic process" (Fradenburg's words) of a number of writers and artists whose work bears witness to how we respond to the anxiety that attends our first experience of change. So distinctive and inimitable is Fradenburg's neurobiological, clinical, and literary appropriation of Lacan that it's difficult to know if her closing question—"Are we witnessing in our current moment a semiotic transformation of the life sciences, or a biologizing transformation of semiotics?"—refers to a general shift in the state of intellectual inquiry, or if "our current discourse," as she terms it, recognizes her own unique methodology. What is clear, however, is that at the present time we are seeing important disciplinary transformations. A water-themed exhibit held from May-August 2012 at the Eyebeam Gallery in Chelsea, New York, "Surface Tension: The Future of Water,"[8] brought together

---

[8] "Summer Exhibit: Surface Tension," *Eyebeam.org*: http://eyebeam.org/events/summer-exhibit-surface-tension.

life sciences and artists exploring the imaginative possibilities of science, while also making urgent points about climate change and the politics of water. Eco-aware art has been around for a while (e.g., Andy Goldsworthy, Mark Dion); the difference with "Surface Tension" was in making the science as important as the art. But the discourse of "me" was completely absent from the exhibit.

Fradenburg's "Breathing" argues that, more than ever, we need supple understandings of the emotions, and for this we require psychoanalysis *and* biology *and* art: it's not enough to say that "[l]ove and hate, beauty and fear are more complex than high speed algorithms and non-Euclidean geometry" (Leach 2013). It's not a choice between a scientific explanation on the one hand and a semiotic one on the other; we need both.

The concept of plasticity—that the brain can create new neural pathways in response to experience or damage—is a model of this disciplinary exchange and transformation. Synaptic pruning—developing new connections and pruning away weak ones—is a neurobiological response to change. But that feedback loop is not just neuronal; it involves unconscious processes, and by attending to those processes and recovering their history, I can better understand how I come to be "me."

Fradenburg's argument is therefore also about what it means to be human, about creatureliness. I want to invoke here my colleague Devin Johnston's subtle appreciation of non-human animal culture:

[C]ulture is not limited to humans. It might include anything learned, any information not genetically transmitted. House cats instinctively pounce, but they only learn the art of killing from their mothers. This technique constitutes culture, though far from Arnold's 'sweetness and light.' It must always begin with a mimicry preceding comprehension; from there, a little darkness grows. (Johnston 2009, 25)

To recognize that animals as well as humans have culture is to acknowledge our shared creatureliness. That does not mean that human values are the touchstone for evaluating non-human animal culture (riffing on Matthew Arnold's refined notion of "culture" as "the study and pursuit of perfection") or that we therefore "get" animals because they seem like us. The object is not to shine light into supposed darkness; rather it is to make what seems obvious—animals' apparent kinship with us—murkier, and therefore more challenging.

Darkness teaches us intellectual and sympathetic humility. After all, crow song "is . . . an emotional cipher, never cracked by our own needs and wants" (Johnston 2009, 25). I like the ambiguities of "cracked": besides code-cracking, I hear cracked apart, broken into, broken down, cracked open like a nut, cracking on (moving fast), crazed or crazy, and even the medieval musical term for "sing loudly," as in the mid-fifteenth-century Towneley *Second Shepherds' Play*, in which the second shepherd marvels at the angel's *Gloria* announcing Christ's birth: "Say, what was his song? Hard ye not how he crakyd it? / Thre brefes to a long?" (Stevens and Cawley 1994, ll. 946–947). The shepherd cannot understand what the angel is singing because it's just too other, too removed from his experience for him to presume to understand it, but he is in genuine awe. That's not an argument for not seeking scientific causes; it's an argument not to impose our understanding on the other.

CONCLUSION: "BREATHING" AS FORM

György Lukács observes that "Form *is* reality in the writings of critics; it is the voice with which they address their questions to life" (1974, 8). Respiration is also a way of addressing questions to life. What then do we make of the form of Fradenburg's "Breathing"? Like the rhythms of respiration, imperceptibly regular or perceptibly irregular, Fradenburg's essay moves in and out; it breathes in molecules of science, of psychoanalysis, of clinical practice, of daily life, of literature, of experience, and all of these inhalations are exchanged in the mix to create a new form. Written in the present tense, the essay's unique connections and insights unfurl like the lungs, or a skein of breath curling in the air. Its form is distinctly that of the *essai*: a trying out, a testing of ideas, a mode of inquiry in and of itself, an "event," in Jean-François Lyotard's sense (Lyotard 1994, 81). Like the future anterior, her essay's full impact—what it will have meant—will arrive belatedly. It is concerned not with pronouncing a verdict but with what Lukács described as "the process of judging" (1974, 8). It brilliantly shies away from what Theodor Adorno, writing on the essay as form, called "the violence of dogma" (1984, 158). "It does not begin with Adam and Eve but with what it wants to discuss; it says what is at issue and stops where it feels itself complete—not where nothing is left to say" (Adorno 1984, 152). For Adorno, "[l]uck and play are essential to the essay" (1984, 152). "Breathing," too, is playful; above all it risks itself with *tuché*, the chance encounter. "Breathing" addresses its questions to life because that is both the reality of its form and its way of staying alive.

REFERENCES

Adams, P. (1996). *The Emptiness of the Image: Psychoanalysis and Sexual Differences*. London: Routledge.

Adorno, T.W. (1984). "The Essay as Form," trans. B. Hullot-Kentor and F. Will. *New German Critique* 32: 151–171.

Augustine (1982). *The Literal Meaning of Genesis*, Vol. 2, trans. J.H. Taylor. Mahwah: Paulist Press.

Beckett, S. (1970?). *Breath* (1969). Gambit: International Theatre Review 4.16: 59.

Benson, L.D., gen. ed. (2008). *The Riverside Chaucer*, 3rd edn. Boston: Houghton-Mifflin.

Brown, G. (1991). "Anorexia, Humanism, and Feminism." *Yale Journal of Criticism* 5.1: 189–215.

Connor, S. (2008a). "Whisper Music." Online: http://www.ste venconnor.com/whispermusic/.

Connor, S. (with Enzo Manseuto) (2008b). "Inside and Outside Voices." [An interview with Enzo Mansueto for *Rodeo* magazine (Milan), marking the publication of *La voce come medium. La storia culturale del ventriloquio,* trans. Massimo Gezzi, Rome: Luca Sossella, 2007, Italian translation of *Dumbstruck: A Cultural History of Ventriloquism*. An edited version of the interview appears as "Le Voci Dentro e Fuori di Noi," *Rodeo* 43 (2008): 66.] Online: http://www.steven connor.com/dumbstruck/interview2/.

Derrida, J. (2000). "Hostipitality," trans. B. Stocker with F. Morlock. *Angelaki* 5.3: 3–18.

Dolar, M. (1996). "At First Sight." In R. Salecl and S. Žižek, eds., *Gaze and Voice as Love Objects*, 129–153. Durham: Duke University Press.

Filippelli, M., R. Pellegrino, I. Iandelli, G. Misuri, J. Rodarte, R. Duranti, V. Brusasco, and G. Scano (2001). "Respiratory Dynamics During Laughter." *Journal of Applied Physiology* 90.4: 1441–1446.

Florence, B. de (2011). "Lacan and Topology." *Lacanian Works*: http://www.lacanianworks.net/?p=126.

Forsyth, D. (1921). "The Rudiments of Character: A Study of Infant Behavior." *Psychoanalytic Review* 8: 117–143.

Freud, S. (1962). *Three Essays on the Theory of Sexuality*, trans. J. Strachey. New York: Basic Books.

Freud, S. (1990). *Inhibitions, Symptoms and Anxiety*. In *The Complete Psychological Works of Sigmund Freud: The Standard Edition*, ed. J. Strachey, trans. A. Richards. New York: W.W. Norton.

Freud, S. (1999). *The Interpretation of Dreams*, trans. J. Crick. Oxford: Oxford University Press.

Galloway, J. (2003). *The Trick Is to Keep Breathing*. London: Dalkey Archive Press.

Herakleitos (1976). *Herakleitos and Diogenes*, trans. G. Davenport. San Francisco: Grey Fox Press.

Hornbacher, M. (1998). *Wasted: A Memoir of Anorexia and Bulimia*. New York: HarperCollins.

Horstmann, C., ed. (1887). *The Early South-English Legendary from Bodleian MS. Laud Misc. 108*. EETS os 87. London: Trübner & Co.

Johnston, D. (2009). *Creaturely and Other Essays*. New York: Turtle Point Press.

Jones, E. (1931). *On the Nightmare*. London: Hogarth Press.

Kierkegaard, S. (1989). *The Sickness Unto Death*, trans. A. Hannay. London: Penguin.

Lacan, J. (1962/63). *The Seminar of Jacques Lacan: Book X: Anxiety*, trans. C. Gallagher, rev. M. Cherou-Lagreze. Online: http://www.lacan inireland.com/web/?page_id=123.

Lacan, J. (1989). "The Subversion of the Subject and the Dialectic of Desire in the Freudian Unconscious." In *Écrits: A Selection*, trans. A. Sheridan, 323–360. London: Routledge.

Lacan, J. (1979). *The Four Fundamental Concepts of Psycho-Analysis*, ed. J.-A. Miller, trans. A. Sheridan. London: Penguin.

Leach, J. (2013). "STEM and the Humanities: A False Dichotomy" [2013 Graduate College Distinguished Lecture, University of Illinois], *National Endowment for the Humanities*: http://www.neh.gov/about/chairman/speeches/stem-and-the-humanities-false-dichotomy.

Lovett, P.B., J.M. Buchwald, K. Stürmann, and P. Bijur (2005). "The Vexatious Vital: Neither Clinical Measurements by Nurses nor an Electronic Monitor Provides Accurate Measurements of Respiratory Rate in Triage." *Annals of Emergency Medicine* 45.1: 68–76. [Online: http://www.ncbi.nlm.nih.gov/pubmed/15635313]

Lukács, G. (1974). *Soul and Form*, trans. A. Bostock. Cambridge, MA: MIT Press.

Lyotard, J.-F. (1994). *The Postmodern Condition: A Report on Knowledge*, trans. G. Bennington and B. Massumi. Manchester, UK: Manchester University Press.

McLane, M.N. (2012a). "My Chaucer/Kankedort." In *My Poets*, 7–12. New York: Farrar, Straus, and Giroux.

McLane, Maureen N. (2012b). "My Impasses: On Not Being Able to Read Poetry." In *My Poets*, 13–25. New York: Farrar, Straus, and Giroux.

Meech, S.B. and H.E. Allen, eds. (1940). *The Book of Margery Kempe*. EETS os 212. London: Oxford University Press.

O'Hara, F. (1995). *The Collected Poems of Frank O'Hara*, ed. D. Allen. Berkeley: University of California Press.

Plath, S. (2005). *Ariel: The Restored Edition*. New York: Harper-Collins.

Salecl, R. and S. Žižek (1996). "Introduction." In R. Salecl and S. Žižek, eds., *Gaze and Voice as Love Objects*, 1–4. Durham: Duke University Press.

Sharon-Zisser, S. (2004). "Male Homosexuality in Both Sexes: Freud, Fliess, and Archaic Sexuality." *Gender Forum* 9: http://www.genderforum.org/fileadmin/archiv/genderforum/maleaccounts/zisser.html.

Stevens, M. and A.C. Cawley, eds. (1994). *The Towneley Plays*, Vol. 1. EETS ss 13. Oxford: Oxford University Press.

Wolf M., S. Naftali, R.C. Schroter, and D. Elad (2004). "Air-Conditioning Characteristics of the Human Nose." *The Journal of Laryngology & Otology* 118: 87–92.

4: Life's Reach

Territory, Display, Ekphrasis

Strength issues from the tongue, for death and life depend upon the powers of the tongue, if haply it is aided
by the . . . principles of facial expression and gesture.
                              Geoffrey de Vinsauf, *Poetria Nova*

Sensations arising from the interior of our body are subject to the same metaphoric transformations as are sensations arising from the external world. In this sense we
can speak of a corporeal imagination.
   Arthur Modell, *Imagination and the Meaningful Brain*

Consider the following real-estate advertisement:

Hand craftsmanship is evident throughout this
spacious home, from the steel and glass doors that
frame its ocean views, to the hand hewn hardwood
floors, custom crown mouldings and fine cabi-
netry found in almost every room. The stunning

library, paneled in rich walnut, has a handsome fireplace and built-in entertainment center. Bright and inviting, the gourmet kitchen opens to the ocean view family room with fireplace and breakfast nook. The upstairs master suite, with its oceanside balcony, romantic fireplace and beautifully appointed bath, is truly a private sanctuary. Each of the four additional bedrooms have their own full baths and enjoy either ocean, mountain or garden views. The lovely outside entertaining areas include an extensive seaside terrace as well as more private and intimate patios for the enjoyment of family and friends. This is a unique and very special home in the very best of locations, at the beach in Montecito.[1]

$25,900,000.00

This example of twenty-first century ekphrasis will, I hope, remind us that while ekphrasis is a means of mak-

---

[1] From a local real-estate flyer; see also "New Montecito Sea Meadow Escrow: 1453 Bonnymede Drive," *Santa Barbara Beach Blog*, March 5, 2013: http://santabarbarabeachblog.com/new-montecito-sea-meadow-escrow-1453-bonnymede-drive/.

ing objects sublime, it can for that very reason, in habitats other than *les beaux arts*, sound a fondly domestic note. Action at/from a distance means that the territory is always open to and affected by what exceeds it, and vice-versa. The $26 million home in Montecito—an unincorporated area just south of Santa Barbara—is an extraordinarily luxurious nest, in a temperate and beautiful territory, "unique and very special in the very best of locations." If we were to see this ad while checking out real estate in the Santa Barbara area, we might wish we could afford the place, or feel scorn for its excesses, or envy, or just brush past it, as not in our price range, or having an insufficient number of bedrooms. Probably the ad would not remind us of Achilles' shield. But both the ad and the shield aim for the intensity of becoming produced by the territory's extimacies, by movements or "lines of flight" between the familiar and the unfamiliar, between microcosms and macrocosms.[2] Both shield and advertisement mark and re-mark territory; their allure depends on the extimate plasticity of place, as exemplified by ekphrasis's use of cross-modal experience to show us how we look from the standpoint of the Real. Art renders our ways of living "from the standpoint of the Thing"—that is to say,

---

[2] See Deleuze and Guattari (2001) on "lines of flight" and other remodelings of spatial and temporal difference. The secondary literature on ekphrasis is vast; in medieval studies, see Barbetti (2011), and a new collection on medieval ekphrasis that is forthcoming from Ohio University Press, which draws on papers from the workshop on "Ekphrasis in the Middle Ages," Free University of Berlin, Berlin, Germany, February 2010. The first version of "Life's Reach" was presented on that occasion. Because this chapter explores some of the biosemiotic grounds for the emergence of ekphrastic art, I use the term ekphrasis to designate both "thought" and "unthought" rhetorics of aesthetic description. Some of what I have to say here is relevant also to the trope of *enargeia*. Some important books on ekphrasis include Heffernan ([1993] 2004), Krieger (1992), and Mitchell (1995).

from the standpoint of the embodied/unconscious mind, which must project itself into the aesthetic object or event so that the unthought and unknown living process can be seen and heard.

Achilles' shield, as Bachelard might have put it (1994, 183–211), is an immensifying miniaturization of the territory *left behind but valorized* by the assemblage of peoples (Achaeans, Boeotians, Locrians, Argives, Cretans) consequent on Agammemnon's activation of the war machine. The shield claims Achilles for a singular world and way of life (agrarian, pastoral, tribal), but also indicates the living experience of worldness as such; the shield is beyond-Greek, just as Achilles himself, through fame and name, is beyond-Achilles. The shield protects Achilles from the indignity of exchange by cosmographing the hills and fields, streams and oceans, work and play of a meaningful way of living. Agammemnon's statist concerns are de- and re-territorialized by this brandishing of the extraordinary power of living process and the beauty of the forms it generates. The real estate advertisement, similarly, is for a dwelling of a singular nature, and one that could be "ours," but it also evokes a mode of living that escapes certain boundaries. It might be a signifier of and in a history of becomings. If your grandparents had lived there, and lost it in a long-ago property bust, but you remember, as a child, dancing there on the terrace at night, on the edge of the adult world, in an inimitable frock, the ad would likely pluck at your heartstrings in a highly particular way. But even if our associations derive chiefly from books or classic films, or *Lifestyles of the Rich and Famous,* we can never *not* populate such a place in our imaginations, whatever the ethical import of our projective creations. Like the shield, the advertisement strives for the mesmerizing power of an ekphrastic idyll standing out from the frenzied buying and selling, the never-proper nature of property, given off by the real estate section in the newspaper, just as Achilles' shield stands against the calculations and catastrophes of reasons of state.

The stately home in Montecito really is a gorgeous place. It is an "enriched" environment, one in which creatures might well be expected to thrive. Some would say it bespeaks "inclusive fitness." Most humanists would want to avoid sociobiological overtones and say nothing of the sort. But if you were studying flycatcher birds instead of the relationships between ekphrasis and property, it most likely would not enter your head to question whether a phoebe would prefer living the good life in Montecito to a hardscrabble life in Barstow. Certainly Barstow will have its partisans, its lovers of clear skies and open ranges and Vegas just down the lonesome highway—the western scrub-jay, perhaps. And the mansion in Montecito wouldn't interest everyone. It isn't an exemplar of innovative or provocative design; it's a bit too Carmel. It isn't in New York City. Its carbon footprint would likely be significant even after the green renovations so popular with rich home-owners like George Walker Bush.

But the ad insists that variation—beloved by creatures because of its power to signal and thereby intensify affective change and hence liveliness—is all over the house on Bonnymede Drive: three different views, cooler and warmer airs, stronger and lighter breezes, wild or tame waters, particularized spaces (sanctuaries for denizens, and larger, more public spaces for visitors). The ad is at once a domographing and a cosmographing of sentience, doing its best to evoke the paradoxical boundlessness of privacy and the particularity that positions me so I can see all the way to the horizon at the end of the ocean. It "places" me, and by letting "me" drift out to sea and letting the sea enter me, by turning "me" into my ecology and my ecology into me, it makes living *feel* like living.

The experience of place is always already displaced by expressivity—by the representations that show us where we might or might not live—partly because territory is an *effect* of expressivity: "[E]xpressive qualities or matters of expression enter shifting relations with one another that 'express' the relation of the territory to the interior milieu of impulses and exterior milieu of circumstances" (Deleuze and Guattari 1982, 317). In other words, shifts in expressivity, such as changes in style, are markers of the relation of the territory both to affect, and to history. Ekphrasis de-territorializes; as a shift in expressivity (and one that announces itself as such), it pulls up, and changes, stakes. Experience in and of a place, for most kinds of sentience, means co-constructing and participating in *holistic* ecological change, as James Gibson's theory of "affordances" also suggests, wherein behaviors are tightly linked to perceptions of environmental affordances, perceptions that create the environment as extimate. For example, which affordances are offered by my perceptions of the texture of this or that particular soil? How is the scent of *this* soil "in" my brain, evoking, perhaps even by its absence, the red clay dirt I played in as a child? And how will *that* reminiscence affect what I do with *this* garden?

Thus, the ekphrastic object is always already multiply transformed (into words, from the textured surface of a bronze tablet, where the tablet also testifies to the artfulness of metallurgy, the power of patronage, the "richness" of what lies hidden in the earth, and so on), and sentience is further de-territorialized by means of the enhanced *strangeness* of the ekphrastic object. What are, were, its affordances? It is from a lost past, or made by unknown arts, or cosmographs a world that looks familiar but escapes definition. Ekphrasis evokes "the Natal"—the home that is elsewhere, that must always be "found" again, *as must the new home also be found again*, and again. This is true even when the ekphrastic effect relies primarily on the time it takes to tell the (tale of the) object; the moment of the fashioning of the ekphrastic object itself is always over by the time we learn of it, and hence has the potential to invite or counter trauma. Epic's ekphrasis tends to stop us in the tracks of territorial narrative, of migration or colonization or conquest, to remind us of the putative homeland—the source, the natal place that's always hard to find and/or under construction—by re-animating the object that embodies it. Or it evokes the elsewhere (for *Beowulf*, Heroic Age northern Europe) where home began. The movements of peoples begin so many pre-modern narratives in order to affirm that wherever we came from, it was not where we are now; as creatures, we had, for better or for worse, always to (re)make our place and way of life. The meaning of territory *is* its mobility and expressivity; it is multiply determined by psychical, historical, and territorial affordances.

Marking and unmarking place, de- and re-territorializing, are dynamically interdependent expressive actions. Hiding and showing, finding and being found, are the principal reasons for "display" behavior, spectacular performances of the behavioral phenomenon of "taking one's place," as interpreted by Roger Caillois and linked by Lacan to the mirror stage (Caillois 2003, 89–106; Lacan [2002] 2006, *passim*). We make all kinds of meanings out of the interconnections between subjective, social, and environmental ecologies: the meanings of mining and metallurgy, as noted; ornamentation, anthems, refrains, rituals, the mysteries of transpersonality. Even very simple organisms depend on the recognition and construction of patterns, hence on interpretation; and the boundaries between self and other are always permeable, as studies of immune system activity have shown. Communication—if "only" in the form of "entrainment," chemical or electrical—is a fundamental characteristic of living tissue. "Matter already has meaning; it is already informed, organized" (Goux 1990, 228). The open systematicity of language is a very special way of communicating, but it is, first and foremost, *semiotic*, and is therefore linked to (as well as different from) other forms of semiosis—for example, cellular activity. Biosemioticians disagree as to whether and how biological "code" and information-processing really share *significant* features with combinatorial symbolic systems; Marcello Barbieri has championed code semiotics and Thomas Sebeok and Jesper Hoffmeyer a more continuist zoo-semiotics (Barbieri 2009, 221; Hoffmeyer 2009). There is, however, general agreement that, as Hoffmeyer puts it, "semiosis is a fundamental component of life." "[S]igns and meaning exist in all living systems"; in fact, semiotic activity is the sign of life *par excellence.* The near-ubiquity of learning in living process—one thinks of Eric Kandel's sea snails—would seem to support these principles (Kandel 2006, 145 ff.).

What biosemioticians most want to understand is how language *emerges from* earlier kinds of semiotic activity. But is the question well-phrased? For example, does the deliberate cultivation of techniques of living emerge from the workings of non-conscious *habitus*? Or do both derive independently from the *écriture automatique* of living process? These questions are far from settled. But the tight bond between living process and the arts is, for all the reasons we have already explored (and many more), unchallengeable. Lacan describes ancient cave art as "primitive subsistence viewed from the perspective of the Thing," shorn of goods and the Good, of rational and utilitarian pretensions (Lacan 1997, 140). Language is an expressive biocultural activity, activity that *enhances* living process by showing us how we look from the standpoint of the Real—by revealing to us the real circumstances of mortal creatures, in some kind of barely bearable form. Life as the Greeks once perceived it is represented on Achilles' shield; representation does not obscure existence, but magnifies and re-stylizes it on another level. How does life reach so far? From apparently "functional" behaviors to the ornamentation of everything and the scrutiny and social transmission thereof, all of it diagrammed in and on the (face of the) earth? From existing to meaning-making to the arts, and back again: signs of life and the lives of signs are overdetermined, networked phenomena.

As affirmed on many occasions in this book, surviving and thriving are much more difficult to distinguish than utilitarian thought suggests. Biologists know that lab rats and fish negotiate mazes without need of reward; they enjoy SEEKING for its own sake, just as we do (Panksepp 1998, 24–27). Another example: attachment between parent and offspring is a genetically-encoded survival mechanism for many animals, but because it is *also* an affective and artful intersubjective experience, it can fail. It always takes place through lines of flight: in Plath's "Morning Song," the baby tries her "handful of notes; / The clear vowels rise like balloons" (Plath 2005, 5). No organism can survive without the ability to communicate with and interpret its environment, which means, at minimum, information-processing that is subtle enough to respond to constant change. Even the polishing of style and ethos isn't just about polishing style and ethos; it draws on highly trained visual attention, enhanced connectivity, the capacity to listen to multiple "tracks" all at once, the power to bedazzle or at least persuade the reluctant. It's about real-time, improvisational use of "procedural" knowledge, the knowledge of how to do things *live*. Affective range and intensity, relational talent and meaning-making are crucial aspects of living process. As Ellen Dissanayake puts it, "valued states of mind and body such as self-transcendence, intimacy with our fellows, and making and recognizing [meaning] are needs just as much as more 'vital' needs for food, warmth and rest" (Dissanayake [1988] 2002, 132). "Living," simply, *is* an art. States of mind, in turn, are constitutive of territory, and vice versa. "Territoriality is not [a] property of space, but of the way an animal behaves with respect to space" (Smith 1980, 74). Further, space has its own histories of becoming, which intersect with those of subjectivity and sociality. Territoriality is *praxis* and part of the self-operating systems and field of "life."

Putting the unthought known into words is a line of flight, de- and re-territorializing the perceptions and feelings of embodied minds. It enhances neuronal activity, and thereby sentience, by enabling reflection on, and thus calling attention to, the cross-modal and holistic character of moment-to-moment existence. The house on Bonny-mede Drive is *animated* by ekphrasis. It *shows* itself. Its doors *frame*, its kitchen *opens*, its bedrooms *enjoy*. It is not just shelter, but artful and affective shelter. "Hand craftsmanship" evokes "tactile display"—the feeling of polishing, the satisfaction of fit, the intimate attentiveness of touch. Living people made this house, carefully; my hand might touch what they touch, a feeling that substantiates my imaginative experience of the house, whereby "I" become part of its ecology, aware of fine detail. It is like a gift to me—there is feeling in its bones. And it is various as well as recursive: it can be warm ("handsome fireplaces") and cool ("ocean view"). It "has" magnitude ("almost every room," "extensive seaside terrace") and intimacy ("nook," "private patios"). It can provide exteriority and social assemblage ("lovely outside entertainment areas"), but also the interiority that protects "private ritualizations" and "individual maintenance behaviors" ("beautifully appointed bath"; see Smith 1980, 72, 97, 57; citing Huxley 1966). It shelters but also welcomes inside itself a way of living: denizens snuggle in the library, entertained; close friends and family come for house parties and patio lounging; the terrace can accommodate a small orchestra. The house *is* sociable—it's for social beings, it invites assemblage, people meet there, it is a crossroads of energies. It is also *domus, oikos,* like the intricate cavelike nests built by male bower birds, with front gardens decorated in abstract patterns made of beetle shells, flower petals, colored stones, and now the blue plastic spoons brought near their habitats by tourists.

Display—by definition "any behavior specially adapted 'in physical form or frequency to subserve social functions'"—is always about inviting and rejecting, accepting and declining, showing and hiding (Moynihan 1956, 1960; cited by Smith 1980, 7). The values of expansiveness and intimacy, of deep time and the moment, are implied by ekphrastic form: a whole way and history of living and dying that is also singular. Just so are we asked to hear, see, and feel Heorot, Hrothgar's great hall in *Beowulf*, through anamorphosis, from the standpoint of the Thing.[3] The ekphrastic object is nearly always a relic, living on, undead; we meet it between the two deaths, like Grendels's shoulder, arm and claw, which Beowulf hangs from the ceiling in Heorot.

Ekphrastic advertising is common in the legends of peoples; cross-modality evokes their assemblages and crossings, territorializations and lines of flight. Geoffrey of Monmouth's divine honeybee, the goddess Diana, tells Brutus that "beyond the setting of the sun, past the realms of Gaul, there lies an island in the sea . . . and for your descendants it will be a second Troy" (Geoffrey of Monmouth 1966, 65). According to W.J. Smith, "singing"— meaning the full, complex song, not simpler "calls"— occurs when a bird is at "important sites in a territory," either the margins or the nest site. In fact, Smith refers to this as "advertising behavior," especially evident when the bird seeks a "high perch" and makes himself visually as well as sonorously conspicuous, a "risk" he will take in order to be found (Smith 1980, 53). Song is a means of "seeking opportunities for interaction" (Smith 1980, 66–67).

Vocal display is part of territorial behavior for many species, birds and people in particular; it tells you when and whether another creature wants to "go out" with you, to play, to see and be seen, or to see where the sun sets (the ocean view), or whether said creature would prefer to be left alone ("closed all around by the sea," en-nooked), with or without you. Most calls and gestures signal uncertainty, when things are "up in the air," "in process"; they are questions, requests, demands, descriptions and solicitations of affect. We mark becomings: "I love you and want to be near you, but I don't know how you feel about

---

[3] "I don't believe the lines demarcating hall from hut, tribe from state, or nature from culture, have ever been . . . stable or . . . clearly defined": Joy 2005, 11.

me, so I'm approaching you, but sideways, with my neck bent in a certain way, my gaze oblique, to give you time to signal me back, since I'd rather we didn't fight."[4] (This is a rough paraphrase of penguin courting behavior.)

"Information" about states of mind and how to share them is conveyed when an organism "shows" itself, in space, to the Øther. As Damasio's (and Darwin's) conception of "emotion" suggests, emotion is linked to the exteriority of display and reception. To put it another way, emotion is always a function of relationality and expressivity. The plasticity of skin—but also, if differently, of feathers, fur, scales, shells, or gelatin—is a crucial aspect of that expressivity. "[A]rt [does] not wait for human beings to begin" (Deleuze and Guattari 2001, 320). The membranes that process movements within and between the worlds of our living experience are not obviously primary with respect to the ornamentation or elaboration of those membranes, since membranes are always elaborating themselves (changing color, shedding, scarring, thickening, grimacing, reaching, withdrawing). Expression, reception, incorporation, rejection, *all* make use of skin, vellum, paper, screen. The latter are affordances enabling display or camouflage, and are themselves media, and this is true on non-conscious as well as deliberately artful planes of activity.

Through the refrain, we "go" here and there, in and out, back and forth, in splendor or stealth. Two signs thereof are *amplificatio* and *brevitas*; when we "show what we are," as the God of Love says of Alceste in Chaucer's *Legend of Good Women*, we also come *near*; we merge with, or emerge from, our surround. Alceste becomes daisy, and vice-versa, through a simultaneously clumsy and beautifully-detailed description of her costume (see Fradenburg 2002, 195):

---

[4] "Indecisive and vacillating behavior" and the signaling thereof make up most displays (Smith 1980, 71).

And she was clad in real habit grene.
A fret of gold she hadde next hir heer,
And upon that a whyt corowne she beer
With flourouns smale, and I shal nat lye;
For al the world, ryght as a dayesye
Ycorouned ys with white leves lyte
So were the flowrouns of hire coroune whyte;
For of o perle fyn, oriental.
Hir whyte coroune was y-maked al;
For which the white coroune above the grene,
Made hir lyk a daysie for to sene,
Considered eke hir fret of gold above.
(214–225)[5]

When we turn away, separate, watch boats sail away, lose the light, we close up.[6] There are so many reasons to mark one's position, both within and without the territory one is always becoming in and through, since marking also turns territory into organism. Self- or allo-marking—like rubbing one's scent onto one's favorite tanning rock, or singing one's fate therefrom—also, paradoxically, enables pair bonding and "group identification" or "assembly," or simply "bring[s] individuals together," as Smith puts it (Smith 1980, 254). Thus is the transpersonal field constituted.

Honeybees mark rich foraging sites with glandular secretions and the odors of flowers, so effectively that the social function of the dance of the honeybee has been doubted (Smith 1980, 255). But experiments have shown that honeybees will only find a marked foraging site if, in addition to marking, the scout bees also perform the location dance. Why then do they *"need"* the location dance? Possibly the answer is that they do not—or, again, that a

---

[5] All citations of Chaucer's poetry from Benson's (1987) edition, *The Riverside Chaucer*, by fragment, book, and/or line number.
[6] On the poetics of separation in *The Legend of Good Women*, see Fradenburg (2010).

more nuanced understanding of need is required to go further with this question. *Need is always a function of particular ecologies and their expressivities.* Smith concludes that such performances "solicit" attention and assembly—i.e., "following behavior" (Smith 1980, 125). Like Diana's evocative description of Britain, or the amazing chrono- and cosmographia that leads us to virtual fellowship and pilgrimage in the "General Prologue" to Chaucer's *Canterbury Tales*, and the similarly de-territorializing line of flight at the beginning of the Parson's "Prologue,"[7] the scout bee mobilizes not simply a finding of resources, but a gathering of forces, perhaps even a becoming-swarm. The direction and angle of a honeybee's "waggle runs" indicates how its next flight will be oriented with respect to the sun. "Musical" and physiological factors in the honeybee's dance indicate how difficult it will be to reach the new site, and how rich its affordances. These are mobile solicitations of great precision and grace. Just so, the Parson's "murie tale" will, he hopes, be the one to lead us to our true (new) source, the heavens; and the Miller brings up the rear, with his bagpipes. Singing and dancing, vocalization and gesture, are shifters that mark (be)comings and goings, changes of direction, the work and play of living process.

Art works to "make special," by calling (to) *all* of us— our bodily, affective, cognitive, developmental, intersubjective, transpersonal processes.[8] It does so in order to call

---

[7] "By that the Maunciple hadde his tale al ended, / The sonne fro the south lyne was descended/Degreës nyne and twenty as in highte. . . / Therwith the moones exaltacioun— / I meene Libra—alwey gan ascende / As we were entrying at a thropes ende; / For which oure Hoost, / as he was wont to gye, / As in this caas, oure joly compaignye, / Seyde in this wise: 'Lordynges everichoon, / Now lakketh us no tales mo than oon" (IX.1–16).

[8] "We might . . . start to think of literature in particular, and art in general, as functionally related to human personality development. Might we perhaps take this functionality as a clue to the longevity and persistence of art across millennia of human

our attention to the extraordinariness of everyday living praxis, to the vital importance of forms of living we might otherwise mistake for unchallengeable routine, or leave unthought altogether. Making special also always recursively calls attention to its own role in living praxis. Performing, getting attention, being recognized, are ways of staying alive, psychically as well as otherwise. Chimpanzees "perform displays incorporating bowing, bobbing, crouching, kissing, and hand-offering gestures when soliciting reassurance" that they will not anger their significant others if they come close (Smith 1980, 71). Elaboration draws attention to our affect-states and our location, in hopes of shared (or spared) experience to come. "Behavior selection" messages (what a creature will do and how) "move the communicator through space (locomotion), remove it from danger (escape), or keep it near another individual (association)"; supplemental messages say "how likely the selection is to be performed," and how ("partially or fully, weakly or vigorously, and in what direction") (Smith 1980, 71). Creatures want to know what an approach means and how their approaches will be received by others. They want information about affect. So, location, location, location: affect relocates us in space, invites us to draw near, draws us further away.[9] "Critical distance is not a meter, it is a rhythm"—a rhythm "caught up in a becoming that sweeps up the distances between characters," relationality expressed through expansions and contractions, oscillations and impasses: between two animals "an oscillational constant is established . . . . Or else the animal opens its territory a crack for a partner of the opposite sex; a complex rhythmic character forms through duets, antiphonal or alternating singing, as in the case of African shrikes" (Deleuze and Guattari 2001, 320). Everything in life depends on our understanding of how to manage

---

civilization?" (Mar 2009, 127).

[9] See Panksepp 1998, 18, on the "distinct subcortical emotional entities" of "approach and avoidance."

distance: its proper calibration; our reasons for crossing it (impulse, affect, wish, desire); the question of what lies in the way. The figures of boundary and territory underlie all of these. My concern here is above all for the productive force of these figures.

Embodied creatures always seek the feeling of where they are in relation to where everything else of significance is—the field of others and of the Other.[10] To this end, we are born with proprioceptive capacities, meaning that our neural circuitry is always already complex enough to perceive a body in motion rather than unrelated fragments (arm, eye, knee) randomly arranged. I can, from my earliest moments, organize movements and objects into shapes—faces, bodies, things that come toward me or speed away. A moving body is already an organization of fragments of sensory information about velocity, density, intensity. Art is the way we draw attention to the unthought process of creating patterns out of the overwhelming amounts of information we receive from, and generate, within and without ourselves.

The plasticity of the boundary between self and non-self is crucial to our ability to situate ourselves. Life forms cannot form in the absence of the power to discriminate between self and non-self, which means also the power to renegotiate such discriminations on the spur of the moment.[11] Life begins with the membrane, with the doubled surface of a "sac" capable both of *both* insulations and diffusions; self/non-self discrimination makes cellular life possible, but the "walls" around and within cells must be capable of mediation—of osmosis, chemiosmosis, endos-

---

[10] See Lacan [2002] 2006, 77 on "the question of the signification of space for living organisms."

[11] I agree with Félix Guattari that subjectivity remains an important concept, and can be distinguished from the concept of "the individual." "Singularity" refers to the particularity and unrepeatability of each "terminal" (e.g., an organism) through which forces flow (and are processed and transformed); see, for example, Guattari 2000, 34–35.

mosis and exosmosis. The principle of plasticity extends
from the immune system to the organism's awareness of
"self"; it is why we can take in everything from transplanted organs to (information about) the doings of other
creatures. According to Stern (1985, 100–123), Damasio
(2010, 22–26), and Panksepp (1998), we are born with a
"core-," "proto-," or "primal" self which allows us to engage in interactions with what we know to be others, from
a much earlier time (evolutionary as well as developmental) than we had hitherto suspected.[12] Proprioception allows us to "sense" how we might put *this* and *that*
together in spatial, sonorous, and tactile registers simultaneously. It is a powerful interpreter and processor of
stimuli, and without it we can't imagine a body, let alone
what a body might do, and so it is also critical to the extimacy of display. We display in accordance with our understandings, thought or unthought, about the meanings
of variations in the displays of other creatures—the con-
stancy or inconstancy of an approach, the softness or
harshness of a touch—because display is performativity,
in real time, whose purpose is to present a particular animal (or plant) as *exceptional*—both hetero- and homogenous with respect to its kind. The techniques involved in
constructing display are thus also the means for the creation of intersubjective experience, what Weisel-Barth calls
"contingent responsiveness" and "rhythmic correspondences" (2006, 373). Kernberg puts it succinctly: "[G]rad-
ually evolving definitions of self and others [and the surrounding world]. . . . start out from the perception of
bodily functions, [and] the position of the self in space
and time" (2006, 973). I am, in part, *where* I am—at a
certain angle to the sun, nearer to you than the sea.

The construction of models of self and world depends

---

[12] See Panksepp 1998, 20, on the idea that an "extended neural
entity" he calls the "primal SELF anchors organisms as coherent, feeling creatures with a basic form of self-identity." See also
Ledoux 2002, 12.

on our capacity for cross-modal transfer of sensorial experience (Kernberg 2006, 974). Proprioception and cross-modal transfer are mutually supportive; both refer to automatic, unthought interpretations of sensory and affective information. We are able, from our earliest days, to interpret and associate one sensory modality with another. Babies know that loud sounds go with large gestures; if the sound is low, threat is suggested; if high, maybe there will be celebration. Organic experience is holistic; everything happens at once, given a nanosecond or two. Driving wedges between, for example, visuality and sound, or between material patternings of sensory experience and verbal language, has only limited heuristic value. True, discrimination of this kind enables style and medium to emphasize the tension of organic experience, or to make special a particular sensory experience. But style is the result of interactions and connections between affects and sensory modes; tension and assemblage go hand-in-hand. If, as does contemporary neuroscience, we conceive of the brain's various interpretative and expressive capacities as highly, if not always evenly, networked, we can more readily think *relationality* between vision and language, language and affect, affect and sound.

Visuality's priority over language in infant development is often adduced as the reason for the affective power of the image. Even Kristeva—whose work on "the semiotic" and "the chora" remains, in my view, our single best account of proto-verbal experience—uses this priority to plead against the greedy consumption of images in contemporary society (Kristeva 1997, 3–26).[13] But this developmental supposition requires considerable nuance. Fetuses can taste and smell, and they can also hear; hearing is our first way of "directly" experiencing distant phenomena, hence of "sounding out" space, calibrating position, being some*where*. We are always *in* language, even

---

[13] On the register of the "semiotic," see Kristeva 1984, 25–30, and Kristeva 1980, 271 ff.

before we are born, where "in" refers to the spatiality created by sound prior to image;[14] this is one way of understanding the effectivity of the refrain. Newborns show distinct preferences for their mother's voice and for the music and stories they have listened to *in utero*, especially their mother's voice; as Stern points out, this "requires some level of awareness and representation of vitality forms while still in the womb" (Stern 1985, 104).[15] Babies can identify phonemes and syllables and, long before they can talk, whole words; they read lips, facial expressions, and the "intonational contours" of clauses and sentences; they understand the emotional meaning of concordances and discordances between verbal and paraverbal expression. "By cross-modal perception the infant has, simultaneously, the sound of the syllables of the word and the emotional impact of the intonation, and the visual impact from the emotional facial expression"; the affective memory structures that result constitute the basis of the "primary motivational system" (Kernberg 2006, 973). Our inter- and trans-subjectivity emerges from the exercise of cross-modal capacities in early "proto-conversational" exchange.

Ekphrasis is a "spectacular" version of cross-modal sensory and affective patterning. It finds words for the smell, texture, color, pattern, surround, and temporality of an object. It is a "made-special" version of cross-modal experience, and is therefore a very special bid for (joint) attention, absorption, and contact with other minds: "Listen to me looking at this object"—often an object that itself represents a history of inter- and trans-subjective life, calling attention to the artistry of display. Ekphrasis is watching when the song of the territory is sung, the song of living creatures, their rhythms and intensities, comings, goings, and becomings. Song happens when the

---

[14] Mehler and Dupoux's *What Infants Know* (1994) argues that infants are born into "a world of language."
[15] On vitality forms, see Stern 2010, 3 ff.

organism tries to feel (by expressing to the Øther) the un/thought environmental and psychical forces that flow and change through its singularity; song foregrounds extimacy, whenever location, nearness and distance, hence inter/trans-subjectivity, are exigent.[16] Further, neoteny, the very long period of human infantile dependency on others for physical and psychical survival, astronomically raises the stakes of intersubjective experience for our species.[17] This is where Lacan situates the transformation of need into demand: in our early years, vital needs can only be met by making and meeting (the) demands of others and the Øther, such that relationality trumps and becomes the matrix for all aspects of our experience. As noted, display is the means by which we conduct relationality; display exerts force on the openness of living process to transformation, and makes that forcefulness sublime. Certainly, in ekphrasis, plot is suspended and time gives itself over to a certain contemplation of sentient experience. Art is a means of demanding intense focus, but the effects of such intense attention are transformative; when one sees from the standpoint of the Real, one sees that what and how one sees is contingent, transient, and all the more remarkable for that. We cannot feel directly or consciously the ongoing creativity of visual (or any other kind of) perception; artfulness de-territorializes those embodied, unthought activities. Cross-modal experience "fits" us for attending to the display and interpretation of sensory *assemblages,* and therefore complex behaviors and interactions, long before either locomotion or autonomous self-provisioning are possible.

Mental life is co-created in small packets of interac-

---

[16] For example, when "intersubjective disorientation" and anxiety threaten; when spontaneous, rapid, and flexible group functioning is needed; when self-identity is threatened by trauma (Stern 1985, 110–111).

[17] I am not arguing that this temporality constitutes us as categorically different from other life forms, but it is without doubt a notable characteristic.

tion with other minds; people mind-read, engage in cross-modal matching, and move in temporal coordination as they participate in each other's experience. These intricate sensory and affective assemblages involve many different kinds of processing. We find de-territorializing figures like ekphrasis enchanting because these packets create our minds in the first place. As to the question of why we might, at times, prefer the delights of verbal description of an object to gazing upon or touching the object itself, we could say that intensifying the transformative experience of cross-modality, rather than the experience of an object *infra se*, is the goal (or at least effect) of "making-special," and is the means by which our creatureliness is given to us as thinkable. This is, for example, how we form affect-laden memories (like images of the mother that sustain us through the crises of her absences), and theory of mind: knowledge that others have minds like our own, but yet are not our own. The quality of *assemblage* is crucial to these inventions, and hence to consideration of how and why a striking verbal presentation of a striking object might make a difference, and to what.

In the late 1990s, Wilma Bucci multiplied Freud's "dual code" theory of psychic process[18] by arguing for the existence of "unicodes," fragments, lowest-common-denominator units of encoded somato-affective-sensory experience (Bucci 1997, 156). Unicodes are assembled into concrete images. These images have coherence and unity, but—like dream-images or memory-images—possess no capacity for abstraction or self-organization *infra se*. The third mode of processing is that of language, which works both unicodes and images into narratives, associational sequences, and metaphors (for example, one unicode or image can "stand in for" another) that in turn

---

[18] Freud's theory of the complementarity of unconscious ("primary") and (pre)conscious ("secondary") signifying process is most fully outlined in *The Interpretation of Dreams* (1900), e.g., 587 ff.

lead all the way from somatic experience to abstract conceptualization and back again. The open systematicity of language permits highly creative constructions of meaningfulness, such as pronominal systems that position us with respect to one another in very abstract and flexible ways. (Note that "point-of-view" has considerable biological value.)

Language is not an obstacle to paraverbal experience. On the contrary, it is one of our most powerful means of accessing that experience, because language is not language without prosody and the vital experience encoded therein. It is an open system that can multiply and rework categories and associations just as easily as it can use them to reduce arousal. It is a temporal art that *requires* rhythm and intensity to achieve its aims. And it permits action at a distance. The stylization of vitality works top-down as well as bottom-up; cortical systems reach out to brainstem functions and vice-versa. The biological values of neural processing are maximal integration and resilience. It is always a mistake to de-emphasize the importance of *integrating* language and affect, or cortical and non-cortical functions; the *coordination* of right- and left-brain activity, for example, is crucial to language, because left-brain activity, on its own, cannot construe the social meanings or larger verbal contexts of utterances. "Talk therapy," for example, permits us to assign verbal tags to traumatic experiences, and by doing so (through enhanced hippocampal processing), resituate a hyper-real terrifying impression as a bad memory, but still, as a memory—as "past," as *over.*

As noted above, ekphrasis addresses the temporality of our experience in part by calling attention to the affective value of constructed or "found objects," as well as to the details of their construction. A certain vision once meant enough to someone, some community, somewhere, that care, expense, and attention were lavished in the process of re-presenting it, calling attention to it, "showing" how special it is. The image cannot substitute for the vitality of presence; but when nothing else is left to us, it is precious indeed.[19] When the time-consuming activity of making-special is itself made special by re-registration in another mode, we know that transformation, de-territorialization, has taken place. A certain history of reception is in the making. We also know, because of the detail and labor involved, that the vision or activity in question was and *is* affectively meaningful, twice, now three times, over. Thus ekphrasis multiplies and extends the fascination of joint attention—of reading other minds, sharing their visions and the meanings thereof. It makes spectacular the trans-formative power of transduction and translation. Psycho-analysts might think here of Bion's argument that when mother and infant process "beta" elements (compare with Bucci's "unicodes") into "alpha" elements (usable, con-textualized bits of information about somato-affective states and events), they are "*recasting . . . inter- and intra-psychic elements conjoined.*"[20] Intersubjectivity is *ipso fac-to* a meaning-making process.

Western culture has typically been of two minds about the transformative power of communion and com-munication: it means we are vulnerable and makes us anxious; it means we can share experience and change minds. The context of attachment is crucial here: "active quiet," the periods during which infant and mother com-mune and communicate, is how we learn that we love and are loved in turn. There cannot be a more momentous or vitalizing development. Between mother and baby, facial mirroring and mutual gaze attunement lead to shared states of arousal that are transformed into experiential states of euphoria. Our fascination with reading and "see-ing into" other minds is why ekphrastic temporality lends

---

[19] The (neuronal) experience of creating and giving meaning to such images is just as important to this kind of healing or inte-gration as are the images themselves.

[20] On the transformation of beta into alpha elements, see Bion 1962, 4–5.

itself to attunement, rhythmic exchange, and a focus on meaning to and for the other. We love the feeling of trust that the meanings of our displays will be understood and received well, and returned with interest.

Again, this is a certain history of art appreciation. Awareness of the temporality of attunement is likewise crucial to ekphrasis. Can we attune our powers of reception to the meaning-making of a long-ago and far-away carver of lapis lazuli? Jahan Ramazani cites Freud on the *rarefying,* and hence extra-special-making, power of time: "Limitation in the possibility of an enjoyment raises the value of the enjoyment. . . . A flower that blossoms only for a single night does not seem to us on that account less lovely" (Ramazani 1991, 305–306.) Transience is of course not usually a positive value in medieval culture, and yet its connection to beauty is equally if differently evident in *contemptus mundi, ars moriendi,* poems about the ruins of the work of giants, retractions of light songs that pass "sone as floures fayre" (Chaucer, *Troilus and Criseyde,* V.841).

In arguing *for* the aesthetic power of transience, Freud remarks that, "all [the] beauty and perfection [we create] is determined only by its significance for our own emotional lives[;] it has no need to survive us and is therefore independent of absolute duration" (Freud 1916, 306). Still, we readily turn our love of mind-reading to the reading of past and future minds. Art helps us along by maximizing our experience of affective meaning and consequently enriching our memories. "Making special" generates novel patterns, and therefore intensity, and therefore memorability—the same way affective attunement to display elaborates the infant's experience of the senses, affects, and cognition. Most creatures love variation just as much as they love recognition (we oscillate between neophilia and neophobia). SEEKING is just as powerful a drive as conservation, and the power of change to fascinate us is enhanced by our long training in cross-modal intersubjectivity. Spectacular figuration assists both seeking and the processing of trauma through the generation of novel idioms; describing is renovating, even *renovatio*. As Geoffrey de Vinsauf puts it, metaphor delights because it "fluctuates . . . now here and now there, now near and now far; there is a difference and yet there is a similarity"; metaphor comes "disguised, as if there were no comparison there, but rather some new transformation were being marvelously ingrafted" (de Vinsauf [1967] 2007, 34–36).

The *Poetria Nova's* advice is simple: "be various and yet the same." How do we accomplish this work that sounds so simple? Geoffrey de Vinsauf proposes crossmodal artistry. The rhetorician must "see [to it] that a voice managed discreetly may enter the ears of the hearer and feed his hearing, being seasoned with matched spices of facial expression and gesture" (de Vinsauf [1967] 2007, 36). The ancient arts of rhetoric knew all about integration, force, intensity, rhythm. How do we make something memorable? How do we ensure that our thoughts will stay long enough in the minds of our auditors and readers to influence them? "[A] statement merely hops through the ears if the expression of it be abrupt. . . . retard your tempo, so giving increase of words" (de Vinsauf [1967] 2007, 24). In other words, a question of intersubjectivity: how does one "bind" the mind of another? "More sophisticated than natural order is artistic order, and far preferable, however much permuted the arrangement be," says de Vinsauf; art "transposes," making quick things slow (or, sometimes, slow things quick), in order to *make special*, to get attention, and thereby to secure enduring intersubjective bonds ([1967] 2007, 19). This assurance of receptivity and influence is clearly de Vinsauf's goal: "commit not the management of either pen or tongue to the hands of chance, but let prudent thought . . . discuss long with itself about the theme." That is to say, "retard your tempo" ([1967] 2007, 24): do the same thing with your mind that you hope your auditor will do with your words. Display is expression de-

signed to make things happen; it sees us through uncertainty, especially the uncertainties of reading other
minds. We exaggerate in order to get our experience
across to others.

As is well known, other times and places are the
means whereby Chaucer's narrators typically situate themselves in his dream-worlds. Two of Chaucer's dream visions
use ekphrasis to start off their respective journeys, as if to
say that narrative always resituates us, however temporarily, to uncanny effect; questions of time and place must
arise. Both descriptions are imitations of Virgil's ekphrastic treatment of the return of what might rather be forgotten, when Aeneas encounters, in the *Aeneid*, just before
he resettles in Carthage, visual representations of Troy's
fall and its aftermath. It's hard to imagine a more ekphrastic *ekphrasis*, at least in this sense: is there a more
powerful story about the dying of minds one might like to
have known, even or especially of minds that were, fatally,
disregarded (Cassandra, Andromache), than the story of
Troy's fall? Then it is rendered even more painful by its
re-presentation in Carthaginian pictures, because representation reminds Aeneas that he has not yet lost
enough—now he must face (again) shame as well as grief
and defeat (and finally, in Chaucer's renderings of the
story, ill fame). Chaucer's Trojan ekphrases are several
times removed, in an era, as Sylvia Federico (2003) has
shown, much preoccupied with the idea of Troy's "new"
position—London, Troy Novant—and with the power of
media to generate change. So we should not be too surprised that what will follow Chaucer's reprise of Virgilian
ekphrasis will most likely be an effort to know other
minds, or to revive them, or try to make them speak, as in
the almost comically grotesque inhabiting of Ceys's
corpse at the beginning of *The Book of the Duchess.* The
re-territorialization of Troy's story involves a realignment
of forces at the natal "center," where "everything is decided," and hence where we find a realignment of psychical,

historical, and territorial affordances (Deleuze and Guattari 2001, 319).

The Virgilian ekphrasis in *The Book of the Duchess* moves quickly, by comparison with the infinite detail of the Man in Black's description of Blanche: "For hoolly al the storie of Troye / Was in the glasyng y-wrought thus, / Of Ector and of King Priamus, / . . . / Of Paris, Eleyne, and Lavyne" (326–331). This is *brevitas;* though ekphrasis more typically makes use of amplification, here it has a simplifying and concentrating effect, as if so many long years of siege and battle could be grasped all "wholly" by one mind or work. Concentration and dispatch work together here also in the addition of "Lavyne," a highly economical way to include the *Aeneid*: it's as though the narrator were ready to get out of this installation as quickly as possible. Focus serves the purpose of *taking in* as quickly as one can, but *so as to* move on. In the de- and re-territorializing poetics of *The Book of the Duchess,* moving on (from death to life and life to death, from center to elsewhere and back again) is a vital, if not obvious, choice. And to what do we move on? To the representation of an encounter between two minds. This is where we encounter the lavish display characteristic of ekphrastic positioning, instead of in the description of the visual images of Troy's legend. There has been a shift, from the story of Troy, to the sublime object of courtly love, at a time (the later fourteenth century) when the fragility of the elite was manifest. And another shift, to the plane of elegy, and then to the de-territorialized space of the future.

Lavishing—that is to say, display—will not in the end stop time; the power to manifest and mesmerize *depends* on the temporality and spectacularity of emergence. *Brevitas* then must (and does) return, when the Man in Black exclaims, "She ys ded!" The writing is starting to show up on the wall; everything will shift, to unknown ends. *The Book of the Duchess* uses vitality forms (sudden movement, loud noise, exclamation, animation, conversation) to re/create the experience of transformation and emergence. What the narrator has or has not understood about the Man in Black's display remains inexpressible, and yet the encounter is transformative nonetheless, not because, or not simply because, of the Man in Black's sunkenness in memories, but because he tries to share and thus "relive" them.

Virgilian ekphrasis in *The House of Fame* is similarly funny and sobering. The narrator says that,

> . . . as I romed up and doun,
> I fond that on a wal ther was
> Thus written, on a table of bras:
> 'I wol now singe, if that I can,
> The armes, and al-so the man,
> That first cam, through his destine,
> Fugitif of Troye contree,
> In Itaile, with ful moche pyne,
> Unto the strondes of Lavyne.'
> (141–148)

This is an odd kind of ekphrasis: a verbal composition is given visual and tactile power by means of its re-inscription on a brass tablet. It is a refrain ("[t]he armes, and also the man") that sings of, and *enacts*, destruction, survival, rising from ashes, the mobility of territory. Refrain accompanies and is movement, incorporation of new rhythmic elements, lines of fight and flight; *translatio* is rhythmic change, new (verse) forms, forms of vitality and enervation: "and al-so," "if that I can." The figure travels by means of recursion, reversal, multimodality: the text is itself but also the brass work of art being advertised. Yet the power of display is of and in the moment, and (in a sense) self-consuming—a vulnerability (that of life itself) to expenditure. The song of the territory is set in brass and still never stays the same.

Through the "medievalization" of Dido's story we see Ricardian fantasies of imperial dominion from the standpoint of the Real. The *pietas* of remembering powerful minds and stories is evident, but so are all the pitfalls to which theory of mind is prey. Seductive display can influence the mind as powerfully as supernatural potions and aromas; receptive ears, despite or because of their concentration, can fail completely to hear what most needs to be heard, or what shouldn't be heard, and to see what most needs to be seen. This is the burden of Chaucer's comment on Dido's situation: "by Crist, lo! Thus hit fareth: / 'Hit is not al gold, that glareth'" (*House of Fame*, 271–272). Brevitas again: move on; let's waste no more vital energy on fixation. This is another citation, now of a proverb—a circulating message (which is to say, a message), like the epic itself, but a change from epic's rhythms, desublimating beyond the desublimations common to epic, which focus on its accounting methods—necessary costs, the sacrifice of attachments, none of which mean anything to Dido. The circulation of rumor has already deterritorialized her, put her between the two deaths.

Advertising, broadcasting, seeking, de- and re-territorializing: in the "Legend of Dido," in Chaucer's *Legend of Good Women*, there is an ekphrastic description of Virgil's ekphrasis of the paintings in the "maister temple of the toun" of Carthage, "how Troye and al the lond destroyed was" (1026). This is a description of what Aeneas sees—again, a multi-modality, history decanted into percept—and it prompts another complaint about broadcasting: "Throughout the world our shame is kid so wyde, / Now it is peynted upon every side" (1028–1029). At the swirling center of the forces, everything will be decided not (exclusively) by war on and over the earth, but by the de- and re-territorializing force of splendid display and rhetorical craft. The visual poverty of the ekphrasis itself, however, deserves comment. In Chaucer's Virgilian ekphrases, the narrative pressure of separation, abandonment and falling devours so much time that there is little left for captation and reverie. The attention ekphrasis usually commands is rushed along. Arguably, the *brevitas* of these ekphrases results from Chaucer's focus on broadcasting, on the transmission of messages, the means by which what is fixed in place can travel, enabled either by the speed of verbal communication or the overwhelm of an installation ("upon every side"). Perhaps more care should be taken when we retell old stories, but perhaps we can also understand why sometimes we don't want the stories of other people to dwell in our minds: they can be so painful, and pain plays, ultimately, an unmanageable role in the call to assemblage. Misattunement, rather than attunement, displacement rather than homecoming, guides Chaucer's Virgilian ekphrases.

The concern for media and reputation runs through the *Aeneid* and its *sequelae*; it is among the memes associated with semiotic bridging (translation, display, ekphrastic description; membrane, skin, *communication* "between," and constitutive of, inside and outside, affect and expressivity). The tight bond between skin and language has been argued by Robin Dunbar (1993) in his account of the development of theory of mind. Language, he proposes, is an extension of grooming behavior. It allows us to offer soothing intimacies to more than one individual at a time, or while we are doing other things, like walking or foraging; and it informs us of things happening in our absence, which means that we can "track" our lineages, and acquire "a better knowledge database on a larger social network than any nonhuman primate"—that is to say, larger mental maps of possible alliances and troublespots (Dunbar 1993, 174, 176; see also Slingerland 2009). Whether or not one accepts Dunbar's causal explanations, clearly grooming and gossiping are both effective means of fostering relationality. In fact, the two are "complementary," which should caution us, should we still need reminders, against overemphasizing the differences between language and other forms of embodied communication. Dido's vulnerability to the influence of Cupid's fire and, ultimately, to rumor and storytelling, is mediated by her embrace of Ascanius/Cupid, her "greedy" consumption of his beautifully-described beauty, their proximity, their inter-breathing, the delivery of tender loving bodily care (to both Ascanius and Ascanius/Cupid), the erotic intimacy screened by the god's use of the person of the child, and, set suggestively within this intersubjective context, Aeneas's own story-telling, his retelling of a story the queen already knows. It's all about "tidings," as Chaucer also knew.

In evolutionary as well as personal history, we acquire a vocal tract capable of producing speech at roughly the same time we acquire the neo-cortical capacity for theory of mind. As noted, infant research on cross- or multimodal expressivity demonstrates the complementarity of touch and sound, gesture and symbol: we come into the world ready to *correlate* sounds, images, and textures. The many arguments about whether language has its origins in gesture, or facial expression, or vocal cries, are all too atomistic. Not only is the language of *homo sapiens* "not modality specific," but "primate communication [in general] is inherently multimodal, at both a behavioral and neuronal level" (Slocombe 2011, 5.) Several brain regions are devoted to the *integration* of visual and auditory signals (e.g., the auditory cortex and the superior temporal sulcus). The brain also constantly integrates right- and left-hemisphere language functions—respectively, interpretation of the social and emotional contexts of utterances, and "plain sense," grammar and logic. "Paralanguage"—meaningful shifts in intonation, rhythm, bodily expressivity, and the like—is part of primate multimodality; "[r]ather than representing emotional vestiges that need to be stripped from language in order to expose the fundamental cognitive components, these nonverbal signals are part of an important composite message" (Slocombe 2011, 923). When we add to this already rich picture the ongoing olfactory, chemical and tactile transmissions of affect and meaning that accompany so much primate exchange, the power of grooming and gossip to integrate neuronal functions appears all the more impressive (Brennan 2004, 49, 52). Slocombe concludes "that communicating simultaneously through a range of modalities is the skill that truly occupies the functional niche of primate grooming, and not the cognitive aspect alone" (2011, 923). Language is coeval with the robustness of human intersubjectivity, and can thus be understood as an emergence from care practices in more ways than one; that is, at least in our scientific models, ontogeny recapitulates phylogeny once again. The significance of that recapitulation in this instance is that nature always exceeds itself in its expressivity—in its territorializations, as Deleuze and Guattari would have it; and thus is dispelled our fantasy of being able to strip care down to the level of bare life.

Dunbar's linking of grooming, gossip, and the origins of language and theory of mind is consistent with modes of language acquisition in the human infant. Both grooming and idle talk—"phatic communion," chit-chat—are simultaneously pursued by infants and caregivers during the course of language acquisition and the signification and hence passion of the body.[21] Michael Corballis complains that, "one is hard pressed to find any structural principles common to grooming and human language" (Corballis 1993; cited in Dunbar 1993, 697). But, as noted, in infancy, vocal sounds, facial expressions, and touch are all integrated, particularly in those moments of active quiet or proto-conversation, when infant and caregiver exchange gazes, make faces and coo at each other, talk (on the caregiver's side), babble syllabically (on the baby's side), play peek-a-boo games, and so on. Again, language acquisition is inherently intersubjective, as noted in 1963 by Werner and Kaplan, who proposed that infants were motivated to learn language and representation for social reasons, and that cognitive capacity develops only within the context of social bonds. Call sounds or "grunts" more recently have been seen as "a primary prelinguistic vehi-

---

[21] On the phatic function of language see Jakobson 1998, 15, 36.

cle promoting the onset of language" (McCune 1993; cited in Dunbar 1993, 716). There is significant evidence of grunt intelligibility among primates (e.g., vervet monkeys), and of the coordination of grunting with tongue and lip movements of grooming; McCune notes that, "[i]n adult human conversation gruntlike vocalizations persist and are among the forms that indicate continued attention to the speaker on the part of the listener," thus serving "a 'cohesive' function" (McCune 1993; cited in Dunbar 1993, 716–717).

Dean questions whether gossip could possibly be the "adaptation on which society rests," since "much of the time [social information] "is wrong, sometimes intentionally, possibly leading to violent misunderstanding" (Dean 1993; cited in Dunbar 1993, 700). Dugatkin and Wilson similarly associate gossip with the "confusion" and "anarchy caused by cheaters' use of language" (Dugatkin 1993; cited in Dunbar 1993, 701). Rumor admittedly is short on references and research protocols, but social and affective bonding is probably its most important overall function, not the communication of information *per se*. Proverbs, like "where there's smoke, there's bound to be fire," would seem to promote the suspicion Dean fears: "[a]s has been illustrated in every manifestation of the police state," he continues, "vocal contact can devolve to pure suspicion. Foucault's discussion . . . . [of the] Panopticon . . . is relevant here"; "[i]n situations of decreasing job security we have reason to be suspicious of the large numbers of people with whom we interact daily. . . . In situations where we need to talk yet say nothing, perhaps most of what Dunbar would classify as stress-releasing endearment is simply white noise" (Dean 1993; cited in Dunbar 1993, 700).

But white noise *is* stress-releasing for many people. More importantly, the adage "where there's smoke, there's fire" acknowledges that there is always already a *question* about the validity of gossip. Like Dido, we are well aware of the unreliability of the *content* of "social information" and also of its destructive power. We have infinite cautionary tales about the bad things that happen to us when we take gossip too seriously, or overindulge in its guilty pleasures, and the *Aeneid* is one of them. But gossip creates as well as severs social bonds, regardless of the accuracy of the information conveyed thereby. It is by no means clear that contemporary surveillance techniques alone occupy the functional niche of primate grooming and gossip. Only if we idealize "society" as necessarily and exclusively dependent on accurate social information can we dethrone gossip as the "adaptation on which society rests."

Since Dunbar's 1993 report, there has been extensive research on grooming and its ubiquity among animal species. There are tropical undersea spas territorialized by small fish called cleaner wrasses, who eat parasites and scar tissue off other fish, including large predators who under different circumstances would be eating the wrasses. "[I]n the calming atmosphere of the cleaning station, the wrasses approach the bigger fish without fear, darting around their teeth and even into their gills"—so much so that fish start settling down as soon as they start waiting their turn to be groomed, just as I do when I walk into my hair salon (a well-known site of gossip, idle talk, and grooming, extending from forms of swaddling to scalp massage) (Natterson-Horowitz 2012, 165). "Grooming alters the neurochemistry of our brains. It releases opiates into our bloodstreams. It decreases our blood pressure. It slows our breathing," regardless of whether we are grooming or being groomed (Natterson-Horowitz 2012, 166). Despite the ways in which grooming and gossiping can go wrong—for example, by threatening exclusion and defamation—it is also a powerful antidote to the three most common factors contributing to self-injury: stress, isolation and boredom. When we "reach out and touch someone," we draw on the multimodal capacity that allows us to link touch to voice and communication. This is thriving, and it is part of living process. As the Darwinist Alfred Russel Wallace contended, "the popular idea" of the "struggle for existence" as "entailing misery and pain on the animal world is the very reverse of the truth. What it really brings about, is the maximum of life and the enjoyment of life" (Wallace 1891, 40; cited by Dugatkin, 1997, 7). Creatures do not live bare lives, if they can possibly help it. The concept "bare life" is, as Agamben argues (1995), a political fantasy, related to the figure of "the least body of the condemned man" (Foucault [1977] 1995, 29). It is a means of discipline, and ought to clarify for us the profound deprivation and constraint that putatively *laissez-faire* capitalism of the twenty-first century sort has in mind for us and our fellow creatures. We must continue to prize the freedom to make meaning and beauty, to show ourselves and thereby announce, herald, and insist upon the indisputable fact of our common aliveness.

REFERENCES

Agamben, G. (1995/1998). *Homo Sacer: Sovereign Power and Bare Life*, trans. D. Heller-Roazen. Stanford: Stanford University Press.

Bachelard, G. (1994). *The Poetics of Space*, trans. M. Jolas. Boston: Beacon Press.

Barebetti, C. (2011). *Ekphrastic Medieval Visions: A New Discussion in Interarts Theory*. New York: Palgrave, 2011.

Barbieri, M. (2009). "A Short History of Biosemiotics." *Biosemiotics* 2: 221–245.

Benson, L.D., ed. (1987). *The Riverside Chaucer*, 3rd edn. Boston: Houghton Mifflin.

Bion, W. (1962). *Learning From Experience*. London: Tavistock.

Bollas, C. (1987). *The Shadow of the Object: Psychoanalysis of the Unthought Known*. London: Free Association Press.

Boyd, B. (2009). *On the Origin of Stories: Evolution, Cognition and Fiction*. Cambridge, MA: Harvard University Press.

Brennan, T. (2004). *The Transmission of Affect*. Ithaca: Cornell University Press.

Bucci, W. (1997). "Patterns of Discourse In 'Good' And Trou-
    bled Hours: A Multiple Code Interpretation." *Journal of the
    American Psychoanalytic Association*, 45: 155–187.

Caillois, R. (2003). *The Edge of Surrealism: A Roger Caillois
    Reader*, ed. C. Frank. Durham: Duke University Press.

Damasio, A. (2010). *Self Comes To Mind: Constructing the Con-
    scious Brain*. New York: Pantheon.

De Vinsauf, Geoffrey. *Poetria Nova*. Trans. M.F. Nims. Toron-
    to: Pontifical Institute of Medieval Studies, 1967.

Dean, D. (1993). "Vocal Grooming: Man the Schmoozer." *Be-
    havioral and Brain Sciences* 16.4: 699–700.

Deleuze, G. and F. Guattari (2001). *A Thousand Plateaus: Capi-
    talism and Schizophrenia*, trans. B. Massumi. London: Ath-
    lone.

Dissanayake, E. ([1988] 2002). *What Is Art For?* Seattle: Univer-
    sity of Washington Press.

Dugatkin, L. (1997). *Co-operation Among Animals: An Evolu-
    tionary Perspective*. Oxford: Oxford University Press.

Dugatkin, L. and D. Wilson (1993). "Language and Levels of
    Selection." *Behavioral and Brain Sciences* 16.4: 701.

Dunbar, R.I.M. (1993). "Co-evolution of Neo-cortical Size, Group Size
    and Language in Humans." *Behavioral and Brain Sciences*
    16.4: 681–735.

Dunbar, R.I.M. (2003). "The Social Brain: Mind, Language, and
    Society in Evolutionary Perspective." *Annual Review of An-
    thropology* 32: 163–181.

Federico, S. (2003). *New Troy: Fantasies of Empire in the Late
    Middle Ages*. Minneapolis: University of Minnesota Press.

Foucault, M. ([1977] 1995). *Discipline and Punish: The Birth of
    the Prison*, trans. A. Sheridan. New York: Vintage.

Fradenburg, L.O.A. (2002). *Sacrifice Your Love: Psychoanalysis,
    Historicism, Chaucer*. Minneapolis: University of Minnesota
    Press.

Fradenburg, L.O.A. (2010). "Beauty and Boredom in *The Legend
    of Good Women*." *Exemplaria* 22.1: 65–83.

Freud, S. (1900). *The Interpretation of Dreams*. In *The Standard
    Edition of the Complete Psychological Works of Sigmund
    Freud*, Vol. 4, ed. and trans. J. Strachey. London: Hogarth
    Press.

Freud, S. (1916). "On Transience." In *The Standard Edition of
    the Complete Psychological Works of Sigmund Freud*, Vol.

14, ed. and trans. J. Strachey, 303–307. London: Hogarth Press.

Geoffrey of Monmouth (1966). *The History of the Kings of Britain*, trans. Lewis Thorpe. London: Penguin.

Gibson, J.J. (1977). "Theory of Affordances." In Shaw and Bransford, *Perceiving, Acting and Knowing*, 67–82.

Goux, J.-J. (1990). *Symbolic Economies: After Marx and Freud*. Ithaca: Cornell University Press.

Guattari, F. (2000). *The Three Ecologies*, trans. I. Pindar and P. Sutton. London: Athlone.

Heffernan, J.A.W. ([1993] 2004). *Museum of Words: The Poetics of Ekphrasis from Homer to Ashberry*. Chicago: University of Chicago Press.

Hoffmeyer, J. (2009). *Biosemiotics: An Examination into the Signs of Life and the Life of Signs*. Scranton: University of Scranton Press.

Huxley, J. (1966). "Introduction." In "A Discussion on Ritualization and Behavior in Animals and Man," ed. J. Huxley. *Philosophical Transactions of the Royal Society of Britain*, series B, vol. 251: 249–271.

Jakobson, R. (1998). *On* Language, ed. L. Waugh and M. Monville-Burston. Cambridge, MA: Harvard University Press.

Joy, E.A. (2005). "James W. Earl's *Thinking About Beowulf*: Ten Years Later," *The Heroic Age* 8: http://www.heroicage.org/issues/8/forum.html.

Kandel, E. (2006). *In Search of Memory: The Emergence of a New Science of Mind*. New York: W.W. Norton.

Kernberg, O. (2006). "Identity: Recent Findings and Clinical Implications." *Psychoanalytic Quarterly* 75.4: 969–1004.

Krieger, M. (1992). *Ekphrasis: The Illusion of the Natural Sign*. Baltimore: Johns Hopkins University Press.

Kristeva, J. (1980). *Desire in Language: A Semiotic Approach to Literature and* Art, ed. and trans. L.S. Roudiez. New York: Columbia University Press.

Kristeva, J. (1984). *Revolution in Poetic* Language, ed. and trans. L.S. Roudiez. New York: Columbia University Press.

Kristeva, J. (1997). *New Maladies of the Soul*, trans. R. Guberman. New York: Columbia University Press.

Lacan, J. (1997). *The Ethics of Psychoanalysis, 1959-1960: The Seminar of Jacques Lacan, Book VII*, ed. J.-A. Miller, trans. D. Porter. New York: W.W. Norton.

Lacan, J. ([2002] 2006). "The Mirror Stage as Formative of the *I* Function as Revealed in Psychoanalytic Experience." In Lacan, *Ecrits*, 75–81.

Lacan, J. ([2002] 2006). *Ecrits: A Selection*, trans. B. Fink. New York: W.W. Norton.

Ledoux, J. (2002). *Synaptic Self: How Our Brains Become Who We Are.* Harmondsworth: Penguin Books.

Mar, R.A. et al. (2009). "Effects of Reading on Knowledge, Social Abilities and Selfhood: Theory and Empirical Studies." In Zyngier et al., *Directions in Empirical Literary Studies*, 127–137.

McCune, L. (1993). "A Developmental Look at Grooming, Grunting and Social Cohesion." *Behavioral and Brain Sciences* 16.4: 716–717.

Mehler, J. and E. Dupoux (1994). *What Infants Know: The New Cognitive Science of Early Development.* London: Wiley-Blackwell.

Mitchell, W.J.T. (1995). *Picture Theory: Essays on Verbal and Visual Representation.* Chicago: University of Chicago Press.

Moynihan, M. (1960). "Some Adaptations Which Help to Promote Gregariousness." *Proceedings of the 12th International Ornithological Congress (Helsinki 1958)*: 523–541.

Moynihan, M. (1956). "Notes on the Behavior of Some North American Gulls I: Aerial Hostile Behavior." *Behaviour* 10: 126–178.

Natterson-Horowitz, B. and K. Bowers (2012). *Zoobiquity: What Animals Can Teach Us about Health and the Science of Healing.* New York: Knopf/Borzoi Books.

Nims, M.F., ed. ([1967] 2007). *Poetria Nova of Geoffrey of Vinsauf.* Toronto: Pontifical Institute of Mediaeval Studies.

Panksepp, J. (1998). *Affective Neuroscience: The Foundations of Human and Animal Emotions.* New York: Oxford University Press.

Plath, S. (2005). *Ariel: The Restored Edition.* New York: HarperCollins.

Ramazani, J. (1991). "Freud and Tragic Affect: The Pleasures of Dramatic Pain." *Psychoanalytic Review* 78: 77–101.

Schore, A.N. (1997). "A Century After Freud's Project: Is A Rapprochement Between Psychoanalysis And Neurobiology At Hand?" *Journal of the American Psychoanalytic Association* 45: 807–840.

Shaw, R. and J. Bransford (1977). *Perceiving, Acting and Knowing: Towards an Ecological Psychology*. Hillsdale: Lawrence Erlbaum.

Slingerland, I., et al. (2009). "A Multi-Agent Systems Approach to Gossip and the Evolution of Language." In Taatgen et al., *Proceedings of the 33rd Annual Meeting of the Cognitive Science Society*, 1609–1614.

Slocombe, K. et al. (2011). "The Language Void: The Need for Multimodality in Primate Communication Research." *Animal Behavior* 30: 919–924.

Smith, W.J. (1980). *The Behavior of Communicating: An Ethological Approach*. Cambridge, MA: Harvard University Press.

Stern, D. (1985). *The Interpersonal World of the Infant: A View from Psychoanalysis and Developmental Psychology*. New York: Basic Books.

Stern, D. (2010). *Forms of Vitality: Exploring Dynamic Experience in Psychology and the Arts*. Oxford: Oxford University Press.

Taatgen, N. et al., eds. (2010). *Proceedings of the 33rd Annual Meeting of the Cognitive Science Society*. Amsterdam: Curran Associates.

Wallace, A.R. (1891). *Darwinism*. London: Macmillan.

Weisel-Barth, J. (2006). Review of *Nanopsychaonalysis: The Present Moment in Psychotherapy and Everyday Life* by Daniel N. Stern (New York: Norton, 2004). *International Journal of Psychoanalytic Self Psychology*, 1: 127–132.

Winnicott, D.W. (1971). *Playing and Reality*. London: Tavistock.

Zyngier, S. et al., eds. (2008). *Directions in Empirical Literary Studies: In Honor of Willie Van Peer*. Amsterdam: Benjamins.

Ekphrastic *Beowulf*
Defying Death and Staying Alive
in the Academy

Donna Beth Ellard

As Aranye Fradenburg's chapter "Life's Reach" explains, a real-estate advertisement for a luxury oceanside property in Montecito, California and Achilles' shield are both art objects that reflect in microcosm the whole of an ecosystem's thematic expanse:

> . . . both the ad and the shield aim for the intensity of becoming produced by the territory's extimacies, by movements or "lines of flight" between the familiar and the unfamiliar, between microcosms and macrocosms. Both shield and advertisement mark and re-mark territory; their allure depends on the extimate plasticity of place, as exemplified by ekphrasis's use of cross-modal experience to show us how we look from the standpoint of the Real.

The shield and advertisement's ekphrastic descriptions evoke the inaccessible Natal—as Fradenburg writes, "the home that is elsewhere, that must always be 'found' again"—whether that be Greece's pre-Homeric past or Montecito's unaffordable luxury. What maintains the art object's restive presence in these human domains is not its organic surfaces or tactile accessibility, but rather its depth of involvement in our lives. Indeed, Achilles's shield is the most ornamented piece of a new set of armor that has been crafted for him by Hephaestus, blacksmith to the gods. It could not have been forged at a more opportune time. As Patroclus, his dearest companion, lies dead on the Trojan battlefield in Achilles's own armor, Achilles seethes with rage and is ready to return to the fight. However, as we gaze upon the shield as it is crafted at Hephaestus's forge, its beauty gives us pause, and the *Iliad* interrupts blood-soaked and battle-grim episodes with an ekphrastic description of its finely-hammered surfaces. The shield depicts an else-where home: an agrarian world of cattle and sheep, of ploughing and reaping, that surrounds a City at War and a City at Peace; and at the center of (but also encircling) these pastoral and urban places are images of the earth, sea, sun, moon, and stars. As a vision of the Natal, Achilles's shield cosmographs the open territory of the *Iliad* upon the armor of its heroes. Its displays of Grecian self and world are no mere filigree, but art shaped according to the everyday practices of human living and an object that shapes human living into extraordinary practices. Consequently, the shield's ekphrastic displays are inseparable from its protective function in the ensuing, bloody battle, pointing towards its central role in the messy and uncertain business of the Trojan War. Achilles's shield acknowledges that the circuitry between ornament and weapon—art and object—is no mere feedback loop but a transpersonal field and ever-expanding network of de- and re-territorialization.

Achilles's shield is critical to environments subsequent to the *Iliad* because its ekphrasis, as Fradenburg explains, outlines the potential of all crafted things—especially those that have become relics—to function as inter-subjective messengers across time and space.[1] The sounds, textures, and graphics of art objects are cross-modal gestures that ricochet back to us our own display behaviors, our own territorializing moves, our own invitations to or warnings against another's approach. These gestures are communicative. They invite us to engage with one another by engaging with them. Achilles's shield therefore articulates connections between Olympian gods, Greek heroes, and Trojan enemies. Yet the shield continues to function in post-Hellenic environs because, as Fradenburg writes, "the ekphrastic object is nearly always a relic, living on, undead." Its arts, shaped in a time that is already over, point out "a whole way and history of living and dying that is also singular." Though past, the shield reaches out in iron-forged rhetoric towards the future. It occupies an expressive "spaciousness" and an enduring "nowness" that exceed the borders of the *Iliad*'s narrative frame (Morton 2012, 222). As a description that, Fradenburg writes, "mak[es] quick things slow . . . in order to *make special*," it articulates a *lentissimo* that "get[s] attention" and "thereby secure[s] enduring intersubjective bonds" across other times and places. Achilles's shield bridges the distance travelled from the classical past to the post-human present, as Fradenburg continues, in "an effort to know other minds, or to revive them, or to try to make them speak." In the aftermath of Troy, it reminds us of the home that we have lost and to which we will never return. But it also brings to mind "*the new home* [that must] *also be found again*, and again." For this reason, the shield's singularity invites replication: poets and translators from Virgil to Auden have riffed off its description,[2]

---

[1] On the function of literature as "quasi-object" and its relationship to intersubjectivity, see Joy 2012, 162–166.

[2] See *The Aeneid*, Book XIII, ll. 608–728 (Virgil 1990), and "The Shield of Achilles" (Auden 1991, 596–597).

and artists John Flaxman, Cy Twombly, and a host of engravers have transformed its visual texture into fine art.[3] The ekphrasis of Achilles's shield extends the limits of life's reach. Its form enacts, like language, in Fradenburg's words, an "extension of grooming behavior" that "allows us to offer soothing intimacies" to each other, and it is for this reason that the shield helps to support human practices of living. It measures our ability to thrive and survive in association with our art objects. The shield continuously re- and de-territorializes social networks across past, present, and future in relation to art's expanding frame.

Like Achilles's shield, *Beowulf*'s sword hilt, found by Beowulf in Grendel's mother's cave (its blade having been melted by the "hot" blood of the Grendelkin, after Beowulf has slain them) is a piece of war gear and an ekphrastic art object that traces the complex circuitry between thriving and surviving, then and now. And yet, while both shield and hilt are described according to the rhetorical poeisis of ekphrasis, each has a very different production history: the former belongs to epic heroes, the latter to epic monsters. Achilles's shield undergoes protracted, unwavering depiction as Hephaestus sets to work at his forge. We gaze upon it while it is crafted into shape by the *Iliad*'s Homeric voice and the Greeks' Olympian blacksmith. These mutual processes fashion the shield into an object that encodes affective networks of display behavior in excess of its military use. Consequently, the shield functions as a relic that lives on long after the death of Achilles and the fall of Troy. In *Beowulf*, we are presented only with the remainder of a sword, an antique work that circulated previously among giants and has been 'unforged' after battle with Grendel's mother. The

---

[3] See John Flaxman, "The Shield of Achilles" (1821), The Royal Collection; Cy Twombly, "Fifty Days at Iliam: Shield of Achilles" (1978), Philadelphia Museum of Art; engravings in translations by John Ogilby (1660) and Alexander Pope (1715-20).

hilt, too, is a relic. But it is a relic in ruins. It registers a lost past that promises no hope for survival.

As a ruin, the hilt re-frames the living practices impressed upon Achilles's shield as survivor strategies: hostile tactics for navigating the aftermath of battle. In Heorot, as the hilt's surface flashes glimpses of this inaccessi-inaccessible, monstrous past, these glimpses set in motion refrains that urge non-communication and anti-sociability. As Hrothgar looks upon the hilt after Beowulf returns from the bloody mere, and attempts to offer loving counsel to Beowulf, he imagines, instead, the hero's body as a lifeless form which bears the marks of the poem's vicissitudes of collapse, decay, and loss. In ekphrasis, Beowulf the warr-ior and *Beowulf* the poem function collaboratively as human object and poetic artwork that extend together the hilt's territory of ruin across the outer reaches of Heorot and the many halls in which its story is sung. As relics of a lost past, Beowulf | *Beowulf* recall the Natal, a home in ruins to which Anglo-Saxons turn and Anglo-Saxonists return.

"Life's Reach" is an essay about home, or rather, it is about the affective strategies by which we search, find, but never arrive, at one. Its arguments begin at the front steps of Bonnymede Drive, a property that (I think I can say with some certainty) none of us will ever be able to afford. By starting here, with a home that is undeniably material but forever inaccessible, Fradenburg asks us to think about other less locatable nesting sites. These are domains of feeling, sites of intensities—places that, despite their immateriality, "carry the earth with it" and therefore exert an undeniable gravitational pull (Deleuze and Guattari 2001, 312). The elsewhere of home leads us (as it does Fradenburg) towards the unending process of making a place for ourselves that is here, now, in the company of others. These activities are not exclusively domestic. To the extent that "Life's Reach" is about living, it is also about living in the University, a home that can feel as inaccessible as a luxury estate in Montecito.[4] "Life's Reach" offers theory and praxis for staying alive, personally *and* professionally, by encouraging living practices that double as reading practices.

My response to Fradenburg is therefore a case study in searching out and finding home in proximity to the arguments of "Life's Reach." It begins with a close reading of the sword hilt Beowulf brings to Heorot from the Grendelkin's mere, the runic refrains of which prohibit intersubjectivity within and without the poem. The hilt forecloses Hrothgar's attempts at intimacies with Beowulf, and it spurs a critical bibliography rife with scholarly disagreement. Yet by way of these communicative prohibitions, the hilt draws its audiences together all the more tightly. Its refrains transform Beowulf the warrior into an ekphrastic object, a ruin upon which the poem's entire thematic territory is cross-modally displayed. I want to consider what it means to make a home in *Beowulf*'s ruins, literary forms that can seem to gesture, in the future-facing department of English Studies, in the direction of lifelessness for those who cannot read them. I want to argue that these are risks only if we do not acknowledge *Beowulf*'s ekphrasis, an embodied form that exceeds the outlines of Old English poetry.

* * *

When Beowulf presents Hrothgar the sword hilt that he has brought up from the murky darkness of Grendel's mother's mere, it is described as a diluvian artifact:

---

[4] Bill Readings' 1996 monograph, *The University in Ruins*, and the BABEL Working Group's 2012 conference program, "cruising in the ruins: the question of disciplinarity in the post/medieval university" (http://punctumbooks.com/titles/cruising-in-the-ruins) both serve as an oblique call and response to Fradenburg's chapter. And both also reconsider how we dwell in proximity to university systems that provide increasingly less shelter to their denizens.

Hroðgar maðelode,   hylt sceawode,
ealde lafe.   On ðæm wæs or writen
fyrngewinnes: syðþan flod ofsloh,
gifen geotende   giganta cyn,
frecne geferdon;   Þæt wæs fremde þeod
ecean dryhtne;   him þæs endelean
þurh wæteres wylm   waldend sealde.
Swa wæs on ðæm scennum   sciran goldes
þurh runstafas   rihte gemearcod,
geseted ond gesæd,   hwam þæt sweord geworht,
irena cyst   ærest wære,
wreoþenhilt ond wyrmfah.
(1687–1698b)

Hrothgar spoke, he looked at the hilt, the old heir-
loom, on which was written the origins of former
strife, when the flood—the rushing ocean—destroyed the race of giants. They fared terribly. That
was a people estranged from the eternal Lord; the
Ruler gave them a final retribution for that by
means of the surging of water. So it was on that
metal plate of shining gold marked, set down, and
said in runic [or secret] letters, correctly, for whom [or
by whom] that sword was made, the best of swords
[that] was first made with a twisted hilt and serpentine patterning.[5]

As we know from Beowulf's initial encounter with Grendel's mother, this was an "eald-sweord eotensic" ("an old
sword made or possessed by giants," 1558a) that he found
lying in her mere when his own sword Nægling failed
him. Although marked as a weapon of a bygone era, this
"eald-sweord" still proves to be of critical importance.
With it, Beowulf kills Grendel's mother and decapitates
Grendel. Afterwards, the blade melts mysteriously, leav-

---

[5] All quotes are from Fulk et al.'s (2008) edition of *Klaeber's
Beowulf*, by line number. All translations are my own.

ing only the hilt, now a ruined artifact of past battles.

As the remainder of a sword forged among giants and unforged among Grendelkin, the hilt is attuned to monstrous intersubjectivities and mythological strife. The written, spoken, and tactile displays that run across its metallic surfaces mark the hilt as a site of ruin. Upon it is "written" the story of the Flood, which the poem characterizes as "the origins of former strife" ("on ðæm wæs or written / fyrngewinnes"). Allen Frantzen points out that "this is the only story in *Beowulf* transmitted in written rather than oral form," and, in evaluating the etymology of "writan," Frantzen points out its associations with cutting and carving, arguing that the sword is "a text [that] has therefore already been 'cut through': a 'pen' (and engraving instrument) has written on the sword, cutting through the metal to create a text" (Frantzen 1990, 186–187). What inscription, though, is actually recorded? What text might actually be read? Despite the poem's claim to a written account of the Flood, the hilt's markings belie its ties to a historically-documented past. Upon its surfaces are inscribed "runstafas," or "secret letters," that identify the sword's craftsman or owner,[6] but which dematerialize in front of our eyes, fading from characters "marked" and "set down" into the hilt's metal plates to those "said" by voice: ("gemearcod, / geseted ond gesæd / hwam þæt sweord geworht"). These slippages from written to spoken modes confuse rather than clarify, problematizing further the hilt's communicative potential. Its tactile displays are no more reliable. Golden plates ("ðæm scennum sciran goldes"), twisted sides ("wreoþenhilt"), and serpentine patterning ("wyrmfah") invite us to touch its material topographies and to look longingly at its ancient craftwork, but they contribute no further to explaining its history.

---

[6] "Hwam" is a dative, which affords the translation of both "for whom" and "by whom." See Klaeber 2008, 213n1696[b] on the likelihood of a dative of personal agency in relation to this passage.

As a memorial to the Flood, the sword hilt amplifies the communicative impasse that arises from permanent estrangement from God. Its "runstafas," which identify those who are left, broadcast a repeated and urgent message of survival in modes that fade into silence. Although correctly "gemearcod, geseted ond gesæd," this secret sign will never be received because it circulates among those banished from God's sight, thought to be dead, and therefore shut out from the living. As the hilt provides no communicative recourse, the blade functions as an alternative messenger. However, it announces postdiluvian survival by way of violent gestures that dispatch psychic misattunement, intersubjective failure, and anti-sociability. Among giants and Grendelkin, this sword practices living by way of another's dying. It proclaims, "I am still here; you are no longer." In Heorot, the hilt's metalwork artfully signals this refrain. Its cross-modal displays invite us to engage with it after our own battles are over—now that we have survived and can celebrate living together. Still, there is danger in approaching what was once a sword. Although its weaponry can no longer hurt us, its arts can return us to the fight. The hilt's cryptic messages are bellicose gestures that draw us into its ruined and ruinous territory: a site of failed transmission; an affective *domus* that marks life as death; a postdiluvian ecology incompatible with that of Heorot, a "home" (supposedly) of capacious sociability.

Hrothgar's sermon proceeds, syntactically, from its exphrastic refrains—"*Then* the wise one, the son of Half-dane, spoke. All were silent" ("þa se wisa spræc / sunu Healfdenes—swigedon ealle," 1698b–1699b)—and an entire community stands hushed and at attention. Hrothgar sets out to advise Beowulf on how to live as a comfort, consultation, and courage to his people ("to frofre," 1707b), but his mind wanders into the hilt's territory of ruin. Hrothgar turns to recalling Heremod, a Danish king whose appetite for violence brought about the persecution of his own subjects and, in the end, led to his own suffering. Then, he describes an unwise man who, because of his wealth and prosperity, falsely believed that tragedy would never befall him. Rather than sharing his fortune, he hoards it only to be killed in the night by a spectral slayer. In contemplating the lives of both figures, Hrothgar emphasizes that problems in one's own mind lead ultimately to problems in one's own body. In failing to attune themselves to the cross-modal displays of others, both men neither thrive, nor live.

The stories of Heremod and the unwise man draw Hrothgar's mind into intimacy with Beowulf's body. They anticipate an "active quiet" that would allow for the expressive cultivation of love, trust, and mutual understanding between an old king and his young hero. However, as a narrative re-territorialized according to the hilt's refrains, Hrothgar imagines Beowulf's human form in ruins:

> Nu is þines mægnes blæd
> ane hwile;   eft sona bið
> þæt þec adl oððe ecg   eafoþes getwæfeð,
> oððe fyres feng,   oððe flodes wylm,
> oððe gripe meces,   oððe gares fliht,
> oððe atol yldo;   oððe eagena bearhtm
> forsiteð ond forsworceð;   semninga bið
> þæt ðec, dryhtguma,   deað oferswyðeð.
> (1761b–1769)

> Now is the glory of your power but a little while; presently in turn it will be that disease or the sword will deprive you of strength, or the grip of the fire or the surging of a wave, or attack of a sword or the flight of a spear, or terrible old age; or the brightness of your eyes will fail and become dim. Suddenly, death will overpower you, warrior.

Hrothgar's timing is purposefully overstated; it is simultaneously now ("nu"), for a little while ("ane while"), presently, in turn ("eft sona"), and all of a sudden ("semninga"). Hrothgar suspends the presentness of this moment by weaving together half-lines in quick succession with the conjunction, "oððe," a move that acknowledges that the duration of the phrase is the time it takes for an intersubjective exchange between two people to occur (Stern 2012, 42). The formal structures of Hrothgar's language point towards the potentiality of a shared experience that could happen between himself and Beowulf. Yet, its content does not encourage such an exchange. Hrothgar imagines Beowulf's body as a field upon which natural disasters continuously, ekphrastically, erupt. Hostile enemies, sickness, and infirmity encroach upon the safe borders of Beowulf's form, serially, simultaneously, and cross-modally. The fire's grip, the wave's surge, the sword's attack, and the spear's flight enact a catalogue of protracted physical trauma. Beowulf does not make gestures himself but is a rhetorical palette upon which others gesture. The extent of the hilt's de- and re-territorializing powers are revealed in this moment. From the depths of the mythic past, the non-communicative displays of this monstrous remnant of a sword have sounded out a refrain of immense social dysfunction. They re-route Hrothgar's singular attempts at intimacy as a poetic form that kills by putting, according to Fradenburg, "*this* and *that* [disaster] together in spatial, sonorous, and tactile registers." Rather than signaling an opening between minds, Hrothgar's ekphrasis envisions Beowulf as an art object that, like the hilt, has been monstrously transformed into a site of ruin. It articulates the limits of death's throes rather than life's reach.

The hilt remains relevant not only to Hrothgar and his audience at Heorot, but moreover to Anglo-Saxonists, who continue to give it pride of place in *Beowulf* criticism. Because of its status as an "eotensic" sword ("belonging to giants"), many discussions consider the giants of Genesis, Anglo-Saxon folklore, or Norse myth (see, for example, Bandy 1973, 240; Melinkoff 1980, 184; Clemoes 1995, 28n59; Taylor 1998, 123–137), and disagreement emerges as to whether the hilt signals their complete destruction by flood or affords the possibility of survival (Frantzen 1990, 188). The hilt's "runstafas" solicit a further array of possible messages ranging from Heremod's name to a Hebrew inscription (Köberl 1978, 122; Schrader 1993, 141–147); and they point the way towards artifactual analogues. Parsing the hilt's markings has frayed rather than consolidated scholarly opinion, and other Anglo-Saxonists have chosen to wrestle with its textual ambiguities rather than explain them: some argue that they articulate a moment in which the oral poem asserts a textual (or visual) mode (see, for example, Frantzen, 1990, 187; Near 1993, 324; cf. McNelis 1996, 175–185); others emphasize the flexibility of the hilt as a sign meant for open-ended reading (Overing 1990, 61; Lerer 2006, 589; Christie 2012, 288). Despite these interpretative differences, scholars agree that the hilt (re)directs Hrothgar's subsequent narrative. Mary Carruthers (2004, 204) calls it the "inventional, ordering instrument" from which Hrothgar's meditation proceeds, and Sean Pollack (2011, 135) notes that its "wyrmfah" pattern "offers a kind of ironic prophecy of Beowulf's eventual doom" in his fight with the dragon.[7]

I bring up the reception history of the hilt and its relationship to Hrothgar's sermon not to deride or invalidate any of the aforementioned individual discussions, but rather to point out that as a body of scholarship, they are also caught up in the hilt's refrains. Just as Hrothgar and the audience at Heorot are mesmerized by its diluvian story and runic script, critics continue to circle around and gaze across the hilt's artful topographies in order to speculate upon its meaning and significance. These conversations lead to an array of interpretations, but few that agree, and these disagreements highlight methodological differences in Anglo-Saxon studies among its philologists, his-

---

[7] On the question of Hrothgar's ability to read the hilt, compare, for example, Gwara 2008, 182–184 and Osborn 1978, 978.

toricists, materialists, and post-structuralists. One could say that the hilt facilitates scholarly misattunement, communicative impasse, and critical anti-sociability among its academic readers that is similar in kind to that of Hrothgar and Beowulf, but far less deadly in degree. Because the hilt's broken arts have maintained its critics. From its displays have emerged some of the most meth-odologically rich and theoretically variegated streams of *Beowulf* scholarship. Together, they de- and re-terri-torialize the poem, continuously expanding the entwined territory of its arts and the criticism upon those arts.

* * *

While ekphrasis forecasts Beowulf's human death, it quickens his objectal form. Beowulf's body emerges from the stories of Heremod and the unwise man as a disaster-ridden outline that endures, without resistance, a cata-logue of destructive scenarios. Beowulf is suspended be-tween the forces of fire and wave, sword and spear. "It" acquires dimension with each poetic turn. The words "oððe . . . oððe . . . oððe" become a delicate refrain that invite tragedy. Like the hilt, Beowulf is transformed into an art object that has been ruined in its production pro-cess. His warrior's body has been similarly unforged. In ekphrasis, Beowulf is a relic that has become, as Fraden-burg writes, "embellished and artful," restively alive, in death.

The intersubjective experience foreclosed to Hrothgar and Beowulf is sacrificial, so to speak, in that it allows for a greater, expanding intersubjective engagement between all those who gaze upon Beowulf's ruined and reliquary body. Beowulf is shaped according to Hrothgar's lan-guage. It is ekphrastic: a translation, a creative and partial form—an *objet a*—that emerges according to the rhetori-cal operations that express Hrothgar's maladapted desire for intersubjectivity. In ekphrasis, the partial descriptions, creative acts, and unfulfilled desires of Hrothgar are shaped into cross-modal displays that signal a joint endeavor between poetic form and polyamorous desire, changing the world each time we notice it. In ekphrasis, Beowulf circulates in the protracted present: from death to life, from center to elsewhere, in a constant motion that travels ceaselessly between then and now. As a form on the move, Beowulf seeks interactions. It solicits an intersubjective encounter by way of its embodied poiesis. For this reason, his body is an active mediator, a rhetorical agent, or actant, that is "*in the world*" as a "constructer of intersubjectivity" (Joy 2012, 164–165). As we attune our minds to the elaborate refrains that penetrate Beowulf's dying body, they de- and re-territorialize it, generating social associations and a capacious intersubjectivity—a sensuous, felt experience of being together—between the dead and the living who encounter *Beowulf*.[8] Beowulf, the hero and the poem, become, as Fradenburg would say, a twinned site of "shared (or spared) experiences," felt encounters with what it means to be human, frail and vulnerable. As Hrothgar concludes, "deað oferswyðeð" ("death overtakes") all of us, even the most hearty of warriors, and although I will most likely never suffer the battlefield injuries of Beowulf nor the medical conditions of Anglo-Saxon listeners, my body will, nevertheless, fall victim to disease, violence, or the debilitations of old age. It will, one day, be a territory of *and* in ruin. Beowulf's ekphrastic displays show me not only the interdependency of arts and lives that happen to co-exist in the same historical moment, but it also expands that moment into a transtemporal, intersubjective experience between Hrothgar, the audience at Heorot, the poem's Anglo-Saxon listeners, and myself, an Anglo-Saxonist.

Beowulf's refrains communicate more than simply the melancholia of human mortality. Like Achilles's shield,

---

[8] Here, Fradenburg's arguments keep company with those of the New Materialists. See especially Latour (2007), Morton (2012), Bryant (2011), and Harman (2007).

his body evokes the Natal: an illusive, singular ground; an unknown homeland that we seek out, find, and return to again and again. Specifically, the "home" that Beowulf embodies is not Germania (although that is its associated geography) but the felt ecology of a lost heroic age. Like the poem, his human form is a monument that stands in ruins, "haunted by images of destruction and forgetting, of the difficulty of preserving and comprehending the past, and the disruptive and violent potential of memory" (Liuzza 2006, 97). As a haunting presence, Beowulf the hero enjoins *Beowulf* the poem as an open territory that invites trauma, the repetitive compulsions of which herald the poem's many, many translations and popular spin-offs. Robert Zemenkis's cinematic adaptation articulates succinctly the centripetal force of such an invitation when Beowulf presents an enemy soldier with the challenge, "You can't kill me, I'm already dead" (*Beowulf* 2007).

Whether announced by Hrothgar's sermon or in his own voice, Beowulf's vocal displays are a mourning song, a refrain that marks the way towards the heroic homeland from whence we came and where we are no longer. In marking, however, Beowulf's language also solicits us to engage in (im)mortal combat. In this way, it signals possibilities for going forth, together, depending upon where we stand here and now in traumatic proximity to the elsewhere of home. James Earl expresses these calls to sociability when he writes that the poem's "system of relations—of us to *Beowulf*, of *Beowulf* to the Anglo-Saxons, and of the Anglo-Saxons to us—constitutes the meaning of "*Beowulf*" (Earl 2006, 265). And Mary Kate Hurley sums things up precisely when she argues that *Beowulf* is "a *living* poem" because it is more than a poem. It is a "story" and a "performance" that "build[s] a future from the remains of a past . . . Beowulf—in a poem, a play, an opera or a movie—continues to live only so long as the tales goes on, enlarging the 'we' who have heard" (Hurley 2010, §24, §23). Such is the re-homing power of *Beowulf*.

As an ekphrastic literary form, it performs. It displays itself cross-modally in print, on stage, in music, and on film. Beowulf gets our attention, makes us pause, and invites us to join with it as we head towards a home that is always lost and therefore always becoming something more.

* * *

As a poem that is "liquid and supple" (Joy and Ramsey 2006, xl), *Beowulf* has always been that ruin to which Anglo-Saxon scholars turn when we need to make a new place for ourselves in the company of English Studies. Whether we engage with it as philologists, historicists, or critical theorists, the poem is a relic that keeps its Anglo-Saxonists alive. It maintains our active communications within the discipline's critical networks, and it permits discussions between Anglo-Saxonists and other fields and sub-fields. Yet, as *Beowulf*'s forms—its alliterative poetics, its manuscript context, and its attendant Anglo-Saxon milieu—become unreadable to all but a handful of scholars, Old English can feel like the "runstafas" on the sword hilt: arts that are no longer communicative. And as job postings in early medieval fields dwindle, we, Anglo-Saxon scholars, can feel like postdiluvian survivors who cry out into an academic universe that thinks we are no longer relevant, or even present. In the world of popular culture, there is no question of Beowulf's survival skills, but within the Academy the future of its critics appears not so certain. (I note briefly the MLA Executive Committee's 2013 suggestion that its Old English, Middle English, and Chaucer divisions be consolidated into one "medieval" category.) Despite alarming institutional moves,[9] I join with many others in believing that there is cause for real con-

---

[9] The precarious status of medieval literatures in language departments reflects, in miniature, Fradenburg's assessment of the humanities' position vis-à-vis the Academy at large.

cern only if we perceive Old English as a dead language; if we understand its poetics as disembodied forms;[10] if we claim the Anglo-Saxon past as a territory of boundaries fixed by periodization rather than of refrains that ripple through time and space.[11]

When we pause and consider the ekphrasis of *Beowulf*'s sword hilt and Beowulf's dying body, we allow their poetic forms to reach out in rhetoric towards us, and we respond *en face* to those who sit nearby: around a seminar table, at a conference, in our office hours. Yet, we also

---

[10] I point to a forum called "State of the Field of Anglo-Saxon Studies," which appeared in a 2008 issue of the open-access journal, *The Heroic Age* (http://www.heroicage.org/issues/11/foruma.php). All participants identify that the health of the field hinges on the question of communication, and Richard Scott Nokes (2008, §41) writes, "There is enough blame for us all to share for the segregation of Anglo-Saxon studies, but the result is very little conversation going on between Anglo-Saxonists and non-medievalists" because, as he states earlier in a post on his weblog, "20th Century Americanists can read and understand the work of 18th [sic] British scholars, who can read and understand the work of film scholars, but unless they can read Old English or Old Norse, or medieval Latin, or Old Whatever, *there will always be a barrier between us and them. We can understand them, but they can't understand us*" (Nokes 2007, my italics). Nokes advocates, as do co-respondents, Michael Drout and Tom Shippey, that reviving Old English might be effected by turning English departments towards a shared goal of language study. Yet, despite Nokes' lexicon of "conversation," "read[ing]," and "understand[ing]," these urgent cries for literary companionship are inevitably foreclosed as he points out the territorial boundaries: the linguistic "self-segregation" and "barriers" that keep Anglo-Saxonists in the ghetto and at arm's reach from their institutional Others. For Nokes, Anglo-Saxon Studies, like *Beowulf*, is a field that has built its home in the ruins of dead languages. He cannot see a way forward past the linguistic gates that separate it from the Englishes of later periods and their literary scholars because, as Eileen Joy (2008) points out, he does not situate language in the body.

[11] See Davis (2010).

recognize their status as reliquary objects that reach outside of rhetoric, reforming themselves in "stories" and "performances" that exceed the linguistic, literary, and temporal contours of Old English poetry. In ekphrasis, we concede that the hilt and hero are conceptual forms that take on many different shapes, only one of which is found in *Beowulf*. Making a home in *Beowulf* and living among its ruined and ruinous forms is therefore a question of companionablity. Which of its forms do we want to include or exclude? As Fradenburg writes in "Driving Education": "we should, more than ever, understand that *everything* becomes part of our work, one way or another, and therefore *it must always be a deliberate part of our work not simply to think critically about the workings of our own (embodied) minds, but also to reflect upon, and engage, our connectedness to wider communities, because they are always in our work*" (her emphasis). For Anglo-Saxon studies, Fradenburg's statement means that "part of our work" about *Beowulf*—in both our teaching and our research—must be to "reflect upon and engage" those "wider communities" that invest in its more contemporary forms. This requires an embrace of the popular, the non-poetic, and the medieval "-isms" that are often referenced with an undue amount of eye-rolling and heavy sighs by some scholars who don't deem these sorts of reflections as "serious" work. It means de-periodizing our field and perhaps turning away from the appellation, "Anglo-Saxon." Because these O/other *B/beowulf*s are "always in our work" whether we admit it or not. For non-Anglo-Saxonists, and especially non-medievalists, Fradenburg's call for interconnectedness means something much more demanding—for example, that Old English be re-integrated into English departments as one non-precedential version of an ever-changing language and its ever-recursive literature. And that *Beowulf* be taught by non-specialists as a poem valued not as a first, and therefore *reliquary* appendage of a literary past, but as an art object of shimmering vibrancy that vaults towards the future, inflecting the voices of poets and critics, then and now.

In my mind, *Beowulf* is a land bridge between continents divided by literary period and linguistic coding. Like the hilt, Beowulf's mortal and frail form serve as a meta-critical touchstone for articulating how many of us across the humanities feel about the health of our profession. Consequently, I believe that *Beowulf* (and moreover, Anglo-Saxon studies) can help us perform the self-critical "work" that Fradenburg charges us to do if we are to stay alive in the Academy. My field's devotion to elegy, its nostalgia for ruins and remnants, its investment in the gnomic, the runic, and the riddlic—in this academic moment, these professional arts can help us *feel* the ecology of risk. They can serve as a poetic looking glass through which we pass in order to make a new place for ourselves, together, in the Academy. In so doing, we as a profession de- and re-territorialize the time zones that separate literary fields and remap the past as present.

* * *

"Life's Reach" underscores ekphrasis as a poetic form that is keyed to human performance. It shows us how others "commune and communicate" so that we might "learn that we love and are loved in turn." Communion and communication are, in many ways, implicit pursuits of formalism, a way of reading that couples the pleasures of literary aesthetics with the enjoyment of another's company. Like ekphrasis, formalism advocates that we take a long and lingering pause in front of a poem's spacious rhetorical structures. It acknowledges a poem's nowness in our critical habits of writing in the present indicative. It attends to the artful, reliquary status of rhetoric, of a poem and of its criticism. Moreover, we maintain these habits of reading and writing with the desire that a poem's form and our scholarship about it will keep us in the company of others. For this reason, I believe, formalism, or close reading, remains the dominant method of teaching undergraduates how to evaluate a poem despite the fact that it often feels eclipsed by other critical methodologies.[12] In short, formalism is ekphrastic.

To write such a literary criticism is to write ekphrastic scholarship.[13] It is to be more mindful of the artful ties that bind literature to literary criticism. It employs the arts—forces that collapse, interrupt and forestall human narratives—in order to rekindle intimate social bonds and also understanding between scholars past, present, and future. Ekphrastic scholarship joins together a researcher and a research community via an acknowledgement of shared description, desire, and sociability. It is the act of reflecting upon moments of individual vulnerability, mutual co-operation, and uninhibited expression, to name only a few of its modalities. It is a *post-factum* narrative that recounts one's scholarly self in kindred spirit with others and, in so doing, asks implicitly how the production of knowledge facilitates togetherness. Ekphrastic scholarship reminds us that the role of research is not to exclude ourselves from the communities we live and work in, but to more fully integrate ourselves within them. A much more capacious definition of living emerges here, one that draws no distinctions between academic work and life, academic works and lives.

---

[12] Which is not to say that some are not attempting to re-value "close reading" via critical movements such as the so-called "descriptive turn" and "new sociology": see Best and Marcus (2009), Dosse (1999), and Love (2010).

[13] A discussion about the role of ekphrasis in academic criticism has been circulating periodically for several decades within art history, a field dedicated to the study of objects and their forms. See Fort (1996), Wagner (1996), Elsner (2006), and Elsner (2010). According to Elsner, scholarly desire for intersubjective communion is located at the heart of art history, and ekphrasis joins scholars of its philosophical past to those of its professional present in one extended conversation of transtemporal intimacy.

Fradenburg's chapter "Life's Reach" advocates and enacts this. As a sustained, theoretical meditation on ekphrasis that extends its arguments from the cross-modal arts of both the house on Bonnymede Drive and Achilles's shield towards the proprioceptive activities of intersubjective living, its writing "'places' me, and by letting 'me' drift out to sea and letting the sea enter me, by turning 'me' into my ecology and my ecology into me, it makes living *feel* like living." Fradenburg's arguments are intellectually rigorous, but they persuade by way of descriptive, creative, and (at times) poetic language that communicates its points frequently by cross-modal displays of crafted logic. Fradenburg's chapter has the same mesmerizing power of the house on Bonnymede Drive and Achilles's shield, her art objects of inquiry. It makes me pause, feel, and consider my own "intensity of becoming" in the plastic spaces of its criticism. Its argumentative turns make me consider the relationship not just between art and living, but moreover, the extent to which these theoretical lines of flight extend towards and away from my own cross-modal displays and my own intersubjective processes. In so doing, I recognize myself, simultaneously, as a scholar living in the Academy and a person living in the world. And so, I navigate myself, with Beowulf, towards (and away from) "home."

*Research for this chapter was assisted by a New Faculty Fellows award from the American Council of Learned Societies, funded by The Andrew Mellon Foundation.

References

Auden, W.H. (1990). *Auden: Selected Poems*, ed. E. Mendelson. New York: Vintage.

Bandy, S. (1973). "Cain, Grendel, and the Giants of Beowulf." *Papers on Language and Literature* 9: 235–249.

Beowulf (2007). Dir. R. Zemenkis. Sony Pictures.

Best, S. and S. Marcus (1999). "Surface Reading: An Introduction." *Representations* 108.1: 1–21.

Bryant, L. (2011). *The Democracy of Objects*. Ann Arbor: Open Humanities Press, http://quod.lib.umich.edu/o/ohp/975013 4.0001.001.

Carruthers, M. (2004). *The Craft of Thought: Meditation, Rhetoric, and the Making of Images, 400-1200*. Cambridge, UK: Cambridge University Press.

Christie, E.J. (2012). "Writing." In J. Stodnick and R.R. Trilling, eds., *A Handbook of Anglo-Saxon Studies*, 281–294. Oxford: Wiley-Blackwell.

Clemoes, P. (1995). *Interactions of Thought and Language in Old English Poetry*. Cambridge, UK: Cambridge University Press.

Davis, K. (2010). "Periodization and the matter of precedent." *postmedieval*.1.3: 354–360.

Dosse, F. (1995). *Empire of Meaning: The Humanization of the Social Sciences*, trans. H. Melehy. Minneapolis: University of Minnesota Press.

Earl, J. (2006). "*Beowulf* and the Origins of Civilization." In E.A. Joy and M.K. Ramsey, eds., *The Postmodern Beowulf: A Critical Casebook*, 259–286. Morgantown: West Virginia University Press.

Elsner, J. (2006). "From Empirical Evidence to the Big Picture: Some Reflections on Riegl's Concept of Kunstwollen." *Critical Inquiry* 32.4: 741–766.

Elsner, J. (2010). "Art History as Ekphrasis." *Art History* 33.1: 10–27.

Fort, B. (1996). "Ekphrasis as Art Criticism: Diderot and Fragonard's 'Coresus and Callirhoe'." In P. Wagner, ed., *Icons, Texts, Iconotexts: Essays on Ekphrasis and Intermediality*, 58–77. Berlin: Walter de Gruyter & Co.

Frantzen, A.J. (1990). *Desire for Origins: New Language, Old English, and Teaching the Tradition*. New Brunswick: Rutgers University Press.

Harman, G. (2007). "On Vicarious Causation." *Collapse* 2: 187–221.

Hurley, M.K. (2010). "The Ruins of the Past: *Beowulf* and Bethlehem Steel." *The Heroic Age* 13: http://www.heroicage.org /issues/13/ba.php.

Gwara, S. (2008). *Heroic Identity in the World of Beowulf*. Leiden: Brill.

Joy, E.A. (2008). "Goodbye to All That: The State of My Own Personal Field of Schizoid Anglo-Saxon Studies." *The Heroic Age* 11 (May): http://www.heroicage.org/issues/11/foruma.php #joy.

Joy, E.A. (2012). "You are Here: A Manifesto." In Jeffrey Jerome Cohen, ed., *Animal, Vegetable, Mineral: Ethics and Objects*, 153–172. Washington, DC: Oliphaunt Books.

Joy, E.A. and M.K. Ramsey (2006). "Introduction: Liquid *Beowulf*." In E.A. Joy and M.K. Ramsey, eds., *The Postmodern Beowulf: A Critical Casebook*, xxlx–lxvii. Morgantown: West Virginia University Press.

Klaeber's Beowulf (2008). Eds. R.D. Fulk, R.E. Bjork, and J.D. Niles. 4th edn. Toronto: Toronto University Press.

Köberl, J. (1978). "The Magic Sword in Beowulf." *Neophilologus* 71.1: 120–128.

Latour, B. (2007). *Reassembling the Social: An Introduction to Actor–Network Theory*. Oxford: Oxford University Press.

Lerer, S. (2006). "Hrothgar's Hilt and the Reader in *Beowulf*." In E.A. Joy and M.K. Ramsey, eds., *The Postmodern Beowulf: A Critical Casebook*, 587–628. Morgantown: West Virginia University Press.

Liuzza, R. (2005). "*Beowulf*: Monuments, Memory, History." In D.F. Johnson and E.M. Treharne, eds., *Readings in Medieval Texts: Interpreting Old and Middle English Literature*, 91–108. New York: Oxford University Press.

Love, H. (2010). "Close but Not Deep: Literary Ethics and the Descriptive Turn." *New Literary History* 41.2: 371–391.

McNelis, J. (1996). "The Sword Mightier than the Pen?: Hrothgar's Hilt, Theory, and Philology." In M.J. Toswell and E.M. Tyler, eds., *Studies in English Language and Literature : "Doubt wisely" : Papers in honour of E.G. Stanley*, 175–185. London: Routledge.

Melinkoff, R. (1980). "Cain's Monstrous Progeny in *Beowulf*, Part II: Post-diluvian Survival." *Anglo-Saxon England* 9: 183–197.

Morton, T. (2012). "An Object-Oriented Defense of Poetry." *New Literary History* 43.2: 205–224.

Near, M. (1993). "Anticipating Alienation: *Beowulf* and the Intrusion of Literacy." *PMLA* 108.2: 320–332.

Nokes, R.S. (2007). "A Day Late and 99¢ Short." *Unlocked Wordhoard*, January 29: http://unlocked-wordhoard.blog spot.com/2007/01/day-late-and-99-short.html

Nokes, R.S. (2008). "Valuing Anglo-Saxon Studies." *The Heroic Age* 11 (May): http://www.heroicage.org/issues/11/foruma.php#nokes.

Osborn, M. (1978). "The Great Feud: Scriptural History and Strife in *Beowulf*." *PMLA* 93.5: 973–981.

Overing, G. (1990). *Language, Sign, and Gender in Beowulf*. Carbondale: Southern Illinois University Press.

Pollack, S. (2011). "Histories of Violence: The Origins of War in *Beowulf*." In A. Classen and N. Margolis, eds., *War and Peace: Critical Issues in European Societies and Literature 800-1800*, 121–154. Boston: Walter de Gruyter.

Schrader. R. (1993) "The Language on the Giant's Sword Hilt in *Beowulf*." *Neuphilologische Mitteilungen* 94: 141–147.

Stern, D. (2012). *The Present Moment in Psychotherapy and Everyday Life*. New York: W.W. Norton.

Taylor, P.B. (1998). *Sharing Story: Medieval Norse-English Literary Relationships*. New York: AMS Press.

Virgil (1990). *The Aeneid*, trans. R. Fitzgerald. New York: E.P. Dutton & Co.

Wagner, P. (1996). "Ekphrasis, Iconotexts, and Intermediality—the State(s) of the Art(s)." In P. Wagner, ed., *Icons—Texts—Iconotexts: Essays on Ekphrasis and Intermediality*, 1–40. Berlin: Walter de Gruyter & Co.

Fuzzy Logic

Michael D. Snediker

In her essay "Living Chaucer," Fradenburg writes that Chaucer's narrators

> help by serving or seeking rather than knowing. They never understand what's just happened, but Langlandian frustration is bypassed by their willingness to keep on moving, led, for example, by garrulous eagles or puppies so charming as to have real ears and enjoy having the tops of their soft heads patted by plump little poppets. (Fradenburg 2011, 59)

Narrative certitude is supplanted here by an epistemological spaciousness founded on effort and the good intention, if not of helping, then trying to help. The proximity of these forms of "serving or seeking" to understanding illuminates peripheral ecosystems of thought that rightly remind us of the pleasures of psychoanalysis.

As interesting, however, as the affinity between psychoanalysis and a Chaucer narrator's peri-epistemological style is the relation between the latter and those soft-headed, real-eared puppies to which Fradenburg's account of attention somewhat surprisingly and wonderfully turns. The cuteness of these puppies is a salubrious example of a signifier "living on" (Fradenburg 2011, 42; see also Fradenburg 2009), as Fradenburg writes, in the host's mind and body. I wonder to what extent the puppy currently living in my head concatenatingly extends the life of the puppy in Fradenburg's and Chaucer's heads. To the extent that I first came to admire Fradenburg's work as a psychoanalyst and only in the past few years of Facebook discovered her soft-spot and flair for cuteness, I wonder about cuteness as a psychoanalytic subject. How might thinking about cuteness save the Humanities?[1] Less teleologically—insofar as cuteness, like lyric poetry, lives less in plot than in affect and style—how might thinking about cuteness sustain our implication in academic systems, as Fradenburg has so well illustrated in this volume, that seem to challenge if not discourage our capacity for fortitude and vision?

As I was initially composing this in May 2013, my computer was cued to Fradenburg's latest Facebook posting of a baby polar bear in a blue plastic kiddie pool. Meanwhile, at the same time, my favorite photo in Anna Klosowska's happily endless stream of Facebook cuteness was of a photographer in a field of dandelions, with something *like* a baby deer standing on her back like it's the Matterhorn.[2]

---

[1] On "the zany, the cute, and the interesting" in the work of the humanities, see Ngai (2012).

[2] Caveat: this image may be manipulated (via Photoshop or some other such software), and thus the situation and also the species we are dealing with here are "fuzzy," but even as fuzzy delusion, this photo tells us something about our relation(s) to cuteness.

Said photographer's camera looks expensively complicated, but whatever she's photographing is subordinate to the baby deer, not to mention some other very sweet, wombat-looking thing at her side (is this real or Photoshop? does it matter?). The cuteness of the latter is a function of its pudgy lean into the photographer's upper arm. It is the expression of being in cahoots. Even as the photographer is distracted by this disarmingly photogenic little thing, the latter has its eyes on the prize, as though its cuteness partially resided in this appearance not only of companionship, but bright-eyed apprenticeship. The cuteness of the deer-like creature likewise has to do not only with how cute it looks, but with the acuity of its looking, nearly, but not entirely, in our direction. Its slightly less than three-quarter view, like Vermeer's *Girl with the Pearl Earring*, seems inadvertently emphatic: it's a look either of great courage (which would match the Napoleon-audacity of its stance on the photographer's back) or shirking timorousness (as though to confirm our suspicion that the animal doesn't quite know how it got himself into so unlikely and declarative a position). The deer's look, crucially, involves us in the photograph's geometry, just as the wombat's look prosthetically involves the composition from which the photographer's camera is turned away.

The pleasure of the photograph not only doesn't rely on knowing exactly what these animals are (baby deer? baby kangaroo? wombat? dik dik?), it may actually attach to our *not* knowing, as taxonomic specificity cedes to kingdom and phylum of cuteness. Cuteness, in this and most instances, runs adjacent to epistemological form. It is illuminated by the knowledge we bring to it, but only up to a certain point. Mostly, it's self-illuminating, and more to the point, we're addicted to these photos because this self-illumination illuminates some aspect of ourselves. That we respond to cuteness at all proves that we're still capable of responding. The insatiability with which we need to be reminded of our responsiveness, like the endless streaming of photos on Facebook, suggests that we groove to cuteness as though it were something like a drive. Somewhere between drive and pleasure principle, cuteness' epistemological fuzziness is inseparable from our unappeasable desire for more of it. The mechanics of Facebook streaming are fundamental to this system of thinking-feeling; this real-time commons is Mystic Writing Pad writ as group psychology.

The cute object—as opposed to the good object or bad object—sometimes asks that we treat it as though it were something like an infant. Sometimes like an infant, it seems to communicate a message of desire whose content we can only begin to guess. *Why are you barking, what do you want, talk to me*: as often, it is difficult to distinguish what cuteness tries to communicate from what we imagine it's communicating (hence the frequency with which the communication of a cute creature ends up being superseded by cuteness-as-communique). That the cute object's wish for love is inseparable from our own amorous fantasies suggests a network of affective risk and experimentation along the lines of Winnicott's theorization of transitional objects (Winnicott 1971). More than this, the Winnicottian blur of both transitional objects and good-enough mothers suspends the self-shatteringly brittle agon that arises in the fiction of psychical discreteness.

If this blur makes possible the kind of inter-relational, inter-generic, inter-disciplinary work in which the best versions of the Humanities are invested, as Fradenburg argues more than convincingly here in this book, it also cozens us into the possibility of the blurring as its own counter-intuitive discipline. I'm inclined to think about this field of generative peri-thinking in terms of fuzzy logic, partly in the spirit of repurposing a charge to which our most adventurous and important work is susceptible. In the context of Fradenburg's deceptively simple claim in "Living Chaucer" that "even cuteness is about healing," and that it is "inclusive, 'generous'; it requires gestures that invite care and protection" (Fradenburg 2011, 59), fuzzy logic likewise conjures the fuzziness that underlies so many of our own inclinations toward and perceptions of cuteness. And as Fradenburg also writes here in this book, in "Living the Liberal Arts," "if the humanities are 'fuzzy,' and their outcomes and processes difficult to quantify, that is because living is 'fuzzy.' It demands artfulness, experimentation, and hypothesis."

As a non-medievalist, I'm in less of a position to assess Chaucerian cuteness than I'm able to note how seductively ahistorical it seems in the context of both Fradenburg's "Living Chaucer" essay and also Chaucer's poetry itself. Even as I wish I were enough of a Chaucerian that I could compare how I imagine these puppies with however they might be operating in the text, how cuteness works in a medieval context is less interesting for me than the fact that it does at all. After all, as Sianne Ngai beautifully argues, cuteness as we know it didn't nominally exist until the early nineteenth century—the Oxford English Dictionary's first citation of "cute" is from 1834 (Ngai 2012, 59). What were cute things called in advance of the word? I'm interested in the migration of a word that originally denoted sharpness (perceptual and otherwise) into a field from which the knives, as it were, have been removed. Hypothesizing Chaucer's investment in cuteness in advance of the term somewhat mirrors queer theory's incorrigible interest in early modern sexuality in advance of the great Foucauldian hypostasization of sexual discourse. This resemblance makes sense, since cuteness's flirtation with anachronism—the only slightly dubious fantasy that what presently counts as cute would have similarly registered across history—both arises from and gravitates toward the same questions of investment and interstitial being that queer theory continues to help us re-articulate. And if this sort of anachronism is deemed a particular fuzzy logic by certain academics, then the fuzziness of theorizing cuteness nearly constitutes a tautology. One way out of the tautology is to give fuzziness a critical vocabulary of its own, such that when we are accused of—and more importantly, when we practice—fuzzy thinking, our sense of fuzzy is if not less fuzzy, then more articulate. This is to also contribute to Fradenburg's own project in this book to demonstrate that "the arts are not fripperies, but activities for life," and that the humanities "teach human organisms how best to move, and to keep on moving, with maximum power and grace."

* * *

Following Sianne Ngai's observation that cute objects seem to address us in the manner of lyric poems, let's turn to Emily Dickinson, for whom fuzziness and cuteness withstand and inspire lyric scrutiny no less than pain or posthumousness. If I began these pages with an inchoate hunch about cuteness and psychoanalysis, Dickinson helps me understand the contours of that juxtaposition. Specifically, Dickinson treats cuteness—along the lines of most analogously overdetermined psychoanalytic objects—as equivocal threshold between affect and interest. This is to say that cuteness, like Barthes's understanding of adorability, seems to arise from our own disposition when we most wish it to speak to the external qualities of something else:

> [The Adorable] seeks to designate that site of the
> other to which my desire clings *in a special way*,
> but this site cannot be designated; about it I shall
> never know anything; my language will always fumble,
> stammer in order to attempt to express it, but I can
> never produce anything but a blank word, an emp-
> ty vocable. . . . From word to word, I struggle to
> put "into other words" the ipseity of my Image, to
> express improperly the propriety of my desire: a
> journey at whose end my final philosophy can on-
> ly be to recognize—and to practice—tautology. *The
> adorable is what is adorable.* Or again: I adore you
> because you are adorable, I love you because I love
> you. (Barthes [1978] 1996, 19–21)

To the extent that I'm inclined to agree with "this *everything*" (Barthes [1978] 1996, 19) of *A Lover's Discourse*,
I'm left with the sense that I might, in fact, find Barthes's
intro/extrospection smitingly adorable. In this observation, I'm left with the happy suspicion that adorability is
more complicated (which is to say, more sophisticated)
than I'd assumed, and it's this "residual quality" (Barthes
[1978] 1996, 19) of complexity that makes me think that
cuteness and adorability alike might be teased out of their
stammering fumble. It's along these Barthesian lines of
miscible subjectivity and objectivity that the following
Dickinson poem meditates on the difficulty of adjudicat-
ing cuteness as something that happens in the world, or
to it:

> Bees are Black—with Gilt Surcingles—
> Buccaneers of Buzz—
> Ride Abroad in ostentation
> And subsist on Fuzz—
>
> Fuzz ordained—not Fuzz contingent—
> Marrows of the Hill.
> Jugs—a Universe's fracture

Could not jar or spill.
(541, F1426)[3]

Sharon Cameron succinctly notes that, "the unexpected 'Fuzz ordained—not Fuzz contingent—' rescues
the bee from the triviality to which 'Buccaneers of Buzz'
had almost certainly doomed it" (Cameron 1981, 9). The
poem, however, seems less interested in rescuing the bee
than in attending to its escape from the poem altogether.
The rhyme of "buzz" and "fuzz" renders the latter as con-
sumingly ambient as sound, as though the quality of fuzz
that describes both the bee and the pollen it feeds on were
saturatingly intangible as a subliminal message. Everywhere and nowhere, fuzziness describes the poem's resistance to resolution: one's attempt to locate meaning
ends up replicating the bee's own fuzzy hovering in a field
of flowers. Or rather, we hover over the poem, but without the bee's innate feel for pollen. The poem implies that
how one converts its fuzz into meaning is as surprising—
and transfixingly mysterious—as Dickinson's own fascination with the bee, even as it is Dickinson's own fascination, rather than the bee itself, we find most alluring.

After all, the ostentation belongs less to the bees than
to the poet who turns their stripes into gilt surcingles,
who consigns them to the forced kitsch of buzz-pirates.
The fancy ingeniousness of "gilt surcingles" inverts the
logic of Fradenburg's real-eared puppies, in that the bee's
stripes seem so much less real than the bees that we are all
the more surprised when it is the former that survive the
poem as signification floatingly removed from antecedent.
It is the extent to which the bees are unable to weather the
metaphors imposed on them that makes the poem, at
least initially, seem so cute. Dickinson forces her bees into
bee outfits with the same slightly-off self-indulgence with
which people sadistically dress up little dogs in bee outfits.

---

[3] Citations of Dickinson's poetry are to Franklin's (2005) edition,
by page and fascicle numbers.

That a bee's attraction to pollen—or in Dickinson's deceptive alembic, fuzz's queer attraction to fuzz—is potentially indistinguishable from imagination's attraction to itself returns us to the Barthesian problematic of adorability describing one's capacity for adoring. Like Winnicott's good-enough mother, cuteness is an adventure in non-vituperative counter-transference, as well as, in Fradenburg's words, an "enhancement of sentience in the service of relationality," and "we can neither thrive nor survive without minds alert to [such] possibility."

Fuzziness, in this case, isn't constitutive of the bees' cuteness—it's, surprisingly, what they (and we) live on. Or as Fradenburg writes here in "Life's Reach": "Creatures do not live bare lives, if they can possibly help it." The leap the poem makes from the end of the first stanza to the beginning of the second reminds me of Fradenburg's accounts, throughout this book, of striving for survival as it blurs into lyric thriving. We subsist on Fuzz, until subsistence, without warning, is eclipsed by an ever-escalating oddness that survives what Dickinson plangently calls a "Universe's fracture." In true Dickinson fashion, it's not *the* Universe, or even *our* Universe. The indefinite article makes the universe of this penultimate line far more fuzzy than the fuzz itself. Few would argue that the university as we know it, *our* universe, isn't broken; but as Dickinson and maybe Chaucer (and also Fradenburg) know, our swerving attention to the fuzzy world we're making takes some of the sting out of this being the case.

REFERENCES

Barthes, R. ([1978] 1996). *A Lover's Discourse: Fragments*, trans. Richard Howard. New York: Hill and Wang.

Cameron, S. (1981). *Lyric Time: Dickinson and the Limits of Genre.* Baltimore: Johns Hopkins University Press.

Fradenburg, L.O.A. (2009). "(Dis)continuity: A History of Dreaming." In *The Post-Historical Middle Ages*, eds. E. Scala and S. Frederico, 87–115. New York: Palgrave Macmillan.

Fradenburg, L.O.A. (2011). "Living Chaucer." *Studies in the Age of Chaucer* 33: 41–64.

Franklin, R.W. (2005). *The Poems of Emily Dickinson: Reading Edition.* Cambridge, MA: Belknap Press.

Ngai, S. (2012). *Our Aesthetic Categories: Zany, Cute, Interesting.* Cambridge, MA: Harvard University Press.

Winnicott, D.W. (1971). *Playing and Reality.* London: Tavistock.

INDEX

W. dreams, like Phaedrus, of an army of thinker-friends, thinker-lovers. He dreams of a thought-army, a thought-pack, which would storm the philosophical Houses of Parliament. He dreams of Tartars from the philosophical steppes, of thought-barbarians, thought-outsiders. What distances would shine in their eyes!

~Lars Iyer

www.babelworkinggroup.org

ma gia volgena il mio disio e'l velle
si come rota ch'igualmente e mossa,
l'amor che move: i sole e l'altre stelle

O you who are within your pretty little bark,
Eager to listen, have been following
Behind my ship, that singing sails along.

Turn back to look again upon your own shores;
Tempt not the deep, lest unawares,
In losing me, you might yourselves be lost.

The sea I sail has never yet been passed;
Minerva breathes, and Apollo pilots me,
And Muses nine point out to me the Bears.

You other few who turned your minds in time
Unto the bread of angels upon which one lives
And does not grow sated,

Well may you launch your vessel
Upon the deep sea.

Dante Alighieri, *Paradiso*

Made in the USA
Charleston, SC
05 August 2014